The Archaeology of Antislavery Resistance

The American Experience in Archaeological Perspective

UNIVERSITY PRESS OF FLORIDA

Florida A&M University, Tallahassee
Florida Atlantic University, Boca Raton
Florida Gulf Coast University, Ft. Myers
Florida International University, Miami
Florida State University, Tallahassee
New College of Florida, Sarasota
University of Central Florida, Orlando
University of Florida, Gainesville
University of North Florida, Jacksonville
University of South Florida, Tampa
University of West Florida, Pensacola

The Archaeology of
ANTISLAVERY
RESISTANCE

TERRANCE M. WEIK

Foreword by Michael S. Nassaney

University Press of Florida
Gainesville · Tallahassee · Tampa · Boca Raton · Pensacola
Orlando · Miami · Jacksonville · Ft. Myers · Sarasota

First cloth printing, 2012
First paperback printing, 2013

Library of Congress Cataloging-in-Publication Data
Weik, Terrance M.
The archaeology of antislavery resistance / Terrance M. Weik ; foreword by
Michael S. Nassaney.
p. cm.
Includes bibliographical references and index.
ISBN 978-0-8130-3759-2 (cloth: alk. paper)
ISBN 978-0-8130-4472-9 (pbk.)
    1. Antislavery movements—United States—History. 2. Slave insurrections—
United States—History. 3. Fugitive slaves—United States—History.
4. Underground Railroad. 5. Ethnoarchaeology—United States. 6. Archaeology
and history—United States. 7. African Americans—Antiquities. 8. Slaves—
United States—Antiquities I. Title.
E450.W398 2012
326.'80973—dc23   2011037454

The University Press of Florida is the scholarly publishing agency for the State
University System of Florida, comprising Florida A&M University, Florida
Atlantic University, Florida Gulf Coast University, Florida International
University, Florida State University, New College of Florida, University of
Central Florida, University of Florida, University of North Florida, University of
South Florida, and University of West Florida.

University Press of Florida
15 Northwest 15th Street
Gainesville, FL 32611-2079
http://www.upf.com

Contents

Illustrations

Foreword

It would be difficult to identify more central core values in the American experience than justice and freedom. Early European immigrants in the age of discovery appropriated new lands at any cost to practice beliefs unimpeded by divine monarchs and politically oppressive regimes. In New England and the Southern colonies these migrants in turn banned and persecuted those who disagreed with their dominant beliefs. The legacy of a free nation propels people from around the world to seek admittance to the United States in order to realize their social and economic dreams for their children and grandchildren.

Yet Americans have always lived with contradictions that have denied large segments of the population supposedly inalienable rights for various ideological reasons. Women, the working classes, Native Americans, and masses of forcefully displaced Africans brought here against their wishes to work without compensation (now called African Americans) have struggled for the freedom and justice that white, male, land-owning Americans have long taken for granted. Perhaps the most horrific denial of human dignity and equality occurred under the peculiar institution of American slavery—a dominant mode of production from the seventeenth through nineteenth centuries. So pervasive and insidious were the injustices and skewed rationale of slavery that the country still lingers in the dark shadow of racism that legitimized the social hierarchy of repression.

Despite the apparent hegemony of slavery, which was buttressed by legal, political/military, social, and economic policies and practices, people of color and their white sympathizers challenged, resisted, and rebelled against human bondage, because the desire for freedom is universal. A small but adamant minority recognized the demeaning nature of enslavement for both the enslaved and the enslavers and sought to liberate especially the former from the physical and conceptual shackles that compromised their humanity.

In *The Archaeology of Antislavery Resistance*, Terrance Weik surveys the literature that points to the myriad ways in which people opposed an inhumane form of confinement and exploitation that was legally sanctioned for the sake of profit. He notes that colonial ideas concerning the perceived European rights to control foreign lands, maintain social superiority, and distance themselves from local peoples were the strategies that reinforced the development of unfree, unpaid labor. While socio-legal distinctions were initially based on religious beliefs, a racial hierarchy soon arose and hardened, casting people of color into subservient roles in which their physical characteristics prohibited social mobility except in rare instances of self-liberation. Weik employs documentary sources, landscape studies, and a critical reading of the archaeological record to demonstrate the power of the material world to assume greater importance when analyzed in conjunction with other lines of evidence. Moreover, he clearly shows what archaeologists know in their hearts and minds—namely, that covert behaviors such as antislavery resistance are difficult to document in the records of the dominant society but evident, even if subtly so, in the physical residues (or hidden transcripts) that reveal sabotage, escape, rebellion, and daily refusal to cooperate.

Sacred bundles, pathways marking escape routes, hideaways, settlements in marginalized locations, and a range of other physical traces suggest how Americans of African descent sought to create conceptual and material spaces that allowed for autonomy from their enslavers. Efforts to resist were continuous, pervasive, and inculcated at an early age. Separate living quarters inhabited by some captives provided seclusion to socialize youth on coping strategies, feigning ignorance, practicing outlawed ancestral traditions, or expressing outrage at the system. In some instances, these conditions led to escape or exploded into outright rebellion. As Frederick Douglass noted, "power concedes nothing without a demand." The efforts to inhibit escape took various forms, including harsh legal measures such as the Fugitive Slave Laws of 1793 and 1850. The need for legislation suggests that slavery supporters maintained an ongoing battle against such resistance.

Weik perceptively notes that the freedom sought by escaped captives as they established maroon settlements and traveled along the Underground Railroad differed from the freedom of capitalism, which privileges individualism at the cost of communal well-being. For example, the fulfillment that Harriet Tubman experienced from her own self-emancipation was limited compared with her satisfaction at having freed others. Thus, one challenge to studying resistance is the tendency to impose contemporary values on past societies. We must also be cognizant of the diverse and changing meanings of actions and objects, and try to see with African eyes to understand fully the ways in which goods were mobilized in strategies of resistance. Something as simple as a pair of iron fire tongs placed near his maternal grandfather's fireplace reminded W.E.B. Du Bois of his African past and the importance of blacksmiths in African societies. Likewise, symbols and artifact associations must be examined from an emic perspective to avoid interpretive violence that diminishes the agency of those who were fashioning alternate systems of meaning.

At stake ultimately is a better sense of the ways in which people bond through social networks which employ culture to create a new social identity—one based on ancestral foundations, transformed under new social conditions, and distinguished from that of their oppressors. Weik uses the concept of ethnogenesis to frame his arguments for understanding the societies that emerged both in the context of slavery and as individuals distanced themselves from its stifling influence. Self-liberated Africans created new institutions and collective ways of producing knowledge. Although difficult to find, archaeologists have been successful in locating remains of self-liberated African communities. The blending of artifact uses from diverse cultural traditions suggests the multiethnic nature of maroon settlements, which reflects their African, indigenous, and sometimes marginalized European inhabitants. As Weik notes, ethnography, archival sources, and the material record suggest a more complex identity formation at maroon sites which is indicative of cultural hybridization resulting from interaction.

In his detailed case study of Florida Seminoles, Weik has identified material evidence of such interaction in the form of imported artifacts such as ceramics. Though African Seminoles relied on local resources to construct houses, they were linked into broader networks of exchange. Nonlocal goods indicate that African Seminoles were willing to face the risk of re-enslavement or death so that they could benefit from regional exchanges and social networks. Evidence of cultural transformation is also illustrated in their willingness to participate in Seminole Busk ceremonies and rites that restored balance and well-being to the people. Further, the emergence of the African Seminoles was facilitated by their ability to reconcile vastly different cultural traditions. For instance, they incorporated elements of Christianity and African religious worldviews into their belief system.

Throughout his discussion of freedom and antislavery resistance, Weik recognizes that archaeology can assist in developing a discourse that transcends Eurocentric, racist, and document-based models derived from the dominant culture. The archaeological record can also bring sites of resistance to the attention of a larger audience, given the lack of extensive written documentation of many Underground Railroad stations and self-liberated African settlements. Such systematic work can dispel simplistic and uninformed ideas about the presence of tunnels and secret in-house hiding places, yet highlight the importance of individuals and places in challenging the system.

In our own work in Cass County, Michigan, we located the antebellum sites where former African captives from the American South lived and worked. Although many contemporary local people were convinced of the roles that both their ancestors and earlier residents had played in the Underground Railroad, our efforts to recover and preserve the material remains of these peoples' lives made this chapter in local and national history more tangible. The project also heightened community pride by verifying the past participation of locals in assisting those seeking freedom. The evidence of self-liberated Africans in the past serves as an inspiration to presently oppressed peoples since slavery has yet to be fully abolished. It also reminds us of the contradictions that our predecessors on both sides of the color line faced in daily life as they built a nation. The work presented here on the archaeology of freedom and antislavery resistance is central to understanding the foundations of the American experience. We must not forget that there have always been challenges to prejudice and discrimination in America bending the moral arc of the universe towards justice. Yet clearly, the journey towards racial equality, economic democracy, social justice, and liberation has only begun. Archaeology can reveal sites where people struggled, won, or died for such freedom. By commemorating these places we can attain a new resolve about the future direction of our nation, the importance of liberation in American history, and the part archaeology can play in exposing this largely hidden past.

Michael S. Nassaney
Series Editor

Acknowledgments

I would like to thank my ancestors and creator for the chance to be here to assemble these ideas. I am thankful for my wife, Natalie, and son, Akin, who tolerated me during the production of this book. Natalie provided useful advice and editorial assistance at various stages of this project. I am also grateful for the millions of people whose courage, efforts, and visions of freedom resulted in the struggles against slavery that inform this book. Further, I am indebted to Colonel Harris, Mr. and Mrs. Warrior, and various other descendants who patiently retold their ancestors' stories.

I would like to also express my appreciation for the many forms of financial, intellectual, and logistical support provided by Peter Schmidt, Kathleen Deagan, Irma McClaurin, Jerald Milanich, Allan Burns, Steve Brandt, Karen Jones, Pat King, and other faculty and staff at the University of Florida, especially the Anthropology Department. The research that informed this book was greatly enhanced by Al Woods, Donna Ruhl, Ann Cordell, Darcie MacMahon, Elise Lecompte, Scott Mitchell, and others at the Florida Museum of Natural History who generously provided their time and expertise. I wish to thank Brent Weisman for his help in locating sites, understanding Seminole archaeology, finding volunteers, and obtaining logistical support. Much archival evidence that is used in this book was obtained with the assistance of Bruce Chappell, Jim Cusick, and other staff at the University of Florida Libraries' Special Collections. Seed money for research at Jose Leta was provided by the A. Curtis Wilgus Foundation at the University of Florida Center for Latin American and Caribbean Studies. The generous financial support provided by the Florida Division of Historic Resources and the Florida Humanities Council ensured the completion of research on Pilaklikaha. Uzi Baram, Vickie Oldham, Rosalyn Howard, Canter Brown, Jane Landers, and other Florida scholars have provided a helpful network for one interested in African Seminoles and Maroons.

I would like to thank Kofi Agorsah and his Jamaican Maroon Heritage Research Project for providing the financial and logistical support that enabled me to first experience Maroon archaeology and become aware of important scholarship on this subject. Manuel Garcia Arevalo provided logistical support, wise advice, and encouragement during my research trip in search of Jose Leta. A number of other scholars and archaeologists have provided reports, insights, and information that aided my research on the Underground Railroad, antislavery resistance, Maroons and freedom: Robert Paynter, Anna Agbe-Davies, Jamie Brandon, Whitney Battle-Baptiste, Steve DeVore, Alejandra Bronfman, Lydia Wilson-Marshall, Chris Fennell, Leland Ferguson, James Delle, Robert Genheimer, Kurt Jordan, Angie Krieger, Deborah Rotman, Daniel Sayers, Barbara Tagger, Fred Smith, Chris Matthews, Robert G. McCullough, Mary McCorvie, Paul Mullins, and Charles Orser. I wish to also thank Edward Alpers and other Africanist scholars who have provided conference papers and information about escapees who fled from slavery in Africa. In addition, I would like to thank the countless Florida volunteers and publics whose interest and labor enriched this research.

I am indebted to various people for their help with the final stages of this book project. The Department of Anthropology, Institute of African American Research, and various faculty and units at the University of South Carolina provided funding, feedback, and other support that were immensely helpful. I am grateful for the comments of Maria Franklin and an anonymous reviewer, which greatly improved the manuscript. I wish to thank Michael Nassaney for his guidance throughout the book production process. I would also like to express my appreciation for the assistance provided by Kara Schwartz, Michele Fiyak-Burkley, Corey Brady, and the staff at the University Press of Florida. Finally, many thanks to anyone who has helped me but I have failed to mention. Any errors or shortcomings of this book are entirely my own.

1

Introduction

Archaeologists have explored struggles against captivity enacted by free and enslaved people for several decades (Arrom and Garcia Arevalo 1986; Agorsah 1993; Laroche 2004; Orser and Funari 1998; Sayers 2008; Weik 1997, 2009). This book focuses on self-liberated Africans ("Maroons") in the Americas and intercultural collaborative resistance movements (for instance, the Underground Railroad or African-Native American alliances), especially material aspects of them that fall within the period 1600–1865. Despite the temporal focus of this book, I still encourage readers to consider the global dimensions of antislavery resistance, a term that will be used to signify any form of defiance against slavery, not just the activities of abolitionists. Resistance and slavery involve issues that continue to spark debate today, such as racism, cultural survival, self-determination, and inequality. Various forms of evidence illustrate how people of African descent sought to protect their human rights, escape from bondage, and combat exploitation. Their actions varied across different settings and included accommodation, collaboration, autonomy, and militancy.

The chapters of this book are organized thematically, with the goal of addressing the historical background, approaches, findings, and wider significance of the archaeology of antislavery resistance in the Americas. This book will also explore some connections between specific forms of resistance, such as revolts, escape, and the Underground Railroad. As these varieties of antislavery behavior are assessed, various meanings and uses of the concept of freedom will become apparent. Freedom has been defined variously by thinkers, artists, activists, politicians, and laypersons. Simply put, to be free one must have the consistent ability to choose one's livelihood, place of residence, beliefs, and ways of life. On another level, freedom is impacted by people's ability to avoid stress, dependency, and manipulation. If people lack the ability to meet their basic needs and cannot determine how they spend their time, they are missing some aspects of freedom. By exploring worldviews that inform struggles against slavery, the archaeological discourse on antislavery resistance can be shifted from its traditional focus on social relations to broader discussions of belief systems and culture.

Another challenge confronted in this book is how to convey the great historical depth and geographical breadth of African (and allied) actions against slavery. Understandings of these phenomena depend on a wide range of factors, including the approaches to evidence and goals of scholars, descendants, and other commentators. An explicit analysis of the activities, strategies, processes, consequences, and cultural implications of American Maroon societies and the Underground Railroad helps readers think more carefully about resistance and its proponents. As a result, one can come to appreciate how opposition to enslavement was comprised of more than just idiosyncratic events or physical reactions. An additional goal of this book is to provide a detailed case study which captures the complexities and dynamics that animated communities formed in defiance of slavery. By considering Native Americans' roles in African slavery and freedom, the bounds of African, African American, and Native American studies are expanded and challenged. The ambiguities, conflicts, and alliances of the past that have complicated our understanding of these populations shed light on current problems and possibilities for cooperation.

Archaeology is one of many useful discourses that examine antislavery resistance. Descendant communities have cultivated oral histories and traditions and impressed their views onto the landscape with place-names, just as their ancestors did in Africa. While the griots and elders who transmit oral accounts address certain critical moments in history, they do not convey all significant aspects of past lifeways, especially certain types of knowledge that were protected (sacred beliefs or military strategy, for example). The potential fallibility and selectivity of memory and the complexities of intergenerational knowledge transmission challenge any claim that oral accounts are all passed down with precision or completeness across time. Similar issues arise with the use of documentary evidence. Government officials, soldiers, and travelers have provided important written sources that mention the names, numbers, subsistence modes, landscapes, and leaders of antislavery activities. The few existing sketches and maps of freedom-seekers' domains are provocative, since so little is known about the enemies of slavery compared to captive laborers and the people who enslaved them. Yet, like textual and oral sources, the representativeness of many images is open to question, as the creators' (often Eurocentric) subjectivities, biases, and assumptions shape visual representations (Price 1989). Many of slavery's resisters were effective because they were covert, which may have prevented their movements and activities from becoming inscribed in records, portrayed in drawings, or passed down orally. Archaeologists and scholars studying material culture deal with their own challenges and opportunities, which are no less productive or inhibiting than are those faced by historians, ethnographers, oral historians, and other knowledge-producers investigating antislavery resistance.

As a synthetic social science and a relative newcomer to antislavery studies, archaeology has not only contributed new knowledge, but also posed different questions, applying alternate methods of data collection and interpretation. As specialists within the wider discipline of anthropology, archaeologists conduct a range of activities: ascertaining the theoretical significance of material culture and the built environment; explaining the dynamics of past cultures and idiosyncratic human behaviors; analyzing and synthesizing separate lines of evidence; and disseminating the knowledge they generate to public and academic audiences.

Some of the earliest examples of African American archaeology proved quite interesting. For instance, despite the laws prohibiting captive Africans from bearing arms, ammunition found its way into the physical remains of enslaved peoples' cabins. Ascher and Fairbanks (1971) integrated humanistic and scientific archaeological methods in their study of everyday life at Rayfield Plantation, Georgia (circa 1834–1865). They juxtaposed a documentary excerpt about an enslaved person who possessed a gun and contemplated escape with chemical analyses of the lead bullets that they discovered at a "slave cabin." Though they had no explicit conceptualization of resistance to slavery, their inclusion of the excerpt about this enslaved gun holder alludes to the potential for antislavery behavior and points out the inherent contradiction in captive laborers possessing lethal weapons.

From ancient times, a number of slave owners around the world armed their bond persons (Brown 2006: 330–54). The popular image that many have of the plantation slave is of a highly dominated laborer who never would have been allowed to keep guns. However, some slaveholders saw the value of allowing limited arms use if it freed them from having to supply their captive laborers with meat rations or if it protected them or their strategic interests. Thus, we cannot assume that every evident contradiction in the slavery system supports the simple conclusion that resistance or militancy was present.

Arms such as lead shot are one of the few types of artifacts likely to be found whole at antislavery sites. It is also one of the more rare types of artifact found in antislavery sites, as are beads and coins. Despite the challenges of locating material residues of escape, rebellions, or covert resistance, fragments of pottery, glass bottles, smoking pipes, nails, and metal containers hint at a range of possessions. These objects present archaeologists with opportunities to study their functions, their "life histories," their social impacts, and their meanings.

I examine rebellion, marronage, and the Underground Railroad in this book because they are similar types of phenomena and because they were sometimes directly interrelated in particular locations and periods. Some resistance phenomena did share features that crosscut dimensions of culture, time, geography, behavior, and circumstance. One implication of a pan-resistance framework is that it reminds us that we cannot fully understand places of escape or revolt (and neighboring locales) in isolation, even if our research questions, field logistics, and resources force us to focus on one site and topic. However, this is not to say that revolts, escape, and antislavery movements were all interrelated, correlated, or homologous.

For example, enslaved Africans had been escaping from Carolina plantations and other Southern bastions of slavery for nearly one hundred years by the time the Stono Rebellion occurred. Some of the rebels who took part had plans to continue beyond their South Carolina low country captivity and follow the lead of precursors who had obtained a level of freedom in Spanish Florida, at places such as Fort Mose. Deagan and Landers's (1999) work on the history and archaeology of Fort Mose informs discussions of everyday life, cultural identity, and social relations at "Colonial America's Black Fortress of Freedom." Maroons became Spanish colonial allies—as the Europeans granted amnesty to former slaves—in exchange for their service against Anglo enemies in the Southeast. The regional perspective employed by Deagan and Landers in their work on Fort Mose has also been crucial in pointing out the interrelation of

Figure 1.1. Beads from Pilaklikaha. Photo by Terrance Weik.

various modes of resistance and degrees of freedom realized by people of African descent in the colonial Americas. Fort Mose was the product of many European-African alliances, which were fostered by military collaborations, trade, and god-parentage. In the last decade, histories of the Underground Railroad have become more vocal about the need to include Southern routes of resistance and communities of freedom, in contrast to older histories that emphasized slaves escaping to "free" U.S. states and Canada (compare Dubois 1915 and Seibert 1898 to Blight 2004).

The study of freedom initiatives and antislavery resistance resonates with anthropological and historical research on important themes such as sociocultural identity, collective survival strategies, and community-building. Life in communities of formerly enslaved Africans offered opportunities to regain acknowledgement of their humanity, which had been largely denied or reduced by slave societies. The act of community-building indicated that people chose to seek alternatives to the oppressive societies that enslaved them. They sought refuge from exploitation, forced labor, surveillance, denigration, and violent abuse. African American or integrated communities of the U.S. Underground Railroad offered similar opportunities. However, as in the case of Fort Mose, people's ability to express aspects of their African heritage and to live autonomously was not fully or consistently encouraged in some places. Although they are often viewed as failures of militant resistance, many rebellions are significant reflections of the aspirants' quest for liberation or greater independence.

African attempts to reclaim community and resist enslavement are very meaningful to descendants (direct or associated groups) and current laypersons. Maroons and rebels have been an inspiration for past and present oppressed peoples. The symbolic significance of Maroons has been highlighted by activist scholars such as the late Asa Hilliard. His book *The*

Figure 1.2. Yanga statue and author, city of Yanga, Mexico. Photo by Terrance Weik.

Maroon Within (1995) encouraged people to seek both self-determination and self-knowledge in order to overcome racism and realize liberation. Hilliard invokes African thinkers such as Amil Cabral, reminding us that the conflicts of colonial and postcolonial racist societies are cultural, as well as ideological and physical, struggles. Hilliard suggests that Maroon societies were holistic models of socialization that allowed people of African descent to discover their heritage, affirm positive social identities, preserve their culture, and enact healing processes.

Histories of antislavery resistance have been publicly acknowledged and celebrated in the last decade by a number of nations. In the United States, legislation has allocated millions of dollars to support research, site preservation, and exhibitions commemorating the Underground Railroad (Sayers 2004). The National Underground Railroad Freedom Center, a museum in Cincinnati, was built with the purpose of celebrating this covert antislavery network. For decades, Maroons in Jamaica and *Kilombos* (Maroon communities) in Brazil have been recognized as part of national heritage and local oral and artistic traditions (Allen 2004; Abrahams 2006; Harris 1994). In the United States, anthropologists and other scholars have helped organize public exhibitions about Maroons that were part of the Smithsonian's Folk Life Festivals in the early 1990s (Price and Price 1994). In places like Mexico, Martinique, and Guadeloupe, public engagements with the past have taken the form of monuments, commemorative stele, and annual celebrations that commemorate the Africans who fought enslavement (Reinhardt 2006: 140–50, 167, 169, 170).

However, not all aspects of research and remembrance are cause for a celebratory outlook. Just as memories are partially the selective products of erasure and forgetting, parts of the archaeological records of communities such as Palmares have been destroyed by artifact collectors, memento seekers, farmers, and monument builders (for example, to the Maroon leader Zumbi) (Allen 2001: 149). Archaeologists commonly acknowledge that excavation removes part of the archaeological record, making it unavailable for future recovery, at which point better techniques might yield more or better information. In 1994, responding to my inquiry about the value that Jamaican Maroons placed on archaeological findings, a Maroon elder told me that our investigations contributed little to what they already knew of their past. Descendants of people who liberated themselves from slavery also are aware of the political economy of knowledge production.

That is, they know that cultural anthropologists, archaeologists, and other researchers are able to capitalize on their history and local knowledge in ways that generate money, prestige, and other resources (Ngwenyama 2007: 141; Price and Price 1994).

Ultimately, regardless of how we choose to valuate, study, and collect these histories and cultural resources, a central message rings clear: Despite the differences in time, culture, gender, age, and political perspective that differentiated people, each era contains a significant number of individuals and groups who were willing and able to fight and flee from slavery. One might say that the desire for freedom is a universal possibility, even if all members of society do not choose to pursue or realize it.

2

ЗЗЗЗЗЗ

Historical Highlights
of Antislavery Resistance

This chapter provides an overview of the nature and development of freedom-seeking initiatives and resistance to slavery. A vast literature has emerged from anthropologists, historians, and other scholars who have written about self-emancipated Africans (Maroons), the Underground Railroad, and rebellions (Aptheker 1939; Blight 2004; Craton 1982; Gara 1961; Landers 1998, 2002; Price 1975, 1993; Thompson 2006). These works stand aside centuries of chronicles, oral histories, and artistic traditions concerning people who escaped from or fought slavery (Bilby 2005; Harris 1994; Jones 1991; Price 1993; Siebert 1898). New works emerge constantly, as do new mediums through which these histories are expressed and communicated, such as the Internet (http://www.johnhorse.com 2005). Rather than intensively engage the voluminous body of writings and oral expressions that exist, I will identify the prominent themes in the broader literature.

My intention is to use these primary themes to frame later discussions of archaeology, theory, and historic places. Outside of a few examples in the Eastern Hemisphere, most of what follows outlines resistance against enslavement in the Western Hemisphere. By contemplating the geographical, social, and cultural dimensions of historical resistance to slavery, one becomes able to appreciate the breadth and depth of freedom struggles and the potential for archaeological research in different parts of the world. Other important topics, such as cultural identity, African influence, and Native American interactions, will be discussed in later chapters, where their significance is clarified by theories about resistance, community transformation, and freedom.

African and Eastern Antecedents of American Slavery and Resistance

The form and magnitude of resistance were related to the unique expressions of inequality and violence intrinsic to each slave society. The English word "slavery," as typically viewed by people in the West, connotes a number of things, including low status, forced servitude, poor living conditions, and the treatment of people as objects (that is, able to be bought like property and used at the whim of an owner). However, certain generalizations—such as children being marked with an enslaved status if their mother had that status—have to be applied cautiously. Parallels and some intellectual and entrepreneurial precedents for Western ideas of slavery can be traced to the Mediterranean and the Middle East. From these areas, systems of sugar production spread to the Americas, where some slave owners earned extreme profits at the cost of brutal human and ecological exploitation. Scholarship on Roman and Greek slavery has probably taken greater notice of research on the Western Hemisphere than vice versa. An example of its influence can be found on the cover of Page Dubois' (2003) book on Greek slavery, where one finds the whip-scarred back of a man who escaped from enslavement and found refuge with U.S. forces during the Civil War (see also Bradley 1994: 122).

Like slavery, resistance, philosophies of freedom, and liberating initiatives can also be found in antiquity. War and debt were primary reasons for bondage in antiquity, and enslaved people performed a variety of tasks, serving as soldiers or forced labor that tended crops (indigo, cotton, or sugar, for example), built canals, and mined minerals (saltpeter). The Bible, and its many iterations over the centuries, is among the texts that discusses resistance to slavery in Eurasia. As Mendelsohn notes:

> The Old Testament slave legislations (Ex. 21, Dt. 15, Lev. 25) do not mention the case of the fugitive slave although the tendency to run away was prevalent in Palestine as it was in the adjacent countries. When David sent his messengers to procure food from the rich but churlish farmer Nabal, the latter very defiantly inquired: "Who is David and who is the son of Jesse? There be many slaves nowadays that break away every man from his master (I Sam. 25:10). Fugitive slaves were extradited when they fled into foreign countries (I Kings 2: 39f.). In view of these facts how should the Deuteronomic

ordinance (chap. 23:15) "you shall not deliver a slave unto his master who escapes to you from his master" be interpreted? (1946: 82–83)

Conversely, the ancient laws of Hammurabi proclaimed that war prisoners who escaped from neighboring countries and came back to their homeland were to remain free. This was somewhat similar to the American colonial policies that undermined slavery in neighboring colonies or enemy territory (for example, Spanish Florida, or the British freeing Africans enslaved to their former colonists).

In ancient Greece, enslaved people were objectified. Reducing people to the state of objects was an ideological way of denying personal responsibility for slavery. By refusing culpability, free people could avoid guilt over stealing others' freedom. According to Page Dubois (2003: 4), slaves were "epistemologically, socially, and corporally invisible." This objectification is illustrated by the instances in which enslaved people were made into living texts, tattooed with messages from their masters. In one case, an enslaved man's head was imprinted with a message meant to signal recipients to join a rebellion. Tattooing was also a means of marking and punishing enslaved people who fled from bondage (Dubois 2003: 4; compare with ancient Babylonian cases in Mendelsohn 1946). Parallel forms of bodily mutilation can be found in ancient Eurasia, where Scythians and other groups blinded captives to prevent their escape from servitude. Threats of mutilation were also used to prevent women from fleeing forced prostitution (Taylor 2001).

The slave rebel has had a long presence in fiction, including literature in the ancient Mediterranean (Bradley 1994: 120). Classical Mediterranean resistance to slavery has also been alluded to in modern representations of figures such as Spartacus, the leader of a slave revolt whose life is the subject of popular films. Spartacus is present in literature produced during the height of American slavery, such as the works of French writers who created novels and histories about the "avenger of the New World" and the "new Spartacus." These figures were created to entertain the possibility of a leader emerging to help enslaved people rebel against abuses (Troillot 1995: 84–85). From the seventeenth century, self-liberated African "Maroons" appeared in English, French, and Indian Ocean Creole (French) literature, where they became archetypes for pirates, outlaws, or characters "marooned on an island" (Alpers 2004; James 2002: 8, 13, 20–24; Mackie 2005). Mark Twain's classic *Huckleberry Finn* was all the more intriguing for its inclusion of a "runaway slave" as one of the leading characters. Contemporary novels continue to explore Maroon life and struggles in Jamaica and other settings (Cooper 1994).

Alliances between members of slaveholding groups and people who fought against enslavement also occurred in antiquity. Almost twelve hundred years ago (868C.E.), a group of enslaved east Africans known as "Zanj" rebelled against their Arabic captors. The revolt was the product of religious, political, and social issues that made it much more than a "slave rebellion" (Furlonge 1999). The enslaved Zanj joined free Africans, disaffected government soldiers, and local Muslims who were alienated by policies of the ruling Caliphate that imposed excessive taxes and blocked access to land (Popovic 1999). For over a decade, the Muslim-Zanj alliance controlled what is today the heartland of Iraq. Their cavalries and infantries captured cities such as Basra and protected rebel towns. Zanj settlements were comprised of mud brick houses, mosques, markets, treasuries, and other buildings. By 886C.E. the Zanj uprising was destroyed, but it was significant for its long survival and its demonstration of power against one of the most formidable empires in the world.

The four centuries of the transatlantic slave trade were preceded by a much longer series of slave trades that crossed the Sahara, linked east Africa and Arabia, and connected Asia to Africa (Alpers 2006; Harris 1971). Although Africans are often discussed as captives taken to foreign lands of enslavement, there were times when they imported slaves. For example, over a thousand years ago, an Abyssinian kingdom levied one thousand slaves per year from the Arabian Peninsula, which it controlled (Drake 1987). Africa also had its own internal slave trade. For example, within the area today known as Ghana, several forms of servitude existed in the eighteenth century: household servants controlled by small farmers; plantation slavery; porters controlled by merchants; and "court slaves" who served monarchs in domestic or sexual functions (concubines) (Stahl 1993: 42). Within African settings, people became enslaved largely because of debts or wars. Besides labor, people were acquired for use as wives, canoe paddlers, trading agents, and sacrificial offerings (Kopytoff and Miers 1977: 14).

In Africa, in contrast to American chattel slavery, slave status was not generally heritable (Lovejoy 1983). Thus the term "slave" may not be appropriate for all the forms of servitude that existed in Africa. A study that compares nineteenth-century African Americans in the Southern United States with a west African group known as the Fante provides additional support for the argument that slavery differed on opposing sides of the Atlantic. Penningroth (2003: 24, 43) notes that the Fante, neighbors of the Asante, practiced a form of servitude that marginalized people. However, this marginality was sometimes overcome by Africans who forged new social identities and accepted new kinship ties. These new family connections came with rights, access to more resources, protections, and entitlements, as well as obligations such as labor.

Resistance to enslavement in Africa took many forms. In the areas controlled by states such as Asante (Ghana), there were times when enslaved servants of the Asantehene (king) could find refuge in certain sacred groves. In neighboring kingdoms such as Dahomey and central African kingdoms such as Kongo, there were periods early on in the transatlantic trade when indigenous rulers opposed slaving. This opposition would dissolve over time, as local rulers in west and central Africa profited from slave trading. People escaped from bondage on the African mainland and island plantations (Miller 1988). In Gonja (modern Togo), local people fought enslavers who raided their settlements for cattle in the seventeenth and eighteenth centuries. According to oral traditions of a group called the Bassar, their ancestors avoided becoming enslaved by an invading cavalry by climbing hills the horsemen could not scale and rolling boulders on the attackers from hilltop enclaves (Debarros 1998: 71). Research on the Birim Valley, situated one hundred kilometers northeast of the slave-trading site called "El Mina," has suggested that earthworks were constructed as deterrents to slave hunting and kidnappings (Decorse 1992: 166–67). Scholars have posited that slave raiding was one reason for historic depopulation in this region.

Resistance to slavery also occurred in eastern Africa and outlying areas. For instance, in Mauritius, an island east of Africa, about twenty-one hundred people were involved in flight or rebellions that disrupted terrestrial bondage and slave ships between 1642 and 1831 (Allen 2004; Peerthum 2001: 110–12, 117). Archaeologists have begun to do research on Kenya's nineteenth-century self-liberated communities, known as *watoro* in Swahili (Wilson 2007). Although few eastern Africans were enslaved in the Americas, their presence was noted in documents from nineteenth-century northeastern Florida (Landers 1999). Around 1720, an enslaved man from Madagascar led a group of Africans on an escape route from a Jamaican plantation to mountain refuges near Deans Valley (Patterson 1979: 260).

Slavery and Opposition to It in the Americas

For many enslaved Africans, their captivity was not initiated or maintained solely by actions in the Americas. Similarly, resistance did not end after initial attempts at flight or self-defense in Africa. Slavery was the product of an extensive network of slave-trading agents (merchants or companies), slaveholders (including institutions), enslaving forces (bounty hunters and governments), consumers (of slavery's products), transshipment entrepôts, and enslavement events that reached across continents and oceans. While the Middle Passage across the Atlantic Ocean was an experience filled with many horrors and attempts to condition Africans to accept bondage, it was also the setting where captives demonstrated their ability to escape and rebel. Throughout the slavery era, seaports also provided Africans with opportunities and inspiration for escape. Some escapees were shipped by boat in crates, while others became stowaways. Various scholars have illuminated the role of ships and sailing in revolutionary acts, ideologies, and Pan-African communication, both during and after slavery. Gilroy observes:

> It has been estimated that at the end of the eighteenth century a quarter of the British Navy was composed of Africans for whom the experience of slavery was a powerful orientation to the ideologies of liberty and justice. Looking for similar patterns on the other side of the Atlantic network we . . . can track Denmark Vesey sailing the Caribbean and picking up inspirational stories of the Haitian revolution. . . . There is also the shining example of Frederick Douglass, whose autobiographies reveal that he learnt of freedom in the North from Irish sailors while working as a ship's caulker in Baltimore. He had less to say about the embarrassing fact that the vessels he readied for the ocean—Baltimore clippers—were slavers, the fastest ships in the world and the only craft capable of outrunning the British blockade. Douglass, who played a neglected role in English antislavery activity, escaped from bondage disguised as a sailor and

put this success down to his ability to "talk sailor like an old salt."
(1993: 13)

Because of maritime marronage, revolts, and flows of radical ideas, port
cities such as Charleston made free African sailors stay in confinement
onboard ships or in local jails when their vessels were anchored in harbor
(Billingsley 2007: 42).

Underwater and maritime archaeologists who have explored slave
ships have uncovered various things about enslaved people, such as the
wealth that was transported alongside them, and the circumstances under
which ships were destroyed and operated. Shackles are among the archaeological remains of slave ships such as the *Henrietta Marie*. They were
a heavy, flesh-tearing means of physical restraint that facilitated captivity
or punishment. They also hint at the ability of enslaved people to rise up,
attempt flight, or commit suicide (Brownell 2007: 102). Students of material culture have explored the ways in which shackles and chains became
part of abolitionist iconography and literature (songs and slogans, for instance). A famous image of a shackled African on bended knee begging
for freedom was manufactured by the English potter Josiah Wedgwood,
who produced the icon on medallions that publicized the abolitionist
cause. These ceramic (basalt-ware) and metal artifacts were sent to U.S.
citizens such as Benjamin Franklin. Franklin exemplifies the contradictions of the abolitionist cause: though he originally owned slaves, he later
freed them and became a vocal critic of slavery.

One of the most famous cases of successful African maritime resistance
happened aboard a ship called *La Amistad* (Jones 1987; Osagie 2000).
During the Amistad Rebellion, Africans rose up and took control of the
slave ship which was transporting them along the coast of Cuba. The enslaved Africans overpowered the crew and attempted to force the sailors
to take the ship back to Africa. However, the captive sailors succeeded in
guiding the ship toward New England. While self-liberated Africans such
as Sengbe ("Cinque") were ashore bartering for supplies, the *Amistad* was
apprehended by a U.S. naval patrol. It became a matter of international
controversy, as various litigants fought over Spanish rights to the ship
(the owner was from this nation) and the status (free or enslaved) of the
Africans onboard. Because the slave ship was attempting to transport enslaved people in defiance of the abolition of the slave trade, and because of

the efforts of abolitionists, the Africans who rebelled on *La Amistad* were freed and allowed to return to Africa.

Public exhibitions and representations of maritime rebellion have been popular in recent times. For instance, a collaborative project put into service "the *Freedom Schooner Amistad*," a ship that was reconstructed in order to raise people's consciousness about the original vessel and event. The *Freedom Schooner* has sailed around the Atlantic over the last few years, attempting to educate people about the Atlantic slave trade, African American sailing history, and rebellion at sea. Another type of public representation of maritime resistance involves Hollywood portrayals such as *Amistad* (1997). This was not the first film about African resistance to slavery, for *Roots* (1977), *Quilombo* (1987), and *Sankofa* (1993) also prominently feature the theme (Davis 2000). Similarly, plays in nations such as the United States and Brazil have also featured dramatic interpretations of struggles for freedom against slavery. For example, W.E.B. Du Bois created a theatrical production called *Haiti*, which portrayed the Haitian Revolution.

Slavery in the Americas

Slavery emerged in the Americas as a result of numerous conditions, agents, and causes. Ideology was as important as defeat in war or debt in justifying the enslavement of people. Dehumanization and the equation of enslaved people with animals played a crucial role in many societies' systems of slavery. As Kopytoff and Miers' (1977) edited volume on ethnographical and historical perspectives on African slavery reminds us, some of these conditions held for people who were not slaves throughout history. The theologies of various religions, including Christianity and Islam, were appropriated to justify and support slavery. However, rebellions and flight were also inspired by various religions. Many mainstream academics hold that race was a by-product of slavery, or at least its contemporary. Other scholars insist that ethnocentric precursors to race ideas and anti-African sentiments existed for centuries in the Islamic world and Europe (Harris 1982; Davis 2006; Drake 1987; Williams 1955). The enslavement of Africans was also part of wider colonial regimes. Colonial ideas concerning European rights to control foreign lands, maintain social superiority, and distance themselves from local people reinforced the development of unfree labor. Native American responses to colonial interactions were diverse. Indigenous people became enslaved as a result of native and foreign slave traders' raids for human captives, regional wars, devastating diseases, disunity among native groups, and the conversion of native people to materialistic economic beliefs. Colonial slave systems were also driven by martial and transportation technologies, as well as European (and American) demand for commodities. The ultimate character of transatlantic slavery, if one can be determined, has been shaped by two perspectives, which Egerton summarizes: "The debate over whether slave systems in the Americas were a curious variety of capitalism or a modern form of seigneurialism that rested uneasily within the framework of the Atlantic trading world is an old one, and one that gives no indication of resolution" (2006: 637).

Slavery systems varied according to the climates, colonial regimes, demographics, and crops or resources extracted in each locale. Other variables affecting slavery included idiosyncratic events, motives of slaveholders, legal conventions, and commodity trading practices. Resistance to slavery took unique forms in each setting as a result of resistors' decisions about these circumstances. For centuries, crops such as sugar were cultivated in the Mediterranean and Atlantic Islands, setting the stage for the transfer of technology, capital, and organization to American plantations. Although crops like coffee and tobacco were important to certain slavery systems, sugar was the primary focus of many plantations, especially in the Caribbean and mainland South America. In the early 1500s, soon after the first sugar plantations and cattle ranches were established by relatives of Columbus on Española (today the Dominican Republic), enslaved people there began rebelling and escaping (Garcia Arevalo and Arrom 1986). However, Native Americans, not Africans, were the first major population to suffer enslavement in the Western Hemisphere. For this reason, they would also become the first to rebel and escape from Western slavery (Arrom and Garcia Arevalo 1986). Decades of massive indigenous deaths, episodes of local resistance, and changing European sentiments convinced colonial regimes to shift to other forms of native exploitation. For example, *encomienda* systems demanded labor from landbound indigenous inhabitants. Another important result of these factors was that Africans became a new target for slave labor. European attempts to maintain post-conquest control over Native Americans were met with flight and rebellions which occasionally involved Africans (Forbes 1993). European indentured servants also fulfilled colonial demand for workers, and they became "runaways" themselves, sometimes alongside Africans and indigenous people.

Myriad Antislavery Forms

In different places and times, various avenues were taken in quests for freedom from slavery. People used their voices for ideological self-defense, consciousness-raising, and attacks on slaveholding. Letters, speeches, or verbal pleas for emancipation were made to slaveholders and politicians (Harding 1981; Gilroy 1993). Enslaved people forged or acquired passes that allowed them to remain mobile, even if encountered by patrols outside of their work zones (Peerthum 2001: 116). In some places, self-liberated Africans used vocal harassment to distract proslavery forces from noticing Africans (Americans) evacuating from villages under attack and to disrupt attackers' sleep (Katz 1986: 45). Agents of slavery were physically attacked or challenged when enforcing bondage. In retaliation for the abuses they faced, enslaved people destroyed tools, crops, and buildings. More accommodationist methods were also employed, such as people purchasing their freedom or being purchased by family and set free (Billingsley 2007: 44). Enslaved people were sometimes emancipated by their owners' wills (Weik 2008: 110). Similarly, some states enacted laws that granted mass emancipations. Some self-liberated communities built defenses such as pit traps or dead-end trails to confound pursuers. The determination and resourcefulness of armed resisters is exemplified by their willingness to use whatever was available—pebbles, coin fragments, and even buttons—for ammunition when bullets were scarce (Katz 1986: 45). A man in Venezuela who escaped from enslavement to a military officer went a step further by capturing his former master, tying him to a public whipping post, and giving him lashes before the townspeople (Acosta Saignes 1967). In this case, justice or revenge was as important as freedom in determining the individual's method of resistance.

South Carolina was the scene for two of the most unique instances of liberation from slavery. Denmark Vesey, who led the later rebellion named after him, achieved his freedom after winning fifteen hundred dollars in the lottery and bargaining for his own self-purchase (Penningroth 2003: 45). This was during a time when enslaved people were regarded as property, and as such could not legally own anything themselves. Exceptions did exist in the form of laws that allowed enslaved people to obtain personal property if their "owner" granted permission. Despite the existence of prohibitive laws, enslaved people in South Carolina and elsewhere engaged in substantial market activity (Egerton 2006; Hauser 2008). Robert Smalls, who later became one of South Carolina's first well-known black politicians, took advantage of the gaps in the system created by the lack of uniform adherence to laws. Smalls purchased his family while he was still enslaved. His family and friends would later help him capture the Confederate ship that he piloted during the U.S. Civil War. Hence, fortune, economic participation, legal loopholes, and negotiations were a part of the circumstantial universe that facilitated freedom.

The physical environments of antislavery activities were crucial factors in the success or failure of resistance. Inaccessible locations in mountainous areas have been particularly appealing locations for rebels who have defied servitude and political oppression throughout history. Hilly enclaves protected self-liberated communities, escaping groups, and lone escapees in places such as the Sierra de Baoruco (Dominican Republic), the Blue Mountains (Jamaica), and Monte Orizaba (Mexico). Narrow mountain passes, thick brush, and streams added to the burdens (such as hauling heavy cannons or moving large numbers of troops) that slowed proslavery forces in their pursuit of escapees. Wetlands and rivers on the Florida peninsula and the Surinamese interior bogged down bounty hunters and armies sent to capture or destroy African escapees. Grasses at various elevations shielded people, and certain varieties were razor-sharp impediments to slave catchers. Likewise, the rivers, swamps, and forests in the Venezuelan interior protected Native American and Maroon groups (Perez 2002). Whether in highland or lowland areas, vegetation and topography helped people elude pursuers, conduct guerilla warfare, feed themselves, obtain raw materials for trade, and remain hidden.

Revolts were sometimes catalysts for escape and sometimes ends in themselves. Orlando Patterson argued that "Maroon" activities in Jamaica were all inseparable from rebellions. He delineated important conditions that encouraged rebellions: enslaved people constituting overwhelming numerical majorities; low numbers of *locally born* bond-persons, compared to enslaved Africans; large numbers of enslaved persons who shared common ethnicity; rugged conditions conducive to guerrilla war; a high proportion of absentee slaveholders (rarely present or in temporary residence); monopolies maintained by massive business entities; a lack of shared cultural identity or beliefs among the colonial population;

low female-to-male ratios in the European (American) dominant groups (1979 [1970]: 288). Rebellions had international political implications, such as their utility to abolitionists and their consequences for colonial control. As a result, revolts were among the factors that helped convince the British government to end Caribbean slavery (or at least compromise by paying off planters for their slaves and enforcing apprenticeship periods) (Matthews 2006).

Most of the earliest research on African resistance against slavery focused on the Caribbean and Latin America. This may in part reflect the empirical data that exist on the scale and scope of antislavery resistance. However, years of scholarship has demonstrated that significant North American resistance to slavery also existed (Franklin and Schweninger 1999; Landers 1992; Mullins 1979). Herbert Aptheker (1939) documented at least fifty groups or communities of self-liberated Africans (Americans) and various rebellions. His work challenged the idea that people of African descent in the United States (or earlier colonies) were docile and unlikely to rebel against slavery or build Maroon enclaves. The history and anthropology of antislavery resistance and rebellion continues to grow steadily and has expanded to include more of North America's underrepresented role in such discussions (Blight 2004; Egerton 2006; Landers 1990; Lockley 2008; Sayers 2004; Smith 2003; Thompson 2006).

Although a number of contemporary scholars link the Underground Railroad to earlier resistance efforts in other parts of North America, its specific etymology and trajectory—as a public discourse and a form of social action—are rooted in the early nineteenth-century U.S. North and its borderlands. American laws suggest that proslavery supporters maintained an ongoing battle against resistance (for example, the Fugitive Slave Laws enacted during 1793 and 1850). The landscape of the Underground Railroad included attics, barns, belfries, rooms, wood stacks, hay piles, cellars, and churches (Seibert 1898: 63; Vlach 2004). Both men and women, free and enslaved, were involved with it, as is the case with antislavery activities in other times and places. The National Underground Railroad Network to Freedom Act (1997) has promoted the recognition and preservation of hundreds of historic structures and a slowly growing number of archaeological sites, which has been aided by the National Park Service's UGRR Network to Freedom Program (Morrison 1998).

Throughout the twentieth century, an increasing number of scholars came to argue that earlier interpretations emphasizing white abolitionists'

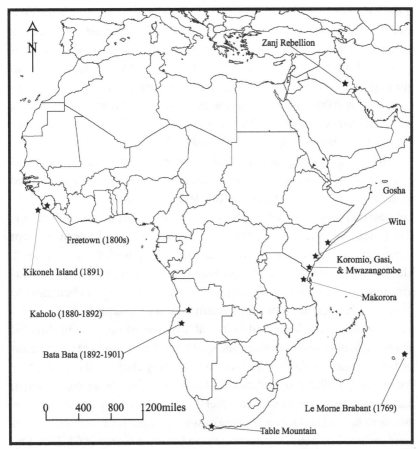

Map 2.1. Select locations of African antislavery rebellion and self-liberation. Map by Terrance Weik.

leading role in the Underground Railroad have to be discarded in favor of a comprehensive view that also recognizes the crucial role of African descendents who were free or who fled to freedom (Gara 1961; Smith 1998). The tactics of leaders such as Harriet Tubman involved publicity and antipublicity (tearing down "wanted" posters) campaigns, armed confrontation, divinely inspired guidance, personal intuition, and pharmaceutical knowledge (for example, paregoric used to sedate babies) (Seibert 1898: 187). The Underground Railroad was connected to other resistance efforts in the world. Some abolitionists in Europe and the Americas communicated and coordinated events. The Haitian Revolution instilled fear in slaveholders and inspired a number of free and bonded opponents of slavery (James 1938; Scott 1985). Associations such as the New York Vigilance Committee, run by leaders such as David Ruggles, established rules of engagement, strategies for maintaining secrecy, tactics to eliminate enemies or traitors, and methods for mobilization. Archaeologists are beginning to consider how they can make contributions to Ruggles' story (Ziegenbein 2009). John Brown, the leader of one of the most publicized rebellions against slavery in North America, helped organize a vigilance association called the "League of Gileadites."

Slavery regimes responded to resistance in diverse ways. Punishments and executions were so cruel as to rival the worst forms of bloodshed found in modern horror films, police television shows, and literature. Dismemberment, burning alive, whipping, confinement in stocks, hanging, attachment to metal collars, branding, deportment, and sale away from family and friends are among the many types of punishments employed. The spectacles of torture and execution that made examples of conspirators and innocents following revolts greatly reduced open challenges to slavery and escape attempts. Eighteenth-century Cuba provides examples of the multiple methods and systematic nature of oppression directed against self-liberated communities: specialized laws were created to control each region; militias were formed to destroy settlements and capture "runaways"; military operations in different regions were coordinated; patrols were well-positioned to observe escape routes; plans and strategies were formulated for each phase of suppression; destroyed settlements were revisited by patrols to prevent reuse (La Rosa Corzo 2003: 250). Despite the multitude of oppressive measures in use and the changing nature of the enslaved majority (for example, the demographic shift in the number of African- to American-born members of the enslaved population), resistance was never completely eradicated in slave societies.

From the Americas to Africa, From Past to Present

For a portion of the enslaved population, consciousness of Africa—memories of homelands, knowledge of a place that symbolized shared heritage, and visions of an alternative haven for freedom-seekers—was never fully eliminated (Stuckey 1985). During and after slavery, self-liberated, free, and formerly enslaved African descendants returned to Africa. The history of Jamaica's Trelawney Town Maroons provides an instance of the relocation of formerly enslaved people back to Africa, though in a less ideal, semi-forced migration. By the 1790s, these western Jamaica Maroons were at odds with colonists and slaveholders (Campbell 1990). After a war with colonial forces, most of these Maroons were deported to Nova Scotia, where they endured the cold climate along with other people seeking a refuge from slavery (Campbell 1993). This case of exile highlights the contradictions inherent within the growing British Empire, which allowed for the simultaneous support of abolition and enslavement, as well as the establishment of colonies populated by African descendants (for example, black former soldiers that served in England's various wars). The War of 1812 and the American Revolution created opportunities for enslaved people to escape by the thousands into the care of British forces, who took advantage of the opportunity to disrupt slavery-dependent U.S. economies. Besides Canada, the Bahamas and Bermuda were destinations for African descendants escaping to British colonial armies. After many frustrations with the climate and economic opportunities in Nova Scotia, the Trelawney Maroons joined "Black Loyalists" and other Africans (Americans) in their migration to the Sierra Leone colony. Another type of back-to-Africa event occurred in the twentieth century, when Surinamese descendants of self-liberated Africans joined a delegation (aided by a scholar) which traveled to west African countries such as Ghana, Togo, and Nigeria (de Groot 1979: 389–98).

Slavery and resistance continue to have relevance for human affairs. Asians and Africans were enslaved into the twentieth century in colonial British holdings such as the "Aden Protectorate" (Miers 2004). Slavery still persists in various parts of the world, despite the history of international efforts against it. The National Underground Railroad Freedom Center, an organization in Cincinnati, Ohio, that commemorates the Underground Railroad, has addressed this global problem in part by supporting a program that creates awareness about the need to eradicate present-day slavery. Indeed, the legacy of slavery can be seen in modern homes in the form of sugar. This product rose to global prominence with the aid of slave labor, and today it is generally found on the labels of packaged foods, though its overconsumption has had costly effects on human health (it is linked to a higher incidence of type II diabetes, among other problems). Specialized markets foster trade in this commodity, and a number of countries depend on the agro-industrial complexes that use sugar to service the human food supply. In places like the Dominican Republic, people still cut sugarcane by hand, load it onto cattle-drawn carts, and endure control and exploitation that are not far removed from some forms of forced servitude.

During a visit to Jamaica in the 1990s, a Maroon descendant explained to me how he (and others from his region) occasionally migrated for work, servicing the sugarcane industry in South Florida. This ironic link between sugar production and migrant laborers whose ancestors had fled from slavery on sugar plantations reflects the reach of long-term, global, political-economic, racialized, and gendered forces of inequality. Harrison's ethnographic research on urban Jamaica points to a range of factors that likely affect Maroon descendants' decisions about labor and migration: U.S. politics that favor sugar producers and neglect to protect the environment or migrant workers in Florida; U.S. and European domination (or intervention) in Caribbean politics and economics; structural adjustment programs that devalue currency and fail to protect local businesses against the powers of multinational corporations (for example, to underprice milk or crops); diasporic drugs and arms trading; economic policies that promote male privilege; "democratic clientelism"; gang and state violence; and the declining viability of island agriculture (2008: 100, 155, 197). Clearly, there remains a need for more reflection on the significance of mobility, resistance, and freedom for the descendants of self-liberated people and other Africans around the world.

Summary

From the preceding historical sketch of captive African labor and slave trading, it is clear that resistance against bondage was a phenomenon that manifested itself in diverse ways around the world, based on a great range of circumstances. Particular social, cultural, environmental, and individual dimensions have to be assessed in order to explain the idiosyncrasies, similarities, and patterns of antislavery resistance in different colonies and countries. While the existence of slavery is a somewhat sad topic to reflect on, in terms of what it says about human capabilities for exploitation and violence, it serves as a useful reminder of the need for vigilant attention to the state of global human rights. It is also encouraging to realize the depth of human ingenuity and will, which have demonstrated great potential for taking advantage of opportunities to realize freedom and pursue social change or justice.

Some self-liberated Africans (and their descendents) realized freedom and returned to the continent of their ancestors. Once there, they had to face new challenges that emerged from colonialism and its post-independence consequences. The fight for human rights has continued into the twentieth and twenty-first centuries, as the descendents of antislavery rebels struggle in political arenas and on battlefields. Attempts have been made to take their land or dismantle communal landholdings protecting them from taxation and speculation (Bilby 2005; Price and Price 1992: 112; Price 1998). Likewise, the descendants of people who were liberated through underground networks or official emancipation continue to struggle against different levels of racial, gender, and/or economic injustice.

For millennia, oral and written sources have informed, aroused, and entertained people with stories and memories of defiance against forced labor. Archaeologists are now in a position to help material culture gain a voice in this discourse. Important themes not raised here (for example, intercommunity politics, economic activities, social organization, subsistence strategies, government, and treaties) will be examined in specific contexts during later discussions of archaeological projects. Likewise, other issues raised by antislavery resistance researchers in the Philippines, China, the Indian Ocean, and Korea may some day attract the attention of archaeologists (Alpers, Gwyn, and Salman 2005; Allen 2004; Alpers 2003; Campbell and Alpers 2004; Salman 2004).

3

Resistance, Freedom, Networks, and Ethnogenesis in Theory and Practice

The aim of this chapter is to develop an anthropological framework that can aid later archaeological analyses and interpretations of antislavery resistance, flight from slavery, and self-liberated African diasporic communities. The best explanations for antislavery phenomena examine the actions, cultural practices, and ideas that animate historical settings and inform theories. I advocate explicitly theorizing struggles against slavery by exploring the role of resistance, freedom, liberation, ethnogenesis, and networks in scholarship and thought on the African diaspora. This "theoretical pluralism" (compare Voss 2008) ensures that discussions are broad enough to cover possibilities and patterns in human behavior. At the same time, this approach suggests ways to avoid weaknesses in previous research, such as the tendency to examine antislavery events according to certain conceptual dichotomies and biases (for example, emphasizing physical resistance over other varieties). By answering fundamental questions, the complexities of resistance against slavery become clearer. How can studies of resistance be used to understand the interpretive and methodological challenges concerning Africans who defied slavery? How might theories of freedom (and liberation) broaden our analyses to contemplate the conditions and ideological contexts of the African diaspora? How did self-liberated African (American) communities operate and perpetuate themselves?

Conceptualizing Resistance

One of the central propositions advanced in this book is that resistance is more than physical acts, defiant thoughts, or conflictual events. It is also a concept that refers to ways that opposition to control, conformity, or destruction are interconnected with other social forces and subjectivities. Furthermore, resistance is not reactionary for all who participate in it (Hegland 2003: 428). This working definition is the product of an intellectual genealogy that will be explored in order to discern nuances and patterns which can be used to interpret evidence, foster analysis, and synthesize findings in the following chapters.

Although this book is more about the nature of resistance than the causes, briefly addressing the latter can illustrate the complexities that inform explanations of human resistance. Slavery involved multiple forms of brutality, violation, and destruction (Painter 1995; White 2004; Thompson 2006: 14, 24, 27), however the harsh physical experiences of "chattel slavery" are only the most obvious reasons why people fled or resisted bondage. Psychological terror and anguish such as that created by the threat or act of being sold away from family and friends was equally damaging. It could both suppress the desire to escape and cause people to flee in pursuit of loved ones. Likewise, free people (European and African Americans) who aided escaped slaves had various motives, some of them self-serving, personal, or uncomplicated. For example, slave owners sometimes harbored escapees from other plantations because they benefitted from the extra free labor that these refugees provided. Enslaved people of the present day continue to develop various methods of coping with, resisting, or escaping debt-bondage, sexual servitude, and other forms of forced labor (Sage and Kasten 2006). Hence, no single generalization can adequately describe people's reactions or initiatives in resistance, nor their engagements with authorities, peers, and indifferent actors.

As my historical synopsis in the previous chapter has demonstrated, resistance has manifested itself in a vast array of forms. Similarly, wider thought on topics such as enslavement, peasant revolts, Native American uprisings, Muslim women, Nepali conflicts with Maoists, and Irish anti-colonialism have moved the discussion from earlier dichotomous categorizations of "passive versus active" forms of resistance to a more nuanced understanding of the wide continuum of relations, beliefs, and behaviors within which resistance operated (Abu Lughod 1990; Delle 1999; Geggus 1982; Hegland 2003; Martin 1991; Patterson 1979; Scott 1985; Shah 2008; Stern 1987).

The study of resistance as an explicit concept for social analysis expanded greatly in the twentieth century, catching the attention of intellectuals, politicians, soldiers, activists, artists, and oppressed people around the world. Human rights and national independence struggles prompted armed and nonviolent resistance, civil disobedience, demonstrations, and other oppositional strategies (Okihiro 1986). Cultural nationalism, vindicationism, and Marxism also prompted academic discourses on resistance (Thornton 1993: 272). Concepts such as agency and concerns for the masses of nonelite people in history have also contributed to the discourse by stressing the need to account for the nonnormative actor in theory as well as by calling into question top-down or elite perspectives that have shaped many primary sources and older ethnographies (Deagan 1982; Leone, Laroche, and Babiarz 2005; Scott 1985). Revolutionaries and scholars have found resistance to be a useful concept for their movements and studies because it shifts the focus of inquiry and engagement from domination to the concerns and acts of less-powerful people. However, it is important to have a balanced perspective that accounts for interactions between different people and interests within ever-shifting webs of power (Foucault 1978, 1982; Abu Lughod 1990).

Resistance is a form of power that is accessible to all people in some way (Hegland 2003: 428; Kondo 1990; Paynter and McGuire 1991: 10; Reed-Danahay 1993; Scott 1990). This insight has come as much from African and diaspora thinkers and liberation-seekers as it has from mainstream theoretical discourses. A case in point is Frederick Douglass, a man who escaped from slavery and became a famous activist and social critic. His "West Indies Emancipation" speech (1857) contains some well-known passages that speak volumes about resistance to North American slavery and other contexts of exploitation:

The whole history of the progress of human liberty shows that all concessions yet made to her august claims, have been born of earnest struggle. . . . This struggle may be a moral one, or it may be a physical one, and it may be both moral and physical, but it must be a struggle. Power concedes nothing without a demand. . . . Find out just what any people will quietly submit to and you have found out the exact measure of injustice and wrong which will be imposed upon them, and these will continue till they are resisted with either words or blows, or with both. . . . If we ever get free from the oppressions and wrongs heaped upon us, we must pay for their removal.

We must do this by labor, by suffering, by sacrifice, and if needs be, by our lives and the lives of others.

This passage represents a sliver in the evolution of Douglass's thought and an excerpt from a larger reflection on notions of progress, Christian values, emancipation, politics, and freedom. But for the purposes of understanding resistance, his particular emphasis on themes such as struggle are important. The notion of struggle is found in the writings of other diaspora and postcolonial writer-activists (such as Cabral 1973), and in historical and ethnographic works, which see the methodological value struggles have for demonstrating the flows, capacities, influences, and other facets of power (compare Abu-Lughod 1990: 47; Scott 1985: 29). A good illustration of these facets can be found in the Comaroffs' (1991) work on colonial religion in South Africa, which uncovers the dialectical interchanges between colonists and indigenous people, each affecting the other's forms of empowerment and weakness.

Archaeologists who have studied resistance have demonstrated that their methods can detect physical remnants of struggle. The "Northern Cheyenne Outbreak" is an example of a resistance event that archaeologists have examined; it involved armed Native American opposition to U.S. military control (McDonald et. al. 1991). Archaeologists excavated an area where a showdown between fleeing Cheyenne families and U.S. soldiers who were sent to return them to a reservation took place. When distribution patterns of bullets at the site were juxtaposed with Cheyenne oral histories and U.S. military records, it became clear how different forms of evidence and different groups' perspectives tell conflicting stories about the nature of historical clashes.

Although dramatic cases such as the Cheyenne Outbreak are alluring, they should not obscure the fact that resistance need not be violent, explicit, formal, or systematic in order to be significant (Abu-Lughod 1990; Kondo 1990; Scott 1985). Enslaved Africans, Asian peasants, and other historical populations engaged in foot-dragging, arson, pilfering, slander, and feigned ignorance in defiance of labor demands or economic inequalities (Hunter 1997: 16; Thompson 2006). Scott (1985: 29, 184) refers to this as "everyday resistance," quotidian acts or social practices that represent masked political expressions, or "hidden transcripts," which are pragmatic responses to the retaliatory powers of governments that enact violent, dramatic domination (compare Reed Danahay 1993). Some archaeologists have also stated their concern for everyday life, claiming that they uncover insights about it in the past, particularly areas of it that were taken for granted, ignored, or unseen by chroniclers (see parallel arguments in Fitts 1996: 69; Scott 1985). Similarly, seemingly inconsequential acts of consumption represent resistance in contexts such as the bedouin society in which Abu-Lughod (1990: 43) observed females secretly smoking. These acts implicated wider social relations involving children who acted as women's lookouts and conflicts rooted in gender-biased codes of morality. Researchers can apply these insights to antislavery resistance by challenging perspectives that devalue certain resistance cases because they failed to create immediate social change, demonstrate military victory, amount to great numbers of physical acts, or take dramatic material form. For the African in flight from slavery, the assistance of unnamed enslaved (as described in WPA and Underground Railroad narratives) or free people, people who may or may not have had strong opinions about slavery, was no less important to their success than were publically militant abolitionists or revolt leaders.

The notion of resistance hidden in subtle cultural expressions or cloaked by daily practices alludes to literal acts and spaces of concealment. Concealment was a primary means of resistance during slavery, and this became manifest as escapees used natural enclaves, buildings, workspaces, vehicles, boats, and shipping containers to hide in or facilitate flight. Material traces of cloaked struggles against control have been discerned by archaeologists working on nineteenth-century Euro-American servants' quarters and cotton mill workers' boardinghouses in the northeastern United States, enslaved persons' covert meeting places in New England, and enslaved African villages in Cuba and the eastern United States. In each of these cases, caches of alcohol were found in hidden or private places, such as subfloor house-pits or waste-disposal areas, where workers could conceal the traces of their resistance to employers' (or slaveholders') moral policies (Beaudry et. al. 1991; Fitts 1996; Smith 2008: 78). These studies demonstrate the capability of archaeologists to detect physical and ideational manifestations of resistant power in residences of the oppressed and marginal spaces.

However, spatial expressions of social conflict have a wider significance that transcends covert consumption and storage and becomes discernable with the help of landscape analyses. The concept of landscape signifies human experiences and relations with environments. These relations are apparent in the histories of modern guerrilla forces and Maroon societies, groups that benefitted from environmental knowledge of rural and urban places, which enabled them to subsist, hide from enemies, and ambush enslavers (Cabral 1973; Perez 2000: 616). A number of people who fled North American bondage attributed their success to the utility of the North Star as a geographical guide (Gara 1961: 60). Beyond these strategic uses, one could study cultural landscapes, intersections of ecologies, worldviews, ways of life, and transformations of the earth (Ashmore 2002; Branton 2009; Ingold 1993). Slave owners used landscapes to project their control over land and people, express their ideology (for example, Georgian mindsets), capitalize on captive labor, and demonstrate their status. Many slave owners maintained their power by convincing captive laborers that slavery's reach and presence was unlimited. Conversely, Africans (Americans) who escaped were motivated by known or imagined places where they could find refuge or release from bondage (Nassy Brown 2000: 341).

Fitts' examination of eighteenth-century New England brings into focus the central importance of proximity in shaping struggles within the institution of U.S. slavery (1996: 57–61). He used oral histories and documents such as probate records to show how slaveholders' co-residence with bond-persons allowed for control through increased surveillance. Distancing and separation were also proxemic mechanisms of hegemony, which materialized in segregationist policies (for example, in churches) that further reinforced control and exclusion. Enslaved persons used their agency to circumvent some aspects of domination. For instance, those who lived in separate quarters used their seclusion from overseers or planters to socialize the youth (for example, on coping strategies), plan resistance, practice outlawed ancestral traditions, and/or express outrage at the system. For long- or short-term escapees, distancing themselves from slavery was one of the most effective ways of finding concealment and relief from oppression. Archaeological approaches to the African diaspora have demonstrated that exploring the landscapes of slavery on broader scales beyond residences further illuminates the wider context of power relations. For example, captive laborers in places such as Jamaica eventually gained some autonomy as they reconfigured their village layouts. However, slaveholders retained their ability to dominate aggregate plantation layouts and regional settlement (Armstrong 2003: 108; Delle 1998).

On the other hand, archaeologists working in Cuba and South Carolina have found that plantation owners actively (re)configured their estates and captive workers' housing to address rebellions and escape (Barile 1999; Singleton 2001).

In the preceding discussions of power, landscapes, and hidden behaviors, glimpses of culture appear that hint at influential factors and tangible expressions of resistance. Culture is a powerful medium through which oppression, resistance, accommodation, indifference, and other aspects of social life are evaluated and enacted (Cabral 1973; Scott 1990: 184; Shah 2008: 490). Some earlier histories of Maroons and slave rebellions framed their discussions in terms of "restorationist" (attempting to re-create African institutions) versus "creationist" (newly created) goals and cultural processes, which in part reflected legacies of the Herskovits and Frazier debates about assimilation and survival in the African diaspora of the Americas (compare Yelvington 1999). Research need not focus on one type of goal to the exclusion of the other, as both were relevant to antislavery activities and self-liberated communities. The importance of both continuity and change has been noted in archaeologies of Native American revolt, nativism, and revitalization (Weisman 2007; Leibman 2008). These tensions will be explored further in chapter 6, in an African-Seminole context.

The challenges of defining resistance and distinguishing it from other behaviors and ideologies become apparent when one considers its interrelation with material practices and survival (compare Hollander and Einwohner 2004: 544). Ferguson (1991) argues that enslaved Africans on Southern plantations created a pottery tradition that included the use of religious symbols (incised x's) that were a form of "unconscious" defiance against a slavocracy that denied the value of African culture. In other words, he posits that the act of potting and religious inscription was an uncalculated expression of African cultural persistence or resiliency. It is difficult to differentiate resiliency and survival from resistance. In the context of many slave societies where African expressions such as drumming were denigrated or outlawed by Eurocentric authorities, culture became a point of resistance. And Ferguson's "unconscious resistance" is not hard to imagine. It could be conceived of like the defense mechanism that raises one's arm to deflect an attacker's unexpected blow. Cultural persistence and self-preservation have been alternative or coexistent motivations for peoples' actions, alongside physical resistance (Ortner 1995: 175). There need not be an either/or basis for evaluating acts or processes that might at first glance appear to be solely resistance. Conversely, all survival is not resistance. Ultimately, Ferguson's archaeological interpretations have to be weighed against the possible relevance of the colonoware pottery marks to Christian symbolism, African American magical practices, and personalized meanings (Gundaker 2001).

These debates about colonoware pottery exemplify the challenges that students of resistance face as a result of the diverse and changing meanings of actions and things. For example, events that are criminalized at one point in time are praised as liberatory at others (Ortner 1995: 175). Similarly, there are cases where the ideological or physical tools of domination are later turned on the oppressors themselves (Comaroff 1985). A long-term view is useful, for resistance is transformed as it engages with shifts in modes of exploitation and balances of power.

The material culture and built environment of antislavery resistance have been stimulating catalysts for intellectual and public discourses about how to understand their role in the past and present. The variant meanings attached to buildings constructed as memorials for John Brown's raid of the armory (reconstructed as an "engine house") at Harpers Ferry, West Virginia, further illustrates this point. As Schackel (1995) notes, "the engine house, occupied by Brown and his followers during his attempted capture of Harpers Ferry, is an unstable socio-cultural symbol among the white community, while it has been a stable icon among the black community." Put another way, the local white community has shifted from largely seeing the Harpers Ferry engine house as negative in the past to today having both positive and ambivalent attitudes toward the historical antislavery event; most publicized African American commentators have consistently seen it as a moral act of liberation from slavery. Archaeologists who study resistance would do well to remain cognizant of the heterogeneity of motivations and backgrounds shaping chroniclers and audiences who give historical actions and artifacts meanings.

A problem in some resistance studies arises from their neglecting to see the complexities of social groups, individuals, and conflicts (Ortner 1995: 177). In other words, beyond the battle between resisters and dominators, there are multiple levels of contention within and between each of these (and other) involved entities. Inequalities and injustices are also potential products of resisters within their own spheres of influence (Brown 1995). Resisters, dominators, and other social actors who fall outside this dichotomy have to be seen in all their intricacy, historicity, subjectivity, and cultural complexity (Ortner 1995: 186; Ortner 1997). Power is not the only goal of resisters, for dignity, identity, and self-expression also move people to confront or circumvent control and oppression (Cabral 1973; Hegland 2003: 428). There are instances where resisters have accommodated or even supported structures of domination. All this is to say that social actors are multidimensional agents whose layered identities and concerns create ambiguities and contradictions, which affect the outcome of any situation.

Resistance can also be conceived of as a product of various modes of knowledge production (philosophy, cosmology, and so forth) that crosscuts the arenas of thought and practice. According to Karenga (2006: 258), resistance is a living tradition that is at the core of the "Africana philosophical enterprise." Resistance, in this perspective, is using the mind to confront and eliminate any form of oppression (based on race, sex, or class, for instance) and to promote creativity and justice. Although their contributions to philosophies of American life and slavery are often neglected, the thinking of some formerly enslaved people deserves attention because of the implications of their reflections on crucial issues such as ethics (McGary and Lawson 1992). For example, Harriet Jacobs, an escapee, noted that "the condition of a slave confuses all principles of morality, and, in fact, renders the practice of them impossible" (quoted in Bradely 1994: 111). Maroon raids against plantations (for recruits or arms) and enslaved people's "theft" of their captors' possessions (such as food) take on a new light when considered from a perspective that accounts for the injustices that they suffered, such as the theft of their freedom. As raids are part of self-liberated people's procurement methods, archaeologists have to be prepared to frame these aggressive acts of economy in their full context, which includes the hypocrisy of slave societies.

Karenga (2006: 263) identifies resistance as an ancient tradition among people of African descent, one that reaches back to the struggle of ancient Egyptians against the invasion of the Hyksos. Classical African civilizations such as ancient Egypt (KMT) are esteemed as the foundation of Afrocentric and (some) Africana studies. However, representations of Egypt have also shaped African descendants' ideas in ways that cast it in a less liberatory light. The story of Moses and the exodus from the oppression of the Pharaohs has had an explicit presence in spirituals, print media, African American church services, and scholarship from the days of slavery and abolitionism to the present (Glaude 2004: 296; Raboteau 1986; Siebert 1898: 185). Antislavery activists such as Harriet Tubman have been identified with the biblical role of Moses. Archaeological views on her life will be considered in a later chapter.

Conceptualizing Freedom and Liberation

Freedom was among the most important motivations that moved Africans and their descendants to fight against the demands of enslavement. Regardless of whether freedom was the central cause of a resistance event, it is useful for gauging the agency of the enslaved and the consequences of life beyond bondage. Freedom can be approached as an ideological corpus that inspired resistance or as a concept for measuring possibilities and conditions. Ultimately, it is best to see freedom as a process connecting ideas, actions, and circumstances, rather than a destination or static state (Hilliard 1985: vi). Kofi Agorsah (2001: xx) situated archaeology in a multidisciplinary dialogue on the global African "journey to freedom" in his edited volume *Freedom in Black History and Culture*. However, it is crucial that we critically examine freedom's (and synonyms such as "liberation" and "liberty") global ideological baggage, which contains contradictions, abuses, and ambiguities. These broad usages will inform my approach by providing an aggregate context for interpretations and a basis for analyses of the causes, consequences, and cultural beliefs that shaped resistance to slavery.

Freedom's theoretical utility is addressed below in my review of anthropological works, which comprise a small part of a larger discourse. As late as 2002, Laidlaw lamented that "freedom is a concept about which anthropology has had strikingly little to say." However, anthropologists have explicitly grappled with the concept for at least three-quarters of a century (Boas 1940: 376; Bidney 1963; Englund 2006; Malinowski 1944). From a cross-cultural, long-term perspective, the meanings and manifestations of slavery and freedom are not self-evident, universally defined, uniformly held, or fixed (Boas 1940: 376; Malinowski 1944: 45; Patterson 1991; Urban 2008: 225). Concepts of slavery and freedom have been debated for millennia, and some scholars argue that the latter's development was dependent on the former (Davis 2006; Fischer 2005: 728; Patterson 1991). For example, ancient Mediterranean iterations of the word "liberty" connote freedom from enslavement and refer to a status that marked free people as possessors of many political rights (Fischer 2005: 7).[1] A number of thinkers have examined various conceptualizations such as libertarianism, "philosophies of free living," spiritual divestment from materialistic desires, mental release from emotional suffering, escapism, and legal or political definitions (Malinowski 1944: 46, 53, 80; Patterson 1991; Fischer 2005: 722–36). As my goal here is not to intensively review histories of freedom ideas, I leave that task to scholars engaged in wider syntheses and criticisms of political, theological, philosophical, and other discourses (for example, Englund 2006: 2–4; Raz 1986; Malinowski 1944: 43–55; Patterson 1991; Skinner 1998).

In the context of colonial societies, the social lines between bondage and freedom were made clear through laws, the use of force, oral and written philosophies, and institutional practices. Whether born free, emancipated, or self-liberated, people had to deal with the bitter reality of persistent racism in "free" and "slave" states. The legislation that made people free did not preclude other customs and laws from curtailing their access to trades or social spaces, restricting their movement, and/ or subjecting them to abuses (Mintz 1996: 34). Slaveholders attempted to rationalize freedom as compatible with slavery by denying that Africans fully deserved human rights (Urban 2008: 224). Nevertheless, histories of resistance demonstrate that captive laborers were not all convinced that their identity was encapsulated in a "slave" status. While ideas of freedom and resistance developed by European (American) philosophers, abolitionists, and slavery proponents may have influenced enslaved people, there is no reason to assume that all peoples' rationales for flight, revolt, or subtler forms of defiance were derived from external sources.

The narratives, public speeches, letters, and oral traditions of formerly enslaved people and free-born Africans throughout the Americas demonstrate that they explicitly contemplated and desired "freedom" (Thompson 2006: 40–42). In the aftermath of the U.S. Civil War, formerly enslaved people told officials that they hoped freedom would bring them access to land, opportunities for political and economic participation, and protection from forced labor (Foner 1994: 458). Mintz (1996: 37) suggests that enslaved Africans from the Caribbean began to exercise freedom in the pre-emancipation period, as they developed skills, made decisions, and formed aesthetics about foodways, transforming their own cultures and those of their masters. Fischer's (2005: 86) history of American freedom uses a similar logic to interpret figurines excavated in Virginia and made by enslaved African ironworkers. While the juxtaposition of freedom and contingent forms of agency risks oversimplifying both concepts, the comparison reminds us of the leverage that enslaved people marshaled and the slaveholders' dependency on their laborers' skills.

No elaborate philosophy was necessary for people to realize why they were at least slightly better off free from enslavement. For enslaved Africans, experiences with confinement, hard labor, brutal punishment, and deprivation were tangible enough to force them to contemplate the usefulness and necessity of freedom (compare Foner 1994, and Shah 2008: 489). Similarly, Stefansson's (1940: 387, 410) anthropological critique of early twentieth-century history and philosophy challenges linear, universalist assumptions about intellectual evolution, arguing that "liberty" was neither an invention of the Greeks nor exclusively the product of highly abstract thought or "civilization" (compare with Fischer 2005: 3). This critique is important because current discourses on early freedom thought emphasize the absence of a freedom concept in ancient non-Western societies and the evolution of ideas from Greek, Roman, and Enlightenment philosophers (Patterson 1991). It has been suggested that precolonial Africans, Asians, and "First Nations" (Western Hemisphere) lacked freedom because they did not have words or concepts for it, because many embraced some form of forced servitude, and/or because citizens prioritized principles of collective responsibility that derived from religion or kinship (Patterson 1991; Fischer 2005: 4–5). Stefansson writes in response to this argument, "you do not invent the thing you have." His primordialist perspective is similar to Thompson's (2006: 46) view that an innate, "primary desire for freedom" motivated Africans to escape from American slavery. Critics of primordialist positions argue that freedom has been continuously (re)invented and socially constructed within the span of human existence (Patterson 1991). However, we need not confine our explanation of African resistance and liberation to a social- or cultural-determinist conceptualization, for personal beliefs are as important as social values in shaping behaviors.

An obvious place to look for factors and motivations that helped people free themselves from bondage is in the minds of enslaved Africans. Personal or cultural memories of pre-enslavement daily life, government, resistance, and mobility in Africa may have reminded diasporans that there were alternative social experiences that fostered well-being and acknowledged their humanity. Although the irony of African participation in slavery is often raised in scholarship, debt-based labor and other varieties of servitude and inequality were glossed by most chroniclers, who were quick to apply the label of "slavery" to relations they saw during the transatlantic slave trade (Lovejoy 2000: 14). While harsh forms of bondage did exist in Africa, there were also cases (for instance among the Yoruba) where some towns within slave-trading regions prohibited slavery (Reis and Mamigonian 2005: 92). Another representation of antislavery resistance involves a Yoruba cultural heroine named Moremi, who is celebrated in oral traditions and festivals in Nigeria and the United States. Moremi is credited with helping to end the enslavement of her people (from the city of Ife) by infiltrating her enemies' settlement and then divulging their foes' attack plans to her peers. Even if polities in African regions later reversed their stance or only outlawed enslavement of their own townspeople, we cannot assume all Africans owned slaves or condoned bondage. Miers and Kopytoff suggest that African perspectives complicate dichotomies which scholars usually make when juxtaposing freedom and slavery:

> In most African societies, "freedom" lay not in a withdrawal into a meaningless and dangerous autonomy but in attachment to a kin group, to a patron, to power—an attachment that occurred within a well-defined hierarchical framework. It was in this direction that the acquired outsider had to move if he was to reduce his initial marginality. Here, the antithesis of "slavery" is not "freedom" qua autonomy but rather "belonging." (1977: 17)

In this quote we see the significance of power rising to the fore, echoing earlier discussions in this chapter about the embedded nature of resistance in wider social relations. The notion of "belonging" has to be carefully conceived if it is to aptly characterize various African societies. Conversely, it is important to consider a wider spectrum of historical African social formations, including egalitarian societies (Weissner 2002).

African worldviews significantly shaped captive and free people who came to the Americas during the slavery period. One such belief system that archaeologists have taken a strong interest in is that of central African Kikongo societies. Archaeological discussions have centered on items called *minkisi*, bundles of spiritually charged implements ranging from carvings to assemblages of organic materials (animal bones, quartz, shells, roots, and so on) (Fennell 2007: 44). They are embodiments of

Figure 3.1. Moremi statue, city of Ife, Nigeria. Photo by Terrance Weik.

divine force, expressions of cosmology, and symbols of sacred agency that have existed for centuries in central Africa (Fennell 2007: 56). Devotees or priests of the ancestor or spirit embodied in the *minkisi* used divination to get messages from spirits, find solutions to problems, enact healing, gain (meta)physical protection, or call forth retribution. Ethnographical and historical studies suggest that meanings were also derived from literal (such as grave dirt signifying ancestors) or metaphoric symbols (such as white minerals signifying purity and the spirit world) in the *minkisi* contents or containers. For Leone (2005), *minkisi* and other spirit bundles (comprised of sanctified mundane objects like crystals, polished stones, and marked potsherds) that he and others have excavated from places such as Annapolis, Maryland, are religious manifestations that facilitated cultural resistance to capitalist slavery and alienating ideologies of individualism. Sacred bundles countered the ideological forces that moved people to compartmentalize their lives (disconnecting them from nature, divinity, and other people) and to become ruled by the artificial rhythms of clocks and materialist consumer aspirations, which created within them an insatiable demand for goods (for example, matching dinnerware sets) (Leone 2005). By contrast, African (American) sacred bundles facilitated ancestral veneration and communication within a spiritual community. The bundles also provided a medium through which people could imagine or invoke (through querying spiritual guidance) decision-making and well-being.

Leone (2005) sees these spiritual media as motivators that inspired African Americans to evade state surveillance, cultivate ancestral worldviews, and challenge Eurocentric collective opinions, which were reinforced by mass media. The bundles promoted freedom by encouraging people to express alternative identities that rejected the impositions of slave society (such as racist definitions of Africans and low status). Further, the bundles facilitated secretive rituals that promoted personal achievements and communal activity. Conversely, as Fennell warns (2007: 81), sacred bundles were also used for malevolent purposes. Thus, these sanctified bundles had a range of meanings, uses, and effects. Likewise, one must be wary of monolithically generalizing about the presence of *minkisi* without acknowledging that many other enslaved African ethnic groups also brought beliefs regarding similar sacred objects to the Americas.

Many Africans were brought to the Americas from homelands heavily influenced by Islamic political and religious institutions (Gomez 1998: 70–77, 106). Their names alert us to their presence as "runaways," "drivers," and laborers on Southern U.S. plantations. Although Islam helped promote slavery in Africa for centuries, it also spread revolutionary ideas about Jihad and explicit ideas about manumission. These beliefs may have catalyzed resistance in other parts of the diaspora, such as nineteenth-century Bahia (Brazil), where Muslims revolted against slavery (Reis and Mamigonian 2005: 92).

Some African diasporans adopted notions of freedom from European deistic Enlightenment thought, natural rights doctrines, pietistic

Christian religion, and ideas about social revolution (Harding 1981; Aptheker 1972; Thompson 2006). Fabian captures the essence of European philosophies of liberty, which impacted both people of African descent and early anthropological approaches:

> The theoretical foundations for modern anthropology were laid in Enlightenment and romantic thought . . . in a confrontation between two movements. Freedom, the philosophies argued, was a condition for emancipated citizens to exercise their faculties of reason and moral choice; romantic thinkers, while accepting this as a matter of principle, celebrated freedom as the prerequisite of artistic creation and as the essence of historical process. Both movements faced a problem (and proposed various solutions): How could they maintain these convictions in the face of necessity (of natural law) and destiny (as embodied in tradition)? To make a long story short, the tragedy of anthropology has been that, in its desire to establish itself as a science (or because of being pressured by the powers that be), it came to approach its subject . . . through theories . . . bestowed on it by Newtonian physics and positivist sociology. Anthropology may have started out by thinking of the "human career" in terms of freedom—freedom from animal fear and destructive instincts, from religious or political dictates, from racism and other forms of biological determinism. It may have found in the concept of culture a tool for such thought; yet it always seems to have wound up with determinist, integrationist theories of human action. The most . . . influential conceptualizations of culture . . . stressed necessity rather than freedom in explaining how culture worked, irrespective of individual choice or consciousness, by the rules of a supraindividual logic. (1998: 18–19)

Moreover, Leone (2005)—borrowing from Western philosophers such as C. B. Mcpherson, Hobbes, and Locke—argues that individualism was the most influential motivation in the American Revolution and later U.S. quests for freedom. Individualism is essentially free will and independence from others and impositions of the state, whose function should be to protect individual rights and property. However, it is an ideology in actual practice, a mask that often blinds people to the inequalities promoted by political economies (compare Urban 2008: 228). Ani (1994: 73) goes a step further, arguing that U.S. society has a history of skillfully constructing global ideologies that cloak aggression under claims of defense, hide oppression under claims of freedom, and mask imperialism under claims of bringing "enlightenment."[2] Similarly, some of the freedoms codified in postcolonial, revolutionary constitutions and liberation-movement leaders' declarations have failed to protect indigenous and other citizens' rights (Fabian 1998: 19; Harrison 2005; Wolf 1990).

Marimba Ani (1994) argues that Western notions of individualist freedom have advanced an ethnocentric agenda that privileges individualism at the cost of communal wellness. She analyzes Western notions of freedom as they relate to various dimensions of being:

> It is not simply the idea of "freedom" . . . that is valued in contemporary European society but a very specific kind of freedom associated almost totally with the unique European concept of validity and necessity of the autonomous individual. "Freedom," as an attribute of space or time, has no worth so long as it remains in that state. (Ani 1994: 343)

Patterson (1991) cautions against equating European (American) freedom ideals with individualistic forms, for other modes of freedom ideology exist, such as civic freedom (see also Skinner 1998). However, the existence of democracy and civic participation in governance does not ensure that the majority will choose political representatives, laws, and policies that respect everyone's rights and allow equal access to resources (without which, the mere ability to do something is not sufficient to realize one's goals) (Patterson 1991).

Critical African (American) thinkers and the abolitionist movement also helped inspire enslaved people to escape or resist. Antislavery activist David Walker published a denouncement of slavery and used his craft to literally spread the text, hidden in seams of clothes he tailored. Walker's words are full of condemnation for the hypocrisies, moral failings, and denials of U.S. society. His antislavery sentiments promoted a pan-Africanist, universalist vision which argued that people could not claim to live in a state of freedom until their oppressed or enslaved peers were also free. Similarly, Karenga (2006: 246–47) sees Harriet Tubman's biography as a useful medium for reflecting on how people transcended individualistic notions of freedom. Tubman came to the realization that her own fulfillment from self-emancipation was limited compared to the satisfaction derived from returning to slave states to free others. This is an example of how people of the African diaspora redefined freedom, shifting its potential meaning from a process of individual flight to a more communal mode of self-determination. African descendants' collectivist redefinitions of freedom may have also derived from an awareness or subconscious affirmation of ancestral cultural values (alluded to in the above-mentioned concept of African belonging). Ironically, an etymology of northern European words suggests that "freedom's" ancient roots signified friendship and kin-based or communal belonging (Fischer 2005: 3–15). While these meanings persisted in colonists' folkways, they eventually were eclipsed by racialist and slavery interests, becoming exclusive prerogatives for "whites."

Ani's (1994: 343–44) critique of Eurocentric notions of freedom extends to aspects of culture such as landscape. She quotes the work of Dorothy Lee (1959), who contrasts Eurocentric ideas about freeness and freedom with the beliefs of other cultures:

> Space is empty and to be occupied with matter; time is empty and to be filled with activity. Whereas often in other cultures, "free space and time have being and integrity." In evidence of this, Lee goes on to cite examples from other cultures in which "The experience of silence; of the space between and within is meaningful." She speaks of such Japanese perceptions that "persists [sic] in spite of the adoption of western culture and science." Lee continues, "free time, through being recognized as valid existence, can and does contain value." Whereas, "in our own culture it is perceived as the unallocated, the unscheduled, the nothing; and it cannot contain value, as it contains no being." In addition to the fact that they contain no value, "empty spaces" are indeed "uncomfortable" to the European, and he "experiences silence" as either embarrassing or frightening. (Ani 1994: 343–44; she quotes Lee 1959)

This Eurocentric anxiety about unallocated, unused time and space created the rationale for colonial and national policies which led to violent conquests of land and the destruction of wetlands and forests. For antislavery resisters and escapees, the consequence was that they lost vital physical cover and protection.

Currently, anthropological discussions of freedom are often intertwined or submerged within broader discussions of human rights, well-being, and politics (Englund 2006). The United Nations Universal Declaration of Human Rights prescribes a number of literal "freedoms" that safeguard free expression, protect socioeconomic wellness, and cultivate civil liberty. Group rights are also ensured in this creed, which is an important attempt to provide a baseline for protecting people from the violence created by national governments, authoritarian leaders, corporations, and paramilitary forces (Harrison 2005). Some groups have found that their struggles to practice their cultural beliefs without state interference coexist with their attempts to gain citizenship rights and access to resources and heritage protection (Wolf 1990: 150). This kind of struggle for support or recognition led some self-liberated Africans to become state agents (for example, African Seminole Maroons who became scouts or buffalo soldiers for the U.S. cavalry) or sign treaties with colonial governments that obligated them to turn in other escapees (such as eighteenth-century Jamaican Maroons).

On one hand, these Maroon treaties could be viewed as opportunism and betrayals of a universal right to freedom. At times, Maroon forces were used to suppress rebellions or other existing Maroon groups (Thompson 2006: 266). On the other hand, the treaties also indicate self-liberated Africans' attempts to achieve long-term security and obtain arms, supplies, or breaks from costly wars. The motives of colonists and slaveholders in many treaties were not to simply bring about peace—they hoped to gradually encumber Maroon polities and keep them divided from their enslaved peers. However, generalizations about Maroons' and colonists' commitment to treaties are questionable, in light of the inconsistencies concerning Maroon capture of escapees and colonists' attempts to capture Maroons after they signed treaties. Similarly, free and enslaved Africans have a mixed record of service against Maroons and revolting peers (Thompson 2006: 267–93). Thus, the contradictions of antislavery resistance are not mere ethical shortcomings, but indications of diverse motives, conflicting beliefs, and complicated geopolitics.

Although elaborate plans were unnecessary prerequisites for the emergence of antislavery resistance, they were crucial for effective community-building, rebellions, or integrated justice movements(Hilliard 1995: 54). Planned resistance was a product of individuals' and groups' choices about goals. Raz's *The Morality of Freedom* draws on the old philosophical concept of "positive freedom" to articulate a notion of autonomous choice which moves the discourse beyond mere considerations of the pursuit of self-interest. From Raz's perspective (1986), effective choice also entails one having the capability—physical ability, mental skills, and adequate range of options—to realize autonomy. The quality of a person or group's options depends on social, economic, and technological limitations, resources, and opportunities. Their diverse social organizations, economic strategies, resource bases, and technological capabilities provided many self-liberated communities with the freedom of action to pursue a tolerable if not desirable life (especially compared to slavery). Malinowski (1944: 25) integrates the aforementioned factors into a dynamic working definition: "Freedom can be defined as the conditions necessary and sufficient for the formation of a purpose, its translation into effective action through organized cultural instrumentalities, and the full enjoyment of the results of such activity." In other words, freedom is a process. The process also includes so-called negative liberty, the classical philosophical concept that evaluates the presence or absence of freedom based on the options open to people within social systems or legal structures (Carter, Kramer, and Steiner 2007: 3–4). It is best to avoid over-investing in the positive-negative liberty dichotomy, as both approaches to freedom have overlapping concerns, and both are useful (Fischer 2005: 3). The methodological implication of this discussion is that one could do a cost-benefit accounting of resisters' situations to assess their capability of achieving liberation and the quality of their freedom. This type of approach is a useful starting point for a larger project that could eventually engage a broader and more intricate discourse (see examples in Carter, Kramer, and Steiner 2007).

Ethnogenesis, Transformation, and Identity in Self-Liberated African Communities

Various approaches and concepts have been used to explain the organization and development of Maroon societies: evolutionary typologies (such as tribe, chiefdom, and state), confederacies, cultural mosaics, African-centered nations, political-economic social structures, and document-based claims about monarchies (Kent 1965; Price 1975, 1979; Thompson 2006). In the last decade, ethnogenesis has become one of the primary theories used in ethnographic and historic research on self-liberated African cultural dynamics, social formations, and identity (Bilby 1996; Weik 2009). Similarly, community-building is one of the critical issues that has shaped the development of theory about Underground Railroad landscapes in the United States (Leone, Laroche, Babiarz 2005: 8). Freedom and liberation are prerequisites for any community whose members seek to direct their own socialization practices or foster cultural creativity (Fabian 1998: 19; Hilliard 1995; Malinowski 1944). These factors are important whether we focus on social (re)production within new group formations or within situations of oppression. Ethnogenesis is valuable for analyses because it forces scholars to think about social complexities and mechanisms of collective transformation, as opposed to simply assuming that these self-emancipated communities were replications of African-based models of society, creolized subgroups of early African American cultures, or chaotic outliers of slave society. African influences, experiences during enslavement, and innovative practices all created self-liberated communities.

Some proponents argue that ethnogenesis has roots in nineteenth-century polygenesis models which were proposed to challenge monogenetic ideas of nationhood and biological purity (Moore 1994, 2001; Voss 2008: 33–37). In the century that followed, two approaches came to exist in anthropological and historical writings, which I will refer to as the identity and social-process variants of ethnogenesis theory. Even though each of these ethnogenetic approaches differs in emphasis, they overlap in content and focus.

The group identity emphasis of some ethnogenesis approaches focuses on ways that culture is used to create social identities (Barth 1969; Roosens 1989; Whitten 1976). This variant investigates the complexities of identity-formation processes rather than assuming that blood relations or primordial bonds are the sole or primary factors determining identity. The newness of groups, or "neoteric societies," is an important point stressed by supporters of this type of ethnogenesis theory (Gonzalez 1988; Mulroy 1993a, 1993b). Social groups ascribe identities to individuals based on select cultural traits which produce expressions of "ethnic" identity (Barth 2000). Fennel (2007: 35) nicely summarizes other concerns of ethnogenetic identity approaches, which deal with the "solidity, permeability, or disappearance of . . . social group identities and their associated boundaries in different settings over time."

The social-process version of ethnogenesis theory was carried forth by the work of Sturtevant (1971), who devised a model based on ethnohistoric examinations of the Florida "Seminole Indian." Sturtevant noted several major ethnogenetic formation processes: group and settlement formation on colonial frontiers; periodic changes in socioeconomic relations and social organizations; opportunistic alliances and trade with European colonists, slaves, and Native Americans; group fissioning and factionalism; fluid settlement in clan-based camps; and the development of different groups from social interchange, cultural mixture, and conflicts. Sturtevant also pointed out that group identity came about through "ethnonymy," the naming and identification of ethnic groups by governments, chroniclers, or other outsiders. Ethnonymies make claims about cultural groups (for example, determining who is a member) and represent them as stable entities which exhibit solidarity. Sturtevant showed that different sources—such as government officials, Christian missionaries, tourists, soldiers, and anthropologists—have been partly responsible for the genesis of "Seminole" peoples, because they have shaped our assumptions about who is "Seminole." Descendants and their ancestors have rejected, affirmed, and remained ambiguous about the ethnonym "Seminole," even as linguists and others affirm the label (see also Sattler 1987). Wickman (1999) argues that the autonomy of Maskoki (for example, Creek) settlements and those of their descendants who became "Seminole," along with the existence of unique indigenous worldviews, has disrupted chroniclers' limited picture of them.

Moore's (1994) conceptualization of ethnogenesis criticizes older social models for assuming that language, cultural beliefs, and biological characteristics coevolve, passing down through different generations and changing at constant rates (compare with Sattler 1996). He stresses the need to recognize more rapid cultural changes and unpredictable events. Similarly, Mulroy (1993b; 2004) argues that the flexibility of ethnogenetic processes involving the "Black Seminole" has allowed them to survive and resist destruction in the borderlands of the United States. Ethnogenesis theories have helped to challenge static, monolithic, isolationist theories of culture, while also modeling diverse agents and processes of transformation (Armstrong 2003b; compare Ortiz 1940). Scholarship on other parts of the world such as Japan and the former Soviet Union suggests that ethnogenesis models have existed outside of the American historical context that shapes much available literature (Hudson 1999; Sturtevant 1971).

Alongside the benefits are the potential limitations of ethnogenesis theory. For instance, proponents tend to heavily emphasize sociocultural change while neglecting organizational factors (Weik 2009). In addition, researchers' focus on regional models has impeded understanding of individual settlements by encouraging scholars to over-rely on fragmented historical details and conditions that fit the model. At the same time, there has not been enough examination of the model's fit with social features in each period of a group's or settlement's existence (Weik 2009). Ingold's (1999) and Gundaker's (2001: 132) criticisms of archaeological landscape and creolization theories (respectively) also apply to ethnogenesis: the time aspect of ethnogenetic social dynamics and cultural processes, or their "temporalization," has been less explicitly conceptualized. Some of these weaknesses are exacerbated by the low level of supporting documentary, material, and oral evidence. Ethnogenesis is often applied to groups who demonstrate the ability to survive and create societies in the face of oppression and harsh circumstances. However, colonial societies and imperial nations have created race, class, gender, and ethnic identities that demarcate lines of privilege, structure resource flows, enact inequality, and reinforce sociocultural solidarity in ethnogenetic ways (Deagan 1996, 1998; Bell 2005; Voss 2008: 37).

Rethinking organizational principles will require building on observations about mechanisms by which people encourage collective life and perpetuate their settlements. It will also require transcending compartmentalized and determinist conceptualizations of politics, economics, religion, subsistence, and other practices. Military and strategic organization were crucial aspects of society that fostered leadership and planning through institutionalized and ritualized means in self-liberated Brazilian (Palmares), Jamaican, and Surinamese populations (Price 1969, 1989). In Jamaica, this led to the ascription of titles to male leaders (for example, "Colonel Harris") and various traditions about the powerful war "science" that helped the heroine "Nanny" overcome her foes (see various chapters in Agorsah 1994; compare Bilby 1996).

One goal of my model-building that I share with proponents of anthropological archaeology is to devise the most holistic picture of self-liberated communities, one that accounts for the broadest range of human activity within and beyond primary institutions and structures, accounting for known and likely relations, products, and beliefs. Classic ethnographic methods in nineteenth- through twentieth-century anthropology approached social organization in ways that largely emphasized synchronic observations about social structures. Theorists have sought to escape the limitations of social models based on snapshots of historical or ethnographic observations. The active role of individuals and groups in creating dynamic "structuring structures" is another important component of a social model (Giddens 1979). These structures provide a set of standardized relations and beliefs that order behavior and mobilize people, regulating their routines and setting terms for collective participation (Bourdieu 1977). The existence of structures, however, does not suggest that they worked perfectly or in every event. At the same time, it is important that we recognize the potential of resistance groups and their structures to create or defy inequalities (Brown 1996).

Models of self-liberated African communities would also benefit from some recognition of the problem of coalition-building. How did groups create coherency despite the potential divisions that arose from linguistic, religious, personal, cultural, and political distinctions between various African, European, and American-born participants? In instances where differences of opinion or interest led to conflicts, means of dispute resolution would have been necessary.

The mechanisms or activities that lead to enculturation and socialization are also key components of the organizational principles at work in a society that perpetuates itself. Ethnographic and historic studies of African and Native American societies suggest that there are various methods for socializing citizens (Andah 1988; Hilliard 1998; Martin 1989). Rites of passage and initiations have marked time and enculturated society members as they took on the responsibilities and identities of their peers, engaged deities, and underwent (meta)physical transformations. Newcomers and children in self-liberated African communities needed special attention because of the uncertainty of their future commitment to the community, and because of the potential dangers posed by people who purposefully or carelessly divulged sensitive information (such as the hideout's location) to outsiders. Oaths were given in certain historical Maroon communities as a strategy to ensure residents' loyalty. While the above-mentioned activities can be found in ethnographic and historical communities, they should not be taken as a formula for what is or was found in all settlements or at all times. In practice, most communities probably had some of these features, but varied according to the idiosyncrasies created by individual choices, social relations, and environmental circumstances.

Scale is another important analytical issue in social modeling. Kenneth Bilby's (1996: 119–41) comparative analysis of Maroon societies in Jamaica and Guiana illustrates that both family and intervillage (for example, clan relations) scales of community play important roles in the various expressions of Maroon ethnogenesis. In order to further thinking about the maintenance of communities at multiple scales, it is useful to bring in another issue, the operation of networks.

Freedom and Resistance Networks

Networks are important features of social movements and communities of resistance. Since Radcliffe-Brown's musings in the 1940s, anthropologists have recognized that networks are useful theoretical frameworks for illuminating the meanings, elements, and mechanisms animating webs of human interaction (Lomnitz 1977; Orser 1996: 31). More broadly, network theories have been developed to suite the specialized needs of the social, technological, and physical sciences (Castells 1996; Knappet 2005: 65). *Social* network theories are my main concern here, for they are the most relevant to the issues involved in resistance to slavery. Simply put, a social network is a set of connections between individuals that facilitates mutual support and the flow of people, information, objects, and relationships. Scholars have examined fundamental attributes of social networks, including density, geographic scope, specialization, functions, sensitivity to other networks, degree of formality, and duration. Research has also explored the nature of participants' commitments to networks, their social proximity, and the types of ideas shared by networkers. Themes such as memory, historicity, friendship, health care, kinship, and capitalist production have featured prominently in studies (Murakami and Middleton 2006; Wellman 1999). Today, a wide range of network theorizations guide anthropologists, sociologists, and other scholars (Law and Hassard 1999). For example, Green, Harvey, and Knox (2005) investigated the intersection of place-making, communication technologies, and European Union projects, illustrating the complications that challenge the integrity and conceptualization of networks.

Much work remains to be done to map out the material remnants of antislavery resistance activities, so that they can be factored into traditional archaeological concerns with the networks connecting homes, temples, paths, roads, waterways, and environmental features (compare Orser 1996). Archaeologists find social networks useful to study given that they often shape physical networks, thereby actively molding the built environment (roads are a good example). On the other hand, environmental features such as rivers form networks that have long influenced settlement patterns and human mobility. Artifacts, particularly commodities, move along "directed networks" such as roads in "orderly and purposeful" ways (Orser 1996: 133). Archaeologists have generally focused on exchange networks rather than other dimensions of social networks (Aswani and Sheppard 2003). However, some archaeologists are attempting to apply actor network theory and semiotics as a more comprehensive conceptualization of the linkages between people, objects, and meanings (Knappett 2005).

Social networks such as the one that connected U.S. abolitionists circulated dishes, jewelry, and other forms of material culture, carrying forward symbols and texts condemning slavery (Fischer 2005; Guyatt 2000). Churches and religious organizations facilitated networks which supported the Underground Railroad, as well as later social movements of the civil rights era and the "Velvet Revolutions" of late twentieth-century Europe. Networks have served social movements in various ways: by implementing recruitment, providing support to activists, and advertising issues which helped supporters identify with activist issues (Passy 2003: 21–22).

Networks were also important for captive laborers and other people who fought against slavery. Some enslaved Africans negotiated for more flexible work conditions, which were possible through being "hired out" to other employers or slaveholders. This practice created opportunities for economic benefits and challenges to slaveholders' power. Egerton (2006: 632) notes, "Planter polemicists certainly recognized that the underlying danger of hiring out was not that it allowed for petty theft, but that it created an illicit network of trade and communication that could prove disastrous to white control." The Underground Railroad is often described as a clandestine network. Laroche (2004: ii) eloquently observes that "The image of the solitary man, escaping slavery on foot, aided by white abolitionists working within a loosely organized network, gives way to nuanced understandings of the elastic, reticulated network of routes, and methods of subterfuge employed by African Americans and their accomplices required to sustain the Underground Railroad movement."

The legacy of resistance networks still resonates with the public in the twenty-first century. Entrepreneur George Fraser (2004) sees networking as "a new Underground Railroad" for African American communities.

Fraser notes that precedents exist, such as "Free Frank McWhorter," who freed himself and his family from slavery through business ventures and started a black town that supported the Underground Railroad (Walker 1983). He defines networks as support systems and states of mind that marshal knowledge, resources, and influence. Fraser (2004) notes how networks have historically affected social change, uplifting communities ravaged by intergenerational inequalities. Networks empower individuals to achieve their goals and mobilize capital for economic success. Fraser sees African heritage as an important point of departure for envisioning descendants' networks. African ideals that he references, such as communalism and egalitarianism, are worth exploring because they are present in historic African (American) communities. More effort needs to be invested in discovering the extent to which these values were transferred through intergenerational beliefs or independent invention in the Americas. Fraser points out that networking is no guarantee of success if it is pursued in isolationist or parochial ways. Networks need not be exclusive creations of any one community, as self-determination can be furthered by working with outsiders and foreigners (Fraser 2004: 135).

Conclusion

The multidimensional nature of resistance, freedom, networks, and ethnogenesis cannot be understated. Thus, an important theoretical thread of this book is that simplistic statements about these concepts can distort the complexity of the phenomena that they represent by promoting dichotomous thinking, ignoring contradictions, and undervaluing the full range of responses and initiatives that drove people to oppose enslavement or achieve long-term self-determination.

Various commentators suggest that resistance is situated in a universe of relations, meanings, and countervailing forces, all of which constitute the flow of power. Even the most successful resisters have had to continuously grapple with the transformations that perpetuate systems of domination. Archaeological evidence and landscapes offer fruitful media through which these dynamics can be tracked, but researchers must be prepared to uncover their subtle or dramatic material traces. Archaeologists have grappled with resistance for decades, largely in response to the resonance of Marxist or political-economic theories, or because they were studying explicit resistance events. Archaeologies of resistance continue to emerge, especially in the contexts of Native American or African American studies.[3] The concept of resistance has fallen out of favor with some scholars, probably in part because of their assumption that it is a reactionary behavior or that studies of it overemphasize the domination-resistance polarity (compare Hollander and Einwohner 2004: 534). But other scholars continue to explore its merits, shortcomings, and manifestations (Sivaramakrishnan 2005).

While we should be wary of simply equating resistance with the existence of free thought or freedom-seeking behavior (compare Abu-Lughod 1990: 42), freedom still has a number of merits: as a conceptual gauge of the relative progress of resisters, and as a point of departure for examining the discourses and motivations of Africans in the diaspora. To understand enslaved or self-liberated Africans' viewpoints on resistance and cultural practices of freedom, we have to look to historically contemporaneous African, European, and American worldviews, personal beliefs, and actions.

A global perspective on resistance, freedom, and liberation suggests that they all are contested, historically contingent, multisemous phenomena (Englund 2006: 2–9; Wolf 1990: 16). These ideas have inspired generations of people to rise up against slavery, colonialism, and other forms of oppression. However, they have also been co-opted by nations and revolutionaries in ways that appropriate their ideological force for the sake of privileged beneficiaries, or that trivialize their usage and neutralize critics (Englund 2006: 3, 9). Another problem with modern notions of freedom is that certain (for instance, human rights) activists have promoted elitist, top-down, outsider-driven approaches that propose to teach people freedom, as opposed to learning how insiders have defined their own common good. But these failings should not discourage continual reflections on freedom as a useful tool in the pursuit of human well-being, a foil for social criticism, and a starting point for visions of self-determination.

Explicit discussions of freedom are relatively new for archaeologists. Two archaeology conference symposia featured papers on issues such as Native American autonomy, colonial entanglement, African American consumption, institutional racism, racist violence, pipe-making, subfloor pits, underrepresented archaeological practitioners, Euro-American historical icons, and Maroon societies.[4] "Freedom" has been a popular part of numerous book titles, but many writers have dealt with the general condition or status of free(d) people rather than the idea or causes of freedom. Nonetheless, archaeological works are appearing that demonstrate the utility of liberty in holistic explanations of social relations, material culture, ideology, and landscapes (Leone 2005).

In contrast to freedom, ethnogenesis has been more fully embraced by archaeologists. Ethnogenesis has been a prominent theoretical framework in studies of African and Native American community-building, anticolonial struggles, and antislavery resistance (see contributions in Hill 1996). The most informative approach synthesizes the identity and social-process variants of ethnogenesis theory. While ethnogenesis continues to provide a viable basis for conceptualizing societies, aspects such as social structure are in need of more formal consideration.

The idea of social networks is also prominent in antislavery resistance studies. Religious, familial, and other types of social networks must be more intensively examined by archaeologists if their field is to demonstrate its unique contributions to anthropological antislavery studies. The fundamental characteristics and material culture of networks need to be more effectively measured with methods that address the difficulties which covertness and countercultural life posed for antislavery activities and community-building.

Notes

1. I use freedom and liberty (liberation) interchangeably, following Fischer's (2005) observation that English speakers came to use both liberty and freedom to signify similar, overlapping things. In the epilogue to *Freedom: Its Meaning*, Schneider (1940: 655) notes that freedom is usually discussed in philosophical or scientific contexts, while liberty is usually considered in discussions of social rights and institutions. Historical usage in the African diaspora needs a more systematic, comprehensive analysis to discern whether African descendants untangled the terms, or if they envisioned a dualism that positioned these words in more polar ways.

2. Similarly, U.S. constitutional freedoms and the democracy that has been their steward have historically failed to protect the rights of a significant number of citizens, not to mention the enslaved people who lived within the early nation (Wolf 1990: 10–11).

3. See the papers on plantation rebellion, antislavery battles, self-liberated Africans, and African American religion in the 2008 Society for Historical Archaeology symposium on Archaeologies of Resistance.

4. See the Society for Historical Archaeology conference on political and economic aspects of freedom in 2006 and the American Anthropological Association conference symposium "Alternative Freedoms: Vantages from Historical Archaeology" (2009).

4

Archaeologies of Self-Liberated
African Communities

This chapter explores the research trajectory of Maroon archaeologies and discerns the role of material culture in discourses and social practices associated with self-liberated African communities. I use the terms "Maroon" and "self-liberated" interchangeably, as they both reflect usage by descendants and scholars as well as debates about the words' meanings and racializing valences. Some protest that "Maroon" is a dehumanizing construct, although certain descendants continue to give the term positive connotations (Weik 2009). This chapter proceeds thematically and geographically with the intention of building on analyses of specific locations and syntheses of the archaeology of African diasporic resistance (Orser and Funari 1998; Weik 1997, 2004).

Africans who escaped from slavery had to decide whether they would seek refuge in temporary hiding places or long-term communities (*gran marronage*) that they founded. Archaeologists have mainly focused on sedentary or semisedentary settlements, largely because of the difficulties of finding the relatively ephemeral material evidence from mobile groups of self-liberated Africans. Newer research is developing location models to address the gap in knowledge about temporary refuge sites (Norton and Espenshade 2007). Documents, oral histories, and oral traditions from across the Americas indicate that Maroons sometimes fled with items such as axes, guns, machetes, and extra clothes (Landers 1998; Price 1983: 89). While raids on plantations, enemy troops, and settlements also helped communities acquire supplies, oral histories suggest that there were times when self-emancipated people rejected both colonial overtures for peace and the material gifts that were given them in order to secure treaties (Price 1983: 93–94). Many self-liberated Africans, such as documented groups in Suriname and Florida, were opportunistic. For example, some Africans recovered weapons and supplies abandoned by Euro-American armies or slave catchers, including goods that enemy soldiers (attempting to prevent their reuse) discarded in rivers. In addition, formerly enslaved rebels carefully considered the implications of self-sufficient local production and regional trade. Entanglement in capitalistic economies and colonial, white-supremacist societies created dependencies and opportunities for co-optation or betrayal, often leading self-liberated Africans to destruction (Flory 1979). These conditions shaped the material evidence available at each historic place where people attempted to create liberated communities.

A Historical Synopsis of Maroon Archaeology

Archaeological research on self-liberated Africans has spanned half a century, with the Americas receiving the vast majority of attention. From the days of slavery to the present, self-liberated peoples and their descendants have taken note of their ancestral lands, the graves of their ancestors, ruins of their old settlements, and the material culture that they abandoned and discarded. Post-slavery landowners, artifact collectors, and other publics have also taken note of the physical remnants of communities of resistance (Campbell and Nassaney 2005: 16).

During the 1950s and 1960s, archaeologists made their first efforts at seeking out the physical remains of self-liberated Africans who allied with European forces at a place chroniclers referred to as "Negro Fort," located on the Florida panhandle (Griffin 1962; Poe 1950). In the 1970s, historians and soldiers began systematic studies of refuges for Africans who escaped from slavery in the Caribbean (Agorsah 1993). By the 1980s, archaeological projects were studying self-liberated Africans in the Caribbean and North America from anthropological and historical comparative perspectives (Arrom and Garcia Arevalo 1986; Smardz 1985). Early scholars were most concerned with providing material evidence of documented events, discerning functional aspects of settlement layout, and providing descriptions of general material evidence. Archaeologists were concerned with the ethnicity of resisters and the culturally specific behaviors (especially African) that could be connected to artifacts and features. During the 1990s, archaeological research expanded into South America (Brazil and Suriname). In this period, archaeological theory and methods

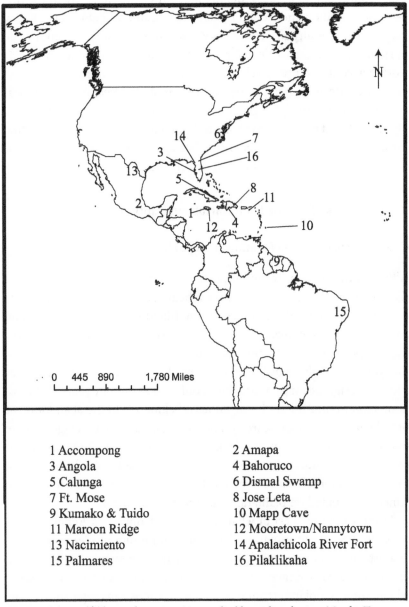

Map 4.1. Select self-liberated communities studied by archaeologists. Map by Terrance Weik.

1 Accompong
3 Angola
5 Calunga
7 Ft. Mose
9 Kumako & Tuido
11 Maroon Ridge
13 Nacimiento
15 Palmares

2 Amapa
4 Bahoruco
6 Dismal Swamp
8 Jose Leta
10 Mapp Cave
12 Mooretown/Nannytown
14 Apalachicola River Fort
16 Pilaklikaha

transcended site-focused, local perspectives and embraced world systems while continuing to address identity and African heritage. With the impetus of legislation and federal money that became available in the 1990s, Underground Railroad archaeology also got underway, largely in the northern United States. In the new millennium, scholarship and field-work has continued to develop in new areas such as Mesoamerica and east Africa. Regional perspectives, ethnogenesis, landscapes, and political economy paradigms have guided methods and theory, while more sophisticated field methods involving technologies such as GIS (Geographic Information System) have emerged. The approaches and discoveries of these investigations are explored in this chapter.

Archaeologies of Escape from Caribbean Captivity

Colonial Española (The Dominican Republic)

Although the Haitian Revolution is the most publicized uprising against slavery in the Americas, significant rebellions and communal attempts at liberation occurred elsewhere on the island during Spanish colonial control. Spanish colonization in northern Española was one of the earliest European attempts to colonize a part of what they came to know as the Americas. Columbus's establishment of the settlement at Isabella resulted in a significant presence, but it only lasted for four years. Sickness, poor support, mutiny, and indigenous rebellion led to the abandonment of Isabella. New DNA research on burials from La Isabella suggests there may have been a number of Africans at this settlement. On the southern coast of the island, Columbus's kinsmen witnessed a similar challenge to Spanish colonial control when a slave rebellion, one of the first in the Americas, erupted on plantations near Santo Domingo.

In the southwest part of what is today the Dominican Republic, field research has sought remains of a small community of *cimarrones* (the Spanish term for Africans who escaped from slavery). Communities of self-liberated Africans were known in Española as either *Manieles*—which some scholars attribute to an indigenous language source—or *palenques*. *Palenques* existed in several mountain ranges in the south central and western portions of the Dominican Republic. The mountains that bordered Haiti (formerly St. Domingue) also served as a refuge for later African rebels against French slavery. West of the plantation belt that surrounded colonial Santo Domingo lay the Sierra de Bahoruco, the mountain range where historian Bernardo Vega (1979) conducted a field investigation of a palenque. The mountains of Bahoruco also provided refuge for a Native American leader named Enriquillo who had engaged in a war against the Spanish colonists in the early sixteenth century.

Vega (1979) investigated a cave site on the southern edge of the Sierra de Bahoruco, an area where chroniclers said that *cimarrones* lived by the seventeenth century. Vega's goals involved augmenting documentary findings with physical evidence. He discovered bones and modern materials on the surface of the cave floor, but no dateable artifacts. In 1995, Weik (no date) conducted a follow-up surface survey of the cave, the plowed neighboring fields, and the dirt road near the cave. Weik employed surface observation strategies because artifacts are commonly found on the ground level at colonial and precolonial period settlements. Weik found no artifacts during his survey. Failed attempts at locating self-liberated African (and Native American) communities are not unique to the Dominican Republic, for scholars studying Maroons in places like South Carolina have met with similar frustration (Dawson, personal communication, 2008). Although it is not popular to discuss unsuccessful fieldwork in print, writing about failed searches conveys to future scholars the challenges of this type of research, the risks of focusing on one or few areas in the early stages of a project, and the need for better site-prediction strategies.

Weapons, pottery, and other items found on the surface of cave sites in the eastern Dominican Republic have been interpreted as possessions of *cimarrones* (Arrom and Garcia Arevalo 1986; Weik 2004). However, the conditions of discovery that produced these items are in need of greater scrutiny. The caves from which they were recovered may have more to offer to future investigators who are able to apply a greater range of data recovery techniques. The stratigraphic context, material culture (besides weapons which researchers have focused on), and use life of these caves have to be addressed before the artifacts can be securely attributed to *cimarrones*, as opposed to Native Americans, pirates, hermits, or other types of individuals who sought secluded refuges. For example, surface finds are not the strongest form of data because their stratigraphic position makes it hard to confirm that they were found in situ (that is, left by the original artifact user versus someone who found them elsewhere and moved them to a new location unrelated to their original use). Artifacts found in sealed soil strata are more likely to have preserved spatial contiguity, which helps archaeologists establish close temporal associations between material culture and the inferred identities or behaviors of people who used the cave. Further, excavated artifacts found in an undisturbed soil matrix are more likely to be useful in establishing relative dates for Native American or locally made artifacts, which often lack firmly known production dates. In a later section, the benefits of more substantial cave excavations will be addressed in another Caribbean context.

By the mid-sixteenth century, the Spanish had conquered the eastern part of the Dominican Republic, the last area to become subject to colonial domination. Archaeological remains have been found at estates such as Sanate (west of Higuey), which were built by some of the twelve thousand Africans enslaved on the island at the time (Chanlatte Baik 1978; Manon Arredondo 1978; Vega and Deive 1980: 151). Native Americans and Africans worked side by side on local sugar plantations. The majority of Africans who escaped from slavery on Española did so from the plantation zone around the city of Santo Domingo. By the mid-sixteenth century, there were around three thousand *cimarrones* on the island (Deive 1989: 43).

At a place called Jose Leta, far from colonial settlements, a tiny group of escaped Africans established a hideout. The exposed, jagged limestone landscape helped protect this band from slave catchers and encroaching plantations. The extremely sparse material culture of Jose Leta is not surprising in light of the few documented *cimarrones* in eastern Española during the colonial period. Two brief archaeological projects attempted to recover remains of Jose Leta's self-liberated African inhabitants. The best documentary evidence of *cimarrones* in the region involves a sixteenth-century rebel known to chroniclers as "Juan Criollo," who lived in the mountainous area east of the town called Higuey (Arrom and Garcia Arevalo 1986: 46).

During the 1980s, a pedestrian survey was conducted by Garcia Arevalo and his research team. Farmers and artifact enthusiasts alerted Garcia Arevalo to the presence of pottery and other finds in the area. Garcia Arevalo's goals were largely to supplement the known history with new material evidence and to see if any potential existed for more developed studies. During surface surveys of plowed farmland (interrupted by numerous rock outcrops), they recovered geometrically incised, locally made ceramic pipe bowls, copper bracelets, stone tools, fragments of Native American pottery such as griddles, pig remains, and metal weapon parts (mostly blades) (Arrom and Garcia Arevalo 1986: 48). Garcia Arevalo obtained radiocarbon dates that suggest the artifacts were deposited sometime between the 1640s and the 1790s.

During the mid-1990s, a surface and subsurface archaeological survey was conducted with the goal of identifying the settlement's layout and boundaries and examining the spatial implications of community formation (Weik 1997b). Fifteen shovel test pits were dug on a grid covering a thirty square-meter area that had the highest concentration of surface artifacts. The rocky terrain must have affected the former inhabitants' ability to ground structures or create pits for hearths or trash; these types of features were not visible in excavated soils. Most artifacts were found from surface level to a depth of twenty centimeters below the surface. Meillacoid and Chicoid pottery were the most numerous type of artifact recovered in this study, although a copper fragment was also found (Weik 2004). These Native American pottery types straddle the colonial and pre-colonial eras (circa thirteenth to sixteenth century), making it difficult to say what portion may have been used by Maroons. Without in situ Native American and colonial artifacts that can be linked to *cimarron* activities, habitation periods, or material traces of identity, it is difficult to make strong arguments about the existence of self-liberated Africans.

Collectively, the archaeological projects at Jose Leta confirm the presence of people who lived there sometime during the last seven hundred years (Weik 2004). While Garcia Arevalo's team discovered dated colonial artifacts, their provenience issues (found on the surface, in cultivated upper soil strata) raise concerns about whether there could have been sufficient disturbance to affect radiocarbon dating. The fact that subsequent subsurface survey has not produced a better range of like artifacts reinforces Garcia Arevalo's original argument that a small band occupied the site for a short period of time. Since there is no specific evidence of a documented group of *cimarrones* living in the area during the seventeenth or eighteenth century—the periods for which Garcia Arevalo has radiocarbon dates—we are left with questions regarding the identity of the inhabitants of Jose Leta. However, it is possible that undocumented *cimarrones* inhabited the locale; written sources should not be the only measure of historic presence. The remoteness, extremely thin soils, and rocky nature of the place make it likely that only the most desperate people would have lived there. People rebelling against slavery certainly make good candidates, as do Native Americans who inhabited the island before and after the conquest. Today the area is used primarily for pasturage or small-scale farming, but few farmers venture into the hilliest areas near Jose Leta. If self-liberated Africans chose this location, it would not be unusual, for swamps and other environments provided similar challenges for people who fled to them from slavery.

If we evaluate *cimarrones* using a conceptualization of freedom as an idealized spectrum gauging relative conditions and potentials for autonomous action and planning, then we are able to discern the valence of consequences facing Jose Leta's residents. The benefits that derive from the self-determination to make choices about one's residence were balanced by the need to limit one's choices to areas far from preestablished settlements. The advantages gained from the region's rough terrain—an impediment that slowed down or stopped bounty hunters or attackers—were matched by difficulties that these environmental features would have created for self-liberated people. They had to navigate over hilly lands, expend considerable energy tilling thin soils and hunting among forested, jagged stone outcrops, and traverse vine-choked trails. Some of the benefits of distance and protective seclusion from authoritative surveillance had to be assessed against the lost opportunities for exchange (of knowledge or goods) that resulted from social isolation.

It remains to be seen if the small size of certain self-liberated groups was a conscious decision, an unintentional circumstance, or an ongoing process (of member selection, for instance). The material implication of living in small groups was that it would have been easier to remain hidden and cover their material imprint. Strategically, having fewer people to organize might have made it easier to mobilize in resistance to (or flight from) parties of attacking bounty hunters. Further, groups had to assess their supplies and the carrying capacity of their region. This type of assessment process led the Jamaican Maroon leader "Cudjo" to express reluctance at requests to take in refugees from eastern Maroon settlements who sought his aid after Nanny Town was destroyed in the 1730s (Campbell 1993: 92–93). More studies of ethnographic and historical data are needed in order to shed light on the interplay between purposeful behavior, ecological relationships, and organizational processes affecting communities of resistance (Hilliard 1995; compare Hollander and Einwohner 2004, and Malinowski 1944).

Barbados

The colonial context of slavery in Española was similar to that of places like British Barbados, another important location where archaeologists have studied resistance. For instance, Barbados was one of the earliest Anglo colonial holdings in the Caribbean, and Africans on the island often escaped in small numbers. Unlike Española, Barbados was a small island with a high population density, making it one of the harder places for enslaved people to find freedom. Map iconography and colonists' accounts suggest that by the 1640s, Africans were escaping from Barbados' sugar plantations and hiding in woods and caves (Handler 1997).

Fred Smith's (2008) research on the archaeology of alcohol at "Mapp's Cave" illuminates social and material aspects of African people's slavery experiences, transatlantic cultural beliefs, and resistance to enslavement. Mapp's Cave is on the eastern end of Barbados, far from the earliest plantations. This remoteness, in addition to the presence of seventeenth-century European artifacts (such as clay jars), is the main evidence for the argument that a thirty-three-meter-long cave and an adjacent limestone sinkhole were used as a refuge from slavery. The sink and two rock shelters located inside it are separated from the cave by a low stonewall. Few features were uncovered from excavations of the sink and a pedestrian survey of the rock shelters (Smith 2008: 104–20). A large number of early and precolonial Native American (Suazoid) pottery sherds, shell fragments, and stone tools were found, suggesting that Maroons (and perhaps Native Americans seeking refuge from slave traders) recycled indigenous tools.

During the latter half of the seventeenth century, the area around Mapp's Cave became situated on the edge of a plantation (owned by a man named "Mapp"), less than a kilometer from the "big house" of a neighboring slaveholder. Smith (2008) suggests that the cave and sink were used by enslaved Africans as a temporary refuge during this period. Documentary evidence hints at the possibility that enslaved people from the neighboring plantation used the cave and sink as a habitation during a major rebellion. Later, enslaved people could have used it during impromptu gatherings and crises (like hurricanes). The few features, lack of precise dates for locally made pottery, and nonexistent soil strata differences all prevented Smith (2008: 105–12) from discerning the number and span of habitation periods.

Most objects found in the cave were European-made items dating to the eighteenth and nineteenth centuries, such as ceramics, nails, and roof tiles. The quantity of alcohol-related items found in Mapp's Cave, such as green glass spirits bottles, was over triple the proportion found on contemporary Bajan plantations. Locally made and imported red-paste earthenwares, which comprise over half of the artifacts at Mapp's Cave, could have been used in alcohol consumption as well as for other types of storage.

Ethnographic and historical texts suggest that indigenous Caribbean and African peoples made various types of alcoholic beverages (for example, from palm trees). Smith (2008) argues that these texts provide analogies for the most likely uses of alcohol-related artifacts at Mapp's Cave: to temporarily forget troubles; to sanctify ritual libations that facilitated some Afro-Caribbean rebellions; and to promote social bonding. Alcohol impacts inhibitions, and slaveholders feared its effects on plantation social control. Drinking had the potential to free bond persons from mental reservations regarding punishment and resistance.

Ultimately, the archaeology of alcohol at Mapp's Cave has generated plausible explanations for behaviors in marginal plantation spaces. However, while Smith's (2008) analogues are reasonable, alcohol could have created other effects. For instance, inebriation impeded people's ability to plot resistance, while alcohol poisoning and addiction destroyed their physical ability to resist or survive. Excessive alcohol use could have created dependency, as some slaveholders gave alcohol rations or gifts (Smith 2008). These caveats aside, Smith's examination shows how alcohol is a useful thematic lens through which to see potential causal factors in defiance, material manifestations of cultural resistance or marronage, and ecological aspects of refuge.

Jamaica

Some of the most frequent and long-lasting Caribbean cases of rebellion and self-liberation occurred in Jamaica. The Africans who escaped from slavery there were largely successful because of their numbers and the mountains that provided them refuge. Numerous rebellions preceded the formation of the major Maroon groups (as descendants identify themselves). Anticolonial resistance initiatives continued to resonate in later years, taking shape in events such as Bogle's Rebellion, an uprising that postdated official slavery but signaled the level of discontent that marked the masses' transition to free status. Ironically, Maroons had a role in suppressing this rebellion. Today, murals, national agencies, portraits, celebrations, monuments, and Jamaica's money commemorate Bogle and a famous Maroon heroine known as Nanny (Bilby 2005: 182–93). During the Spanish colonial period (lasting until 1655), Maroon settlements such as Juan de Bolas emerged. Archaeologists have been unable to locate this settlement (Reeves, personal communication, 1995).

In the 1730s, treaties were signed that established the legitimacy (in some colonists' eyes) of an eastern Maroon group led by a woman known as "Nanny," and a western group who lived in an area called "Accompong" under the leadership of individuals such as "Cudjo." By the late eighteenth century, a third Maroon group was established on the western part of the island. A number of this last group, particularly some inhabiting Trelawney Town, eventually were deported to Nova Scotia and then shipped to Africa. The Maroons in colonial Jamaican enclaves collectively numbered in the upper hundreds to low thousands.

In the 1990s, Kofi Agorsah brought his Maroon Heritage Research Project (MHRP) to fruition in Jamaica. Agorsah's project was the first multiyear endeavor to explore various Maroon communities in a region of the Americas. His project was guided by the central goal to "determine the nature of functional adaptation of Maroon communities . . . over time . . . a search for cultural history . . . rather than a history of 'rebels'" (Agorsah 1993: 167). Agorsah (1993b) was also concerned with studying the maintenance and transformation of African heritage at Maroon sites.

The MHRP brought to light new information regarding Maroon material possessions, site locations, medicinal and subsistence plants, and built environments. Descendents have been an integral part of the MHRP, sharing perspectives on landscapes and oral traditions regarding leaders, weaponry (such as locally made crossbows), and herbalism. Like archaeologists who have done similar research elsewhere, Agorsah discerned a Native American presence in the early self-liberated communities and identified material remains of indigenous precolonial inhabitants in the area (Agorsah 1993: 164). Coins are the main form of evidence that indicates a Spanish-period (before 1655) Maroon presence, at least if the pieces of eight recovered are not heirlooms.

Agorsah's team excavated forty percent of the Nanny Town site, one of the most sacred historic places for descendants. Besides the structure and inscription (see below) left by an invading colonial army, and present-day descendants' identification of the site location, pipe stem dates (1710–1750) have helped establish that the site was the same place referred to as Nanny Town in archival sources (Agorsah 2001: 12). Agorsah (1993b: 169) has noted the complexities of understanding Nanny Town, such as chroniclers' assertions that it had satellite towns and that individuals from Nanny Town also had residence in other towns.

However, important documentary findings have yet to be fully integrated into archaeological methodologies used to investigate Nanny Town. For instance, systematic comparisons could be made of Nanny Town's artifact assemblage and possessions that were recorded by members of a colonial expedition that temporarily conquered Nanny Town. The colonists who destroyed Nanny Town observed objects such as pewter and pottery vessels, arms, linens, and drums (Campbell 1990: 90). Potential exists to juxtapose recorded objects and archaeological remains in order to explore phenomena such as underground exchange or countercultural consumption. In addition, examinations could be made of how spatial distributions, feature attributes, or assemblage characteristics could be used with archival details, such as the "127 huts" discovered by colonial forces, in order to understand the social and cultural dimensions of settlement spaces or the society's "functional adaptations" to the local landscape (compare Agorsah's [1993b: 176] goals to documentary observations in Campbell 1990: 90).

However, like many other archaeological projects, the MHRP was unable to discover the total settlement layout and spatial patterns of behavior at particular communities such as Nanny Town (Agorsah 1993a, 1993b). This lacuna holds true for both the Spanish- and British-period Maroon sites in Jamaica. Structural features have been difficult to locate in many parts of the Americas, although a Brazilian *quilombo* (self-liberated community) named Ambrosio and some North American examples (discussed later) offer exceptions to this generalization (Guimaraes 1990;Castano 2000; Sayers 2008). Around the time of the destruction and occupation of Nanny Town by a British colonial force, at least five stone structures were built. Other finds from this colonial occupation of Nanny

Town include features such as an engraved stone (dated 1735), postholes, a flag post, and artifacts such as ceramics, scissors, bottle fragments, gun parts, and clay pipe fragments (Agorsah 1993b: 174–77). It remains to be seen whether Maroons built or (re)used any of the stone structures.

Agorsah's regional approach to Jamaican Maroons who lived around Nanny Town and a western town called Accompong has uncovered a spectrum of human activity centers that range from the seventeenth to the twentieth century: house platforms, burials, battlegrounds, hideouts, war camps, military trails, and fortifications. His research has discerned local settlement strategies, defensive techniques, and a Maroon settlement typology. By moving between scales of analysis, Agorsah was able to see how the neighboring Seaman's Valley served as a battleground and conduit for the trade relations that involved Nanny Town (Agorsah 1994). The landscape perspective he used at Accompong combined oral history and ethnoarchaeological studies of kinship in Ghana and Jamaica. Agorsah (1994, 1999) interpreted the settlement layout at Accompong as evidence of how African kin relations resonated in the design of Jamaican Maroon towns. He argued that clans were decisive organizing forces determining where people lived and how they fostered solidarity.

Agorsah developed analyses of networks, particularly the travel routes and communication media that constituted regional linkages. His recognition of the significance of networks helped him move beyond creating settlement pattern typologies to theorizing how settlements were involved in dynamic regional interactions and ecological engagements. Many archaeological studies of resistance to slavery have not fully embraced the potential insights of network theories (social and otherwise). This oversight has impeded archaeologists' ability to develop robust explanations for the exchanges that shaped artifact acquisition and the paths and communication vectors enabling flight and rebellion.

Cuba

Cuba had one of the longest-running slavery systems in the Caribbean, and one of the longest records of *cimarron* activity. The mountainous nature of Cuba made it an ideal setting for the formation of numerous settlements. La Rosa Corzo sought to illustrate that Cuban *palenques* (escapee villages) were best understood not as a series of isolated rebellion events by slaves seeking quick refuge, but instead as part of an infinite set of changing circumstances and phases of development or decline (La Rosa Corzo 2003: 11). His research was driven by goals such as discovering the geographical distribution, economic activities, and defensive strategies of *palenques*. Conversely, he also sought out the systems of colonial suppression used against self-liberated Africans.

La Rosa Corzo (2003: 2–3) focused on the eastern part of Cuba because it had one of the longest and most geographically extensive histories of African resistance. His analyses concentrated on the diaries of bounty hunters sent to re-enslave people, especially sources pertaining to the late eighteenth and nineteenth centuries. An examination of diaries and maps led La Rosa Corzo to conclude that most settlements were either short-term camps (*rancherias*) of nomadic hunter-gatherers or *palenques* that relied on subsistence agriculture. Most *cimarrones* did not aggressively raid plantations, hastily seek revenge on enslaving colonists, travel outside of familiar territories, or attract attention to their activities (La Rosa Corzo 2003: 1–11). When attacked, these self-liberated Africans used a fallback strategy, where *palenque* leaders and soldiers held off slave catchers long enough for other *palenqueros* to escape. The most successful *cimarrones* in Cuba retained their freedom by remaining far from slave societies, finding concealed areas to live, and settling in physically inaccessible places. Similar tactics were used elsewhere in the Americas, such as in nineteenth-century Florida.

The archaeological discoveries in eastern Cuba were made at well-documented settlements. La Rosa Corzo (2003: 236, 239) reported finding the physical remains of floors for fourteen out of twenty-six dwellings at the *palenque* called Calunga. Cooking stones and utensils were found along with the floor residues. The habitations were made of light timber and had thatched roofs and dirt floors. The leveled land around these dwelling sites (in a naturally uneven environment) was a key indicator of a *cimarron* presence, as were the alignment of house sites, the presence of large trees, and oral traditions that placed *cimarrones* there. Bounty hunters' diaries describe the dwellings and other landmarks which sit in close proximity to the material culture La Rosa Corzo recovered. The clustering of domestic remains from different households within a vicinity also set the *cimarron* remains off from those of modern settlements, which tend to be arranged in isolated homesteads (La Rosa Corzo 2003: 243). Artifacts found at Cuban *palenques* include buttons, a hoe, machetes, and shackles (Rosa Corzo 2005).

La Rosa Corzo's analysis sheds light on how both the enslavement system and the African resisters were methodical in their approach to adversaries. His detailed examination of the interplay between environmental conditions and the actions of bounty hunters and *cimarrones* implicitly validates the effectiveness of a landscape approach. The success and failure of each group depended on their ability to understand, employ, and adapt to the variations of topography, vegetation, hydrology, and soil qualities.

Saint Croix

A common problem that has frustrated archaeologists studying resistance is how to find self-liberated Africans' hideouts. The challenge is compounded by the fact that many people who escaped from slavery were nomadic, organized in small groups, unable to carry large numbers of possessions, and aware that survival depended on remaining hidden. Much energy has been expended attempting to use maps to locate Maroon sites, which has resulted in both successful and failed searches. Maps can sometimes be misleading, particularly in cases that have suggestive place-names (for example, arroyo de los cimarrones) but which were never inhabited by people. Although some settlements founded by self-liberated Africans still exist, allowing archaeologists to learn a great deal from descendants, many towns are no longer inhabited by descendants or at all (De la Rosa 2003: 21–22). Archaeologists have had to work with these complications while seeking new sources of evidence and methods for locating self-liberated Africans' activity areas.

The island of St. Croix, one of the U.S. Virgin Islands, has been a testing ground for important methodological discussions, GIS spatial analysis, and site-prediction models that have been published in the *Journal of Caribbean Archaeology* (Norton and Espenshade 2007; Ejstrud 2008). Like on other small islands, *gran marronage* (large-scale, long-term settlement) was less likely on St. Croix than maritime escape or anonymous, small-scale settlements (Ejstrud 2008: 5). The mountainous northwestern region, known as "Maroon Ridge," has been examined to narrow down the list of likely eighteenth-century self-liberated African hideouts, many of which only receive vague geographical reference in documents describing them. Norton and Espenshade (2007) have identified explicit field methods and criteria for settlement discovery. They have also proposed using analogies for diagnostic assemblages and site features from unexpected sources, such as alcohol distilling sites that were covertly established in resistance to U.S. Prohibition.

Bo Ejstrud (2008) has brought a European perspective to the archaeology of self-liberated Africans. He and other Danish archaeological researchers on the Galathea expedition have been engaging in one of the latest field projects on St. Croix, which has used cost-surface, view shed, and other GIS applications to determine the high-probability areas where slavery escapees may have lived (Ejstrud 2008). Ejstrud used GIS to model and analyze a wide range of variables: plantation slaveholders' houses from a 1750s map; place-name locations; areas of historical high-density settlement; areas valuable to Africans who escaped from slavery (for their remoteness, rough terrain, seclusion, or low visibility); and environmental characteristics (topography, habitat, and hydrology).

Although such sophisticated methods provide many predictions about high-probability site locations in places such as Maroon Ridge, sites have yet to be found on the ground. However, these St. Croix studies are providing explicit site prediction methods which could be valuable to archaeologists seeking more formal, comprehensive approaches to locating communities of resistance in different parts of the African diaspora. It will be interesting to see how many sites fit the predictions of models based on logical factors (places outside of authority view sheds or in rough terrain), and whether it will be learned that self-liberated Africans used counter-intuitive settlement strategies. In addition, sensitive recovery techniques have to be developed to detect the sparse (low artifact density) and unconventional nature of Maroon settlements. For instance, archival and material culture data suggest that spatial characteristics of settlement layouts or locations do not always conform to expectations that scholars have about pattern (versus randomness) and symmetry (Weik 2004).

Communities in Defiance of South American Slavery

Brazil

Brazil features a multitude of self-liberated African communities and examples of temporary escape from enslavement (Kent 1965; Carneiro 1966; Schwartz 1992). For example, in the Archivo Historico Colonial of Lisbon, Portugal, crown records, governors' reports, and related documents mention at least thirty-five *mocambos* (another name for self-liberated communities) existing from the sixteenth to the nineteenth century. Most settlements lasted two years or less (Schwartz 1979). From the estimates of historians, the largest *quilombo* in the Americas was called Palmares and was located in the state of Alagoas, in northeastern Brazil. From 1600–1690s, between five thousand and twenty thousand people lived in several settlements which constituted Palmares. Early histories argued that Palmares was a kingdom, but later research has proposed alternative theories that suggest its political organization conformed more to state or confederation systems. Palmares had systems of birth rights and status, interdependent political and military leadership, and slavery (Cardoso 1983: 154). African leaders ruled over a culturally diverse population comprised of Native Americans and a few Europeans (Kent 1965; Schwartz 1992: 104, 117). A council of leaders who each represented a settlement helped integrate the wider community of Palmares, allowing collective responses to matters such as defense (Cardoso 1983: 155).

Historical evidence suggests that there were streets, houses, political leaders' compounds, spiritual spaces, fortifications, agricultural fields, smithies, and watchtowers at Palmares (Carneiro 1966; Kent 1965; Orser 1992). More than twelve thousand seventeenth-century artifacts, over ninety percent of them pottery, have been found at Palmares. Like at other American Maroon sites, they also consist of smoking pipe fragments, glass vessel shards, stone tools or debitage, and metal items (Allen 2001; Funari 1999). The ceramics are comprised of locally made, European lead- or tin-glazed, and indigenous Tupinamba wares. One of the most unique ceramic finds is a large *aratu* (Native American tradition) funerary urn. Although it was buried in the soil, it contained no skeletal remains.

A range of goals guided the two major field projects (1992–1993, 1996–1997) that have been conducted at Palmares: assessing the integrity and scope of the material assemblage, discerning the development of local potting, applying an ethnogenetic model to the society, understanding Native American contributions to Palmares, formulating a chronology of the *Palmaristas* (inhabitants of Palmares), and writing a critical historical theory about this community using all available forms of evidence (Allen 2001: 84–87; Orser 1992). Fourteen major artifact concentrations were spread over four kilometers on a hill called the Serra de Barriga (Orser 1992). A variety of testing strategies were employed during the phases of fieldwork, such as pedestrian surveys, shovel test pits, and variously sized excavation units (Allen 2001; Orser 1992). As one might predict from similar projects, evidence for whole structures has been difficult to find, although plenty of hearths, pits, daub chunks, postholes, and other features were identified in excavations (Allen 2001: 110). "Site 1" was subjected to two perpendicular shovel test transects (130×90m). Over twelve hundred square meters were examined from "Site 3" (Allen 2001: 112). A high level of disturbance (from farming and monument construction) and the complicated national identity politics that surround Palmares have hindered field studies in the area. For this reason, we have no clear picture of the spatial organization of Palmares.

Self-sufficiency and regional exchanges shaped the economics of Palmares. Archival and material culture evidence illuminates how people made a living. Farming was a fundamental aspect of the economy, according to visitors' descriptions of abundant crops and fields. Allen's (1994, 1998, 2001) work on locally made ceramics illustrates that trades such as potting largely contributed to the utilitarian needs (such as for cookwares) of *Palmaristas* and to an asset base which allowed participation in regional exchanges. Various other roles, such as priest, herbalist, or warrior, were filled by *Palmaristas*, creating a fully functioning society. The ironworking that chroniclers described at Palmares fits into a wider constellation of manufacturing capabilities and metallurgic skills present at other Maroon sites in Jamaica and the Dominican Republic (Cardoso 1983: 154; Kent 1979: 177; Weik 1997).

Palmaristas' relations with outsiders were complicated and contradictory. They participated in "world systems" and covert trade with local colonists known as "*moradores*" (Orser 1994; Parris 1983). Work needs to be done to discern the degree to which these relations were systematic or formalized, and whether they should be considered networks. Colonial chroniclers tell of African and Amerindian troops helping to quell slave rebellions and attack Palmares. Settlements were named for African, European, and Native American people, which reflects the diverse background of the *Palmaristas*. There is evidence that parts of Palmares were a Native American burial ground, which raises questions about the *Palmaristas'* interactions with outlying indigenous communities. Broader studies are needed to better address the area's relations with enslaved populations and other regional inhabitants (Allen 2001: 160).

Of all the cultural and social streams that converged at Palmares, the African tributaries have been subject to the most investigation and public interest. The word *quilombo* has long been recognized as a linguistic manifestation of African heritage, originating in a political-religious secret society from historic Angola that initiated warriors and integrated diverse ethnic groups (Kent 1965). Kilombos in Angola provided an organizational basis for leadership and resistance, as well as regional power. One of the best-known leaders at Palmares was Ganga Zumbi, whose name has been traced to central African languages. The Kimbundu word *nzumbi* means "ancestral spirit," and if this linguistic meaning resonated in the historical setting of Palmares, it may have spiritually augmented the political legitimacy of the leader.

Archaeologists are arguing for the revision of previous interpretations of Palmares's material culture. For instance, Palmares's geometrically incised clay pipes have great stylistic resemblance to pipes found in Maroon hideouts in Cuba and the Dominican Republic and slavery contexts in Virginia. Orser (1996) had suggested that Palmares's pipes should be interpreted as manifestations of ideas about pipe production that traveled in the minds of potters in diasporic networks. He also suggested that a "mutualist" perspective is useful for modeling pipe production and use, one that focuses analysis on global human connections, overlapping motivations, shared social group features, and world systems. However, Allen (2001: 152) notes that these pipes lack solid provenience information. Thus, the "mutualist" arguments for seeing the pipes as stylistic or symbolic products of slavery-driven diasporic artisan networks may be premature until more work is done at Palmares which can determine the pipe-maker's identity.

Suriname

Anthropologists have long been familiar with the Maroons of Suriname, through works such as Melville and Frances Herskovits' (1934) investigation of Africanisms. However, Richard and Sally Prices' twentieth-century research has produced a broader anthropological project culminating in works on a wide variety of topics: art, social structure, creolization, oral history, multi-vocal historical anthropology, public engagement, religion, onomastics, and gender (Price 1979; Price 1983; Price 1993; Price and Price 1994). Tens of thousands of self-liberated African descendants inhabit the interior of Suriname today, carrying forward their own dynamic body of knowledge, social memory, cultural history, and antislavery narratives.

Historically, Suriname's origins as a place of bondage were partly products of Caribbean connections, in particular to the English colonists of Barbados, who brought slavery there in the mid-1600s. Another island-to-mainland relocation occurred as Kofi Agorsah transferred his Maroon archaeology research interests to Suriname after he terminated pursuit of the Jamaican MHRP.

English colonial domination was relatively short-lived in Suriname, as the Dutch took over in the mid seventeenth century. As plantations expanded, so did the number of people who escaped from slavery, including Native Americans. Self-liberated Africans encountered a wide range of indigenous groups in Suriname's interior (Price 1983). Just after the mid eighteenth century, self-liberated Africans signed treaties offered by a colonial regime eager to seek alternatives to costly wars. The treaties contained stipulations such as the recognition of blood oaths, prohibitions against Maroons providing refuge to other escapees from enslavement, limitations on legally recognized (in colonial eyes) Maroon travel and assembly, and specifications about goods that the colonial authorities were to supply to self-liberated Africans at future meetings. Communities varied in their adherence to these treaties, and many still managed to maintain significant autonomy despite continuous pressure from colonists and slaveholders to submit.

Kofi Agorsah's (2006) investigations of Suriname's self-liberated African history sought to address regional problems such as identifying their modes of adaptation to new environments. He sought data concerning the processes and strategies by which Maroons settled, as well as the shifts they underwent as they transitioned from forests to riverside locations in the later eighteenth century. Agorsah's Suriname research project has stimulated the development of a dissertation on two eighteenth-century locations: Kumako, which is the first Saramaka Maroon settlement, and Tuido, a revered settlement of another Saramakan Maroon group called the Matawai (Agorsah 2006: 196; Ngwenyama 2007: 70).

Ngwenyama's (2007: 70–80, 89) research focused on the two sites and an area that was visited by self-liberated Africans by the early eighteenth century. In the decades that followed, Kumako and Tuido were founded, the former lasting a generation. These two settlements were studied in order to understand the relative influence of African, indigenous, and European culture on Maroon cultural construction, material possessions, and social life. Another goal was to integrate the extensive ethnographic, ethnoarchaeological, documentary, and environmental data made available by previous researchers. Agorsah's (1993) pursuit of a "local rule model"—a theoretical exploration of the relationships between spatial proxemics, settlement strategies, and social affinity or kinship—was also applied in Ngwenyama's (2007) study.

Ethnoarchaeology has generated a range of discoveries concerning the Saramaka Maroons and has addressed the great challenge archaeologists have had in locating structural remains at self-liberated African settlements (Agorsah 2006: 196; Ngwenyama 2007: 147). There is, for instance, a gendered dimension to particular Saramaka construction tasks and household management that ethnographers have also noted (Price 1983).

An archaeological surface survey of Tuido suggests that there is great potential to examine local and imported ceramics, stone configurations, house mounds, and other features that range from colonial times into the twentieth century (Agorsah 2006: 197; Ngwenyama 2007: 169). Investigations at Kumako focused on areas identified from oral and written histories which were most accessible. Kumako appears to be a mounded village, complete with defensive ditches, that is rich in material culture. More subsurface samples of Kumako need to be taken before the full site plan and social organization of space can be discerned. Potsherds, cowry shells, green bottle glass, stone tools, and an assortment of other colonial period objects such as arms were recovered. In one of the numerous pits at the site, Maroon field crews identified fragments of pots that were used for herbal spiritual medicines (Agorsah 2006: 199; Ngwenyama 2007: 192, 254). Radiocarbon dating has identified habitations ranging from two hundred to nearly two thousand years old. A range of local or regional pottery was identified, including some that may have been produced by Maroons.

North American Refuges from Slavery and Colonialism in the Dismal Swamp

Archaeologists conducting research in the "Great Dismal Swamp" (GDS), an area that straddles North Carolina and Virginia, have overcome great obstacles that accompany fieldwork in rural, wetland areas. Over the last few centuries, Maroons, enslaved canal workers (who were forced to drain the swamp), free and bonded African lumberjacks, and Native Americans inhabited the GDS. Elaine Nichols' master's thesis and Dan Sayers' dissertation and journal articles illustrate the groundbreaking research in the area. Nichols' (1985) research on Culpepper Island sought to locate documented Maroon sites and give voice to resistance, a neglected area of African American archaeology at the time. The marginal location of the area and the European manufactured goods and Native American pottery found there suggest that Culpepper Island could have been occupied by Maroons, though questions have been raised about whether Culpepper Island was otherwise inhabited (Sayers 2008). Sayers' (2008) research explored how forced laborers and formerly enslaved Africans dealt with the expansion of capitalism into the "liminal spaces" of the wetland landscapes. In addition, Sayers' team explored site location models that provided field workers with testable targets for probable areas of historic settlement and aided the preservation of cultural resources within the Great Dismal Swamp National Wildlife Refuge (Sayers, Burke, Henry 2008). Self-liberated Africans who found refuge in the Dismal Swamp have been linked to some of the most notable nineteenth-century revolts against slavery in the South, such as Gabriel's and Nat Turner's rebellions (Sayers 2006).

Sayers' research employed novel methods such as "tree-root mass" testing, which involved probing the roots of trees overturned by hurricanes for remains of artifacts and features. In addition, Sayers' team employed standard archaeological techniques such as shovel test pits and block excavations. A few hundred familiar colonial artifacts have been discovered, including items such as lead shot, gunflints, knife parts, white-ware ceramics, dark green glass bottle shards, and fragmented metal (Sayers 2008). Over a hundred features have been discovered in excavation units, including soil stains that hint at the former presence of structure walls, postholes, palisades, and pits. Field schools run through American University continue to explore GDS settlements. Fieldwork has substantiated the presence of numerous islands ranging from fractions of an acre to almost forty acres in size. A number of social forms and settlement strategies were likely used in the GDS. The material remnants of human occupation reflect a time span that extends from the 1600s until the end of slavery, including stone points associated with phases of "disenfranchised Native American" habitation.

Overall, most of the predicted archaeological signatures of free and enslaved African GDS functional centers—ephemerality, low proportion of mass-produced objects, complicated feature patterns, poor preservation, and significant presence of local lithic tools—have been encountered (Sayers and others 2008: 13–22; Sayers 2007). The one exception to Sayers' model is the low proportion of locally made ceramics (Sayers and others 2008: 36). However, in light of the low density of like ceramics found at other Maroon sites in such severe environments, this is not unusual and may hint at nomadism. Alternatively, Sayers and others (2008) suggest that it may indicate a greater dependence on other organic materials such as basketry. If Sayers' (2008: 33) interpretation of aligned postholes as a palisade is valid—versus other possible explanations for the postholes, such as a tightly spaced livestock fence—then it would indicate a considerable investment in defensive works and the possibility that some Maroons were more sedentary in their defensive strategy and lifestyles. More sites containing a substantial quantity of material culture will have to be discovered in order to substantiate claims that the GDS was inhabited by thousands of people.

Scholars may differ in their assessments of Sayers' analyses and interpretations, but most would probably agree that his project is one of the most well-organized, rigorous archaeological examinations of self-liberated Africans. His project has developed prediction models for settlements, located site remains, and analyzed material patterns of the three major inhabitants of the GDS (Maroons, enslaved laborers, and Native Americans), illustrating how self-liberated Africans cannot be understood without reference to neighboring groups and expanding capitalist world systems.

Conclusion

Archaeological research on self-liberated African communities has discovered new details about the breadth of inhabitants' possessions, refined our understanding of the geomorphologies alluded to by chronicled landscapes, and put forth unique explanations about the nature of sociocultural developments.

To date, archaeologists have uncovered over twenty self-liberated African settlements in the Americas. Although my literature review has focused on long-term or recurrent settlements, much work remains to be done to locate documented and undocumented short-term refuges. Chroniclers have described camps in places such as nineteenth-century west-central Florida (Porter 1996). Archaeological site location surveys suggest that self-liberated Africans used much of the available land in each region where they settled, leaving behind physical remnants of various activities (domestic, defensive, or sacred). Spatial patterns have been difficult to discern at individual settlements, in part because field data collection strategies and study areas have not been extensive enough to differentiate many features (such as hearths) indicative of households or activity areas. Settlement patterns vary in each region based on factors such as population size and environmental conditions. In general, each self-liberated group used a variety of defensive strategies, including choosing site locations based on their command of high ground or digging trenches. Settlement distributions varied from the more concentrated structural organization of densely populated Palmares to the sparsely inhabited Jose Leta site.

In general, the material culture of self-liberated communities includes fragments of European tablewares and utilitarian vessels (such as annularware bowls or stoneware jugs), dark green alcohol bottles, gunflints, lead shot, white-clay pipes, precolonial stone tools, glass beads (usually whole), locally made pottery (Native American or Maroon), stone tools (such as hearthstones), and highly eroded metal (such as kettles, knives, machetes, or guns). In many sites, Native American artifacts outnumber or equal those made by Europeans or Euro-Americans. Assemblages at different locations range from hundreds to tens of thousands of artifacts. At this point, it would be premature to compare self-liberated African site assemblages in search of answers to questions about issues such as population size or exchange. More comprehensive studies are needed to produce representative samples amenable to comparative analyses.

The challenges of doing Maroon archaeology are daunting: Agorsah had to fly his crew into Nanny Town; Sayers had to slosh through knee-deep water and fallen trees in the Great Dismal Swamp; Weik and Garcia Arevalo had to ride donkeys and walk across jagged rising limestone to get to Jose Leta; Ngwenyama's crews in Suriname had to use slash-and-burn methods to clear dense forests. Each project has had its share of logistical adversities and complex political negotiations (Allen 2001). For this reason, it is important not to view some of the fundamental silences (for instance, the inability to discern a clear settlement layout with material evidence) in the results of many projects as simple faults of the researchers. The fact that researchers have found self-liberated sites is an accomplishment in and of itself, and the artifacts that have been uncovered provide new, undocumented information on local behaviors and artifact production. These successes have to be weighed against the inability of some researchers to find sites and other potential impedances to the study of antislavery resistance: material ephemerality, chroniclers' imprecise documentation of site locations, inaccuracies of historical maps, and the destructive impacts of post-depositional land use.

Most of the sites that have been examined could be revisited in order to conduct more archaeological fieldwork. There are many other sites that could be explored through traditional or ethnoarchaeological research, particularly in South America. A great number of Maroon communities existed in places such as Colombia and Venezuela, and some are still inhabited (Acosta Saignes 1967; Perez 2000). In order to succeed, researchers will have to commit to prolonged, tenacious field campaigns that overcome some of the same environmental obstacles that self-liberated Africans faced. As anticolonial or antislavery thinkers have suggested, sacrifices and struggles—mental, physical, and social—are important factors in the realization of personal or collective liberty. Scholars studying self-liberated Africans will have to remain cognizant of the fact that they must make sacrifices to realize success, just as their research subjects did in the past.

5

Antislavery Collaborations and the Underground Railroad

Historical collaborations across race, culture, gender, and other lines of human difference defy simple conclusions about antislavery resistance and African self-emancipation in the Americas. Research on antislavery archaeologies of Euro-African (American) collaboration is heavily concentrated in North America, particularly the United States. Research has expanded in the Northeast, mid-Atlantic, upper-middle South, and Midwest. A number of projects have developed, initiated by the impetus of researchers as well as the ebb and flow of national interest in the Underground Railroad. However, investigations of Canada and Mexico suggest that there is much research to be done outside of the United States.

Underground Railroad Research in the Eastern United States

Harriet Tubman's Home

Harriet Tubman was a tireless opponent of slavery, one whose selfless service to African Americans transcended emancipation (Humez 2003: 55, 117; Laroche 2004: v). Since 2002, her former property has been investigated by Dr. Douglas Armstrong (Armstrong and Hill 2009), whose teams (and field schools) have conducted excavations and surveys on a thirty-two-acre property that Tubman owned from 1859 to 1913, when she passed away. Tubman's home was excavated, as was a kiln that produced bricks used in the construction of a house that replaced an earlier structure which burned in the 1880s.

Armstrong's teams have uncovered personal possessions such as a pillbox, pottery (tablewares), glasswares, a toothbrush, and metal items (Armstrong and Hill 2009). The excavations also recovered a calling card plate with Tubman's name on it, a material manifestation of her identity and physical presence (Armstrong 2009). These excavated items shed light on the intimacies of her home life and later years in ways that help bring some balance to public images largely portraying Tubman as a gun-toting warrior actively engaged in liberatory migrations and service to the Union Army. These antislavery actions created a presence that boldly contradicted gender norms of her times (Humez 2003: 5, 32).

Many popular images of Tubman are not particularly concerned with interpretations and representations of her life that could be derived from items such as the sherds of ceramic teacups that were excavated from her property. These tea-ware remnants were part of daily routines and cultural practices of domesticity (Armstrong 2009). The role of commodities like tea in facilitating entertainment is well known. However, this leisure-time beverage was also the product of exploitative global plantation regimes and forces of consumption. Conversely, tea has also been a site of struggle—the Boston Tea Party prompted conflicting views on the ethics or merits of the rebellious act, even among future participants in the American Revolution. Archaeologists may someday explore Tubman's perspective on and experience with tea (or alternatives such as coffee); her use of herbalism, which she demonstrated during her healing work for Union forces during the Civil War; the physical effects of tea (as a tonic, for example) in daily life or confrontational liberatory acts; or the social role of tea in abolitionist gatherings or meetings which planned the liberation of enslaved people.

Tubman's service and activist vision reflect her understanding that struggles for survival and social responsibility were as important as militant resistance in combating a system of inequality. The buildings on her property include John Brown Hall, which housed Tubman's "Home for the Aged." Harriet Tubman ran the home with support from the African Methodist Episcopal church from the 1890s until 1903. Other landscape features include a cistern, a barn, and a pond (Armstrong 2009b). Like other antislavery proponents, Tubman realized that racism and domination were not likely to disappear just because of an emancipatory government decree. Abolitionists and slavery-era activists understood that vigilance was needed to ensure the continuation of rights and autonomy in the post-emancipation era, for laws and the leftover racialized language of constitutions were potential tools that could be used to reinstate injustices such as disenfranchisement (Aptheker 1972: 547–50).

It remains to be seen in what direction Armstrong and his collaborators will take their future research and whether they will formulate formal approaches to Tubman's role (or that of her property) in antislavery resistance. Another potential research topic involves Tubman's long-term struggles against racism and gendered inequality during slavery and the post-emancipation period. These are among the factors that created Tubman's dissatisfaction with the U.S. government, which failed to provide her with fair pension payments for her Civil War service. The government did not see her as deserving of a soldier's pension, probably in part because of her gender. Rather, they chose to allocate her pension based on her cooking and hospital services, a determination which ignored her roles as a scout and intelligence officer (Humez 2003: 68, 109). Although the government responded to her protests by raising her pension, it was not enough to fully help her overcome the destitution that weighed on her in old age.

Future archaeological research will likely show how material culture informs our understanding of Tubman's final years, during which she was coping with poverty and supporting orphans and elders (Humez 2003: 109–17). Will archaeology at the Tubman property produce an artifact assemblage and features containing predictable residues of financial hardship and self-sufficiency (for example, lacking luxury items and containing game animal remains)? Can post-emancipation archaeological studies provide data that will facilitate insightful comparisons of African American political and economic strategies (compare Mullins 1999)? Did the support (food, goods, money, and so forth) she received from Euro-American or African American patrons affect her power to fight racism or run her household (compare Humez 2003: 309, 321, 328)?

Tubman's Travels in South Carolina during the Civil War

Relatively recently, newspapers in South Carolina have represented Tubman as a heroine in the heart of the Confederacy. Tubman, scouting for Union troops, infiltrated the Confederacy and liberated enslaved people at Combahee Ferry (Humez 2003: 54, 56). Tubman's tour of duty ranged from the islands of the Carolinas to Florida (Humez 2003: 49). A classic archaeological problem exists for interpreters of the Combahee Ferry site: can artifacts be linked to a specific event? The post-deposition processes operating on the site, which is situated in terrestrial and underwater contexts, make it complicated to understand and recover data from. Processes of shoreline erosion are just some of the natural forces that disturb archaeological proveniences. Human shipping, dredging, and construction constitute other post-depositional forces that have altered this environment and mixed the archaeological remains from centuries of human activity.

It is no wonder that journalists would take interest in the archaeology of Combahee Ferry. Archaeologists have increasingly noted how their images and data are appropriated at a rapid rate by a variety of media, institutions, and publics. Indiana Jones continues to defy the aging process as another sequel appears in the twenty-first century. Airline magazines, bloody television cop shows, video games, and personal Web sites feature artifacts, archaeologists, and archaeological sites. Newspaper stories about topics such as resistance to slavery are the product of sincere inquiries into the findings of scholars as well as more explicitly political constructions of history (Abrams 2006; Allen 2001: 78). However, the desire to create eye-catching headlines and interesting stories has led to quick news briefs and broadcasts that stretch the possible inferences about artifacts which may or may not be relics of antislavery resistance.

For example, the *State* (October 16, 2005) published a story entitled "Work Uncovers Site Where Raid Freed 700 Slaves." According to journalist Wayne Washington, "Archaeologists have unearthed artifacts they believe pinpoint the location of a Combahee River ferry crossing used in a Civil War raid led by legendary abolitionist Harriet Tubman." *Archaeology* magazine ran a short synopsis of the research in 2006:

A highway-widening project has revealed the ferry crossing where, on a summer night in 1863, Harriet Tubman led Union gunboats up the Combahee River. . . . More than 700 slaves were freed, and Tubman became the first woman to lead a U.S. Army raid. Artifacts from the ferry lodge, including items likely burned during the raid, have been recovered. (10–11)

Underwater and terrestrial archaeologists' work at Combahee caught the attention of local and national media as well as the archaeological community.

A photo in the *State* article (Washington 2005) featured a cannonball and some ceramics juxtaposed with the nineteenth-century sketch of the raid published in *Harper's Weekly*. However, the link between these items and the raid needs clarification with specific reference to their provenience (the location and stratigraphic level at which they were found). These details would help eliminate doubts about whether the artifacts were deposited at this setting at some other point in time, such as during another historic battle or from a dumping event.

Archaeologists at Brockington and Associates, a cultural resource management company, conducted field investigations of an area that included the former Combahee Ferry (Poplin and Watts 2010). They found no strong associations between the Tubman raid event and most of the artifacts, architectural remains, and activity areas that they uncovered, with the exception of a small area next to a highway where they discovered remains of a privy, refuse pits, and ceramics (circa 1830s–40s). The items and features may have been made and used in a period twenty to thirty years before the raid (Poplin, personal communication). Although some of the artifacts could have been passed down or continuously used decades after their production period, they need to be tied more securely to individuals and local contexts that date to the period of the Tubman raid (1863). Archaeologists also need to explain why the items in the privy and refuse pit were likely to have been used by participants in or refugees from the raid at Combahee.

Productive questions could be framed that account for the role of material culture and landscape in the raid. What kinds of items would have been carried (or lost along the way) by soldiers and formerly enslaved people moving from plantations to the docking areas? One African American soldier noted that thousands of dollars worth of property were taken, while Tubman herself described over seven hundred livestock being taken by the soldiers and evacuees (Humez 2003: 60, 299). If more specific documentation of the Combahee war booty recorded by Union officials, soldiers, or evacuees could be examined, this information might provide archaeologists with an idea of what to look for or, with the help of a database, could be used to assess the likelihood that certain types of artifacts were part of the raid. In a letter, Tubman described her frustrations with the long, flowing dress she wore during the raid, which she stumbled on as she carried two pigs for a formerly enslaved woman. The tiny bits—particularly buttons or accessories made of durable materials—of Tubman's torn dress may be among the items that were scattered over the land as the raid commenced. In an interview, Tubman described how people who escaped during the raid fled with whatever was immediately at hand, including cooking pots of rice and belongings bundled in blankets, which they put on their heads (Humez 2003: 246). Rather than "pinpoint *the* location of the Combahee River ferry crossing used in a Civil War raid" (as the newspaper article suggests; my emphasis), archaeologists need to think broadly about how the land and river were used and viewed by the many participants in the raid (evacuees, soldiers, and antislavery agents) or local inhabitants before, during, and after the raid. Little more can be said about the potential of the material culture until the final report on the Combahee archaeological study is completed.

Attempts at recovering submerged remains at Combahee and elsewhere suggest that underwater archaeologists are making contributions to antislavery archaeology. One set of researchers has sought Maroon settlements as part of the Looking for Angola Project (Sarasota, Florida) (Baram 2008). Another group, working on the shore of Lake Michigan, near Ogden Dunes (H.N.N. 2007), has investigated the remains of a ship that they believe slave hunters sunk while it was carrying people on the last leg of the Underground Railroad. These studies remind us that resistance has to be approached with the total physical and social environment in mind, not just the terrestrial part.

Wesleyan Methodist Church, Syracuse, New York

The abolitionist movement in the area surrounding nineteenth-century Syracuse, New York, was promoted by the Wesleyan Methodist Church (WMC), a structure containing seven clay faces on its basement wall which archaeologists believe reflect antislavery sentiments (Armstrong 1998; Armstrong and Wurst 1998). A pastor named Luther Lee wrote about his success in moving over thirty individuals in a month through Syracuse on the UGRR. Archaeologists investigated whether they could shed more light on written sources about UGRR activity in the church and oral traditions which assert that the carved faces were products of UGRR passengers. No written or oral sources indicate the clay sculptors' identities or the dates of the carvings.

Excavations in 1994 demonstrated that the tunnel containing the faces was constructed by the 1850s. Besides the tunnel, the basement contains a bench-like earthen ledge, a furnace, a coal storage area, and a dead end near the carved faces. A brick furnace base and ash lenses, transfer print ceramics, window glass, a broken communion cup, a pencil, and a bead were among the few items excavated (Armstrong and Wurst 2003: 28). Most artifacts can be dated to the period 1840–1870. The clay faces showed signs of carving as well as variations in color, applications (for instance, the presence of candle wax), clarity, and level of completion. The different fingerprints on each face suggest different sculptors were at work, possibly at different times. One face had attributes suggesting curly hair, a probable feature of an African descendant. The date 1817 was carved below this face. Armstrong and Wurst (2003: 30) suggest this date is probably a reference to Frederick Douglass, who was born in the same year. The second face had more of an Afro hairstyle and a nail embedded in it, the function of which (utilitarian or ritual) is not clear. Two faces show evidence of burning, possibly from a fire that occurred in 1898.

The evidence that Armstrong and Wurst (2003) assessed is compelling. However, the fact that the faces are not buried in a soil stratum frustrates any attempt to give them an absolute or relative date. Yet the artifacts and tunnel construction date do fit well with the UGRR's primary operation period. It is plausible that the clay faces are the remnants of people who sought to artistically pass their time in hiding from slavery (Armstrong and Wurst 2003: 32). It seems less likely that these faces were the creations of free people who simply spent their leisure time in such a dark, uninviting place. The clay faces in the Wesleyan Methodist Church (WMC) could be part of the wider corpus of abolitionist visual representation, invoking famous antislavery leadership and less-well-known antislavery proponents or UGRR passengers (Armstrong and Wurst 2003). Drawing on Ortner's (1995) observations about transformations of resistance, one could conceptualize the meanings and uses of the WMC faces and tunnel as products of different individuals or generations of churchgoers. This diachronic view fosters consideration of a number of discrete, simultaneous, or sequential functions and meanings for the clay faces: as educational media, as symbolic tools for indoctrination, or as commemorative busts. Similarly, the lack of numerous sources about the clay sculptors or the creative works of church members begs a question about whether the face-makers at Wesleyan Church may have been uninvolved in the UGRR.

By 1989, the WMC congregation had moved to another location and church ownership passed to a man who was willing to allow archaeological work and conservation of the faces to take place. He also provided funding for conservation. Preservation efforts by the wider community generated nearly a quarter million dollars to conserve the faces (Armstrong and Wurst 2003: 20–25). After fears emerged that the National Underground Railroad Freedom Center in Cincinnati—who supported preservation efforts—would remove the faces from Syracuse, local activists and churches rallied to keep them in the city. The faces have been removed from the church, and are now displayed at the Onondaga Historical Association.

The Thaddeus Stevens and Lydia Hamilton Smith Property, Pennsylvania

Pennsylvania was a location of significant antislavery activity for various reasons. Being a border state between the North and South, and a place with networks of railroads and rivers, it provided the proximity and transportation vectors that aided people on the move. The state was home to humanitarian groups, was the setting of a long list of antislavery events (dating as far back as the 1600s), and was a free state decades before U.S. emancipation. Compelling circumstantial evidence and material remains of possible antislavery activities exist on the former property of nineteenth-century congressman Thaddeus Stevens and his African American colleague Lydia Hamilton Smith (Delle and Levine 2004). While the political efforts of antislavery activists have been of great interest to scholars, it is more complicated to find proof of politicians' participation in the UGRR (Delle and Levine 2004: 137). Nevertheless, Stevens' general correspondence with abolitionists, his opposition to the Fugitive Slave Law of 1850, and his legal services in support of the defendants who fought against the enslavement of people during the Christiana Riot are compelling reasons to associate Stevens with the Underground Railroad (Delle and Levine 2004: 134–35).

Politicians' indebtedness to multiple constituencies has often limited their overt support of legislation deemed radical or their participation in actions that benefit the people who suffer most from inequalities. Similarly, there is a "politics of remembering and avoidance" that affects political and economic leaders shaping preservation priorities in Lancaster, Pennsylvania, the county containing the Stevens and Smith site. Uncomfortable issues such as racial slavery are easily erased from historical narratives that inform the heritage and tourism institutions of many U.S. communities. Since the mid twentieth century, urban renewal initiatives have catalyzed the destruction of historical resources as well as the "salvage" type of impetus that led Lancaster's Historic Preservation Trust (HPT) to seek archaeologists' help in extracting information from the Stevens-Smith site.

The archaeological project's goals were shaped by the HPT's broad interest in identifying artifacts for exhibition, locating biographical information related to notable residents, and (potentially) promoting an inclusionary heritage program that featured an African American woman. Delle and Levine (2004: 139) put the potential for UGRR research on the table. Delle's (1998, 1999) earlier research on Jamaican slavery (including Maroons) and Irish anticolonial struggles against British expansion made him no stranger to resistance histories.

Excavation of the courtyard behind Thaddeus Stevens' former office revealed a series of brick pavements and fill layers which contained nineteenth- and twentieth-century ceramics as well as glass and metal artifacts. It also contained a subterranean cistern that archaeologists argue was a viable place for concealment of escaped slaves. The cistern was partially filled with artifacts (largely ceramics) dating to the late nineteenth century. A square portion of the cistern wall, wide enough for a medium-sized person to pass through, was repaired with a brick pattern that Delle and Levine (2004: 131) interpret as an entryway to a small tunnel. Excavation revealed that this patched area of the cistern was connected to an external trench (marked by distinct soil coloration and composition) which contained artifacts dating to the 1850s. The cistern's repaired wall section and external trench aligned with a patched area in the wall of a neighboring saloon. Another peculiar finding was a spittoon, which was standing upright in the cistern. Other artifacts recovered from the soil inside the cistern date to the late 1890s.

The fact that no major concentration of UGRR-period artifacts was discovered in the cistern is not necessarily a weakness in the argument that it functioned as a hideout. African (Americans) who escaped from

Figure 5.1. Eastern wall of Stevens cistern showing modified "window." Courtesy of James Delle.

slavery usually carried a few essential items with them (food and clothes, for example); it was in their interest to pack light (Gara 1961: 46). Exceptions might have included highly liquid items of exchange (valuables to trade for cash). It is likely that food and drink vessels would have been supplied by hosts, masking the presence of explicit artifacts of resistance. Another benefit of created or unintentional material invisibility was the protection it provided to activists, whose properties were subject to search by bounty hunters and law enforcement officials. It is reasonable to expect that formerly enslaved people and their antislavery hosts would have been resourceful, maximizing the utility of all items at their disposal. Thus, one could hypothesize that an artifact such as a spittoon could have served as both tobacco depository and chamber pot, in an emergency. These are among the reasons why it is difficult to conclude the absence of UGRR activity from a sparse material pattern (compare Delle 2008b: 64). Thus, it is useful to consider the potential insights that could be gained from "negative" or subtle evidence.

The Parvin House, Berks County, Pennsylvania

There are times when the general public and local advocates for historical preservation alert archeologists to the potential for research. In Berks
County, Pennsylvania, a homeowner of the Parvin House property invited
archaeologists to investigate tunnels that family oral traditions assert were
used by agents of the UGRR. Between 2000 and 2005, archaeologists investigated the Parvin House property in order to see if there was any material evidence of UGRR use and to help homeowners preserve possible
UGRR features threatened by road construction (Delle and Shellenhammer 2008).

A few of the Parvins have been definitively linked to the abolitionist
movement and/or to active participation in the Quaker religion and its
organization, the Society of Friends (Delle and Shellenhammer 2008).
Although critics have noted that the Quakers were not universally against
slavery, a number were active in founding abolitionist groups (Gara 1961).
As we shall see, archaeologists have studied Quaker lands with alleged
links to the UGRR in a few states. From the seventeenth century, Quaker
representatives put forth decrees banning members from owning slaves
and calling for an end to slavery. One Parvin family member signed a
decree against slavery before the Civil War began. Another employed
freed African Americans. The African Methodist Episcopal church had a
prominent role in the UGRR, which is significant here because an AME
church is located less than ten miles from the Parvin house. All these
particulars suggest that there is reason to look closely at the possibility of
UGRR activity at the Parvin House property (Delle and Shellenhammer
2008).

Delle and Shellenhammer (2008) found the above circumstantial evidence as sufficient to warrant an archaeological examination of the family's claims. Their data collection strategy involved directly testing a semi-
subterranean cold cellar that had a channel surrounding a small pipe near
its foundation and a recessed area. Excavation pits were also dug in areas
that aligned with the channel or that were positioned on a possible line
between a barn and the cold cellar. No tunnel was found, and the channel
proved to be merely a pipe trench. The archaeologists also monitored the
ongoing road construction, but they found no tunnel evidence.

Over seven hundred artifacts were excavated from the Parvin property, including fragments of refined earthenwares, stoneware, butchered animal bones, a medicine bottle, a blue bead, and metal objects (Delle and Shellenhammer 2008). The artifact assemblage did not provide incontrovertible evidence of UGRR activity, such as abolitionist medallions or a cache of hidden letters. Most artifacts were recovered from the cellar's recess, or "alcove," a 1.5 × 1-meter stone-lined area. Researchers argue that medicine bottles and more expensive pottery—highly useful items that are unlikely to be kept distant from people's residences—and chamber pot sherds suggest that the cold cellar could have housed people escaping slavery. However, it is also possible that some items were cast into the cellar after falling out of active use. The cellar could also have been used for preserving some temperature-sensitive medicines or for general storage (for instance, of pottery that lost its aesthetic or utilitarian appeal).

Although excavations and a D.O.T. road trench provided no evidence for the existence of tunnels on the property, the landowner rejected these findings. Instead of accepting official results, he put forth his own interpretations by appropriating a picture of archaeologists working on the cellar and affixing a caption stating that it was the inside of a tunnel (Delle 2008). Archaeologists also made use of their own form of interpretive creativity by using stories based on oral accounts and UGRR history to interpret material culture from the Parvin House cellar (Delle and Shellenhammer 2008). Delle (2008: 65–67) argues that these narratives have a role in a larger project that can accommodate ambiguity and critically engage authorized public memorializations, social memories, and myths of the UGRR.

Delle and Shellenhammer's (2008) reluctance to rule out the possibility of UGRR activity in the cellar is important because the house and other buildings might be worth architectural or archaeological explorations as hiding places. However, it is important to not bias UGRR testing strategies by overemphasizing methods designed to locate tunnels, as underground areas were often not the main mode of concealment. Similarly, on social and discursive levels, the "underground" aspect of the UGRR did not retain complete integrity. This prompted Frederick Douglass to note that the numerous public accounts and newspaper articles describing the success of the UGRR threatened to "out" the movement and invert the underground metaphor, bringing it "above ground" (Gara 1961: 145; Vlach 2004: 95). Researchers should be careful not to fall prey to the ideological force of the Underground Railroad as a metaphor for a coordinated, high-traffic resistance system. Abolitionists used the UGRR metaphor to enact their agenda of changing policy by changing minds. Some also used it to inflate their successes. Slavery advocates appropriated the UGRR idea to decry the moral problem of theft (of their human property) and the financial losses it created (Gara 1961: 148–55).

Midwestern Movements toward Freedom

Although the northeastern United States and East Coast are privileged in many classical works on antislavery resistance and the UGRR, the Midwest also had a substantial amount of antislavery activity. Archaeologists have studied self-emancipation and resistance to slavery in states such as Illinois, Indiana, Ohio, and Michigan.

Miller Grove, Illinois

In southern Illinois, an area that was hostile to nineteenth-century African Americans, a group of self-liberated and freed African Americans set up a small settlement known as Miller Grove. Although no explicit account of UGRR activity at Miller Grove has been discovered to date, scholars have discovered the presence of local abolitionists who exchanged letters with members of Northeastern antislavery organizations. Laroche (2004: 208–11) used a range of government records (such as the census) to construct a picture of the community. An AME preacher ministered to the surrounding area, and if histories about this denomination's involvement in antislavery struggles are any indicator, activist sentiments may have been propagated at Miller Grove.

Three items named in the will of Joseph Dabbs (a Miller Grove resident) indicate that he was equipped to potentially resist slavery proponents (Laroche 2004: 210): his shotgun could have been used to prevent attack or carry out armed defense; his wagon allowed him or potential UGRR passengers mobility; and his books, including one on laws, provided him with a knowledge base to understand legal structures of inequality and to devise strategies of resistance to these laws (compare Rotman and others 1998: 51 and Laroche 2004: 50, 160, 289). Dabbs' sentiments also become apparent in letters he wrote to abolitionist societies requesting antislavery literature. Laroche (2004: 211) also added that the local abolitionists were part of an organization that actively distributed Bibles. These Bibles were useful to people aspiring to empowerment through literacy (as slaveholders and lawmakers who legislated against African literacy both understood). However, the Bible was an ideological site of struggle, for it contained stories about both resistance to slavery and slaveholding. Thus, its valence (liberatory or oppressive) and wider political impact on the general population (black and white) is hard to assess in singular terms.

Mary McCorvie, an archaeologist working for the Shawnee National Forest, where Miller Grove is located, has led fieldwork there. The main discoveries at Miller Grove include house foundations, wells, gardens, and grave markers. Research has targeted family homesteads of residents such as William Riley Williams and Bedford and Abby Miller. Oral history and documents suggest that a school and a few churches may someday be found by archaeologists (Laroche 2004: 236–37). Other locations in the area, such as a nearby settlement that was a destination and a detention area for people who escaped from slavery, also hold potential to inform UGRR history. Cheryl Laroche (2004: iii, 229) has contributed to studies of Miller Grove, as well as Lick Creek, Poke Patch, Rocky Fork, and New Philadelphia, by employing landscape theory, an approach which has shed light on the potential of strategic natural settings such as ridges and caves to serve as lookout points and hiding places. Laroche (2004: 235) suggests that isolation and inaccessibility were features of Miller Grove which allowed residents to insulate themselves from racism and support the UGRR.

The search for pre-emancipation churches at Miller Grove is important because it may tell us about religious networks linking antislavery ideology, resources, and activists (Laroche 2004). Besides being places where people could find guidance and spiritual engagement, churches were vital hubs of African American connectivity that fostered leadership, literacy, mutual aid, education, entertainment, fund-raising, and political organization (Hunter 1997: 69; Raboteau 1978). Historically, churches have been important refuges from the dangers and sorrows of the world. White supremacists have also understood this and destroyed churches during slavery and in more recent times. As the archaeology of Wesleyan Methodist Church (above) has demonstrated, churches were also potential places of concealment for escapees.

1 Birchtown	2 Combahee Ferry
3 Camp Nelson	4 Harriet Tubman Home
5 John Rankin & John Parker Homes	6 Lick Creek
7 Miller Grove	8 New Philadelphia
9 Parvin House	10 Poke Patch
11 Ramptown	12 Randolph Co.
13 Rocky Fork	14 Stevens-Hamilton Smith Bldgs.
15 Tracadie	16 Wesleyan Methodist Church

Map 5.1. Select UGRR and antislavery archaeological research locations. Illustration by Terrance Weik.

New Philadelphia, Illinois

A multidisciplinary research team and descendants have worked for many years to bring forth the story of one of the first towns to be founded by African Americans (Shackel 2010). New Philadelphia, Illinois, is also a site that fosters reflection on the role of entrepreneurship, a primary means of self and family emancipation for founder Frank McWhorter and his peers. McWhorter and others like him illustrated that the business skills and economic savvy of free people could also be found among enslaved African Americans, who worked for wages, made loans, saved for their children, worried about currency valuation, and set prices for goods they sold (Penningroth 2003: 191; Usner 1999; Walker 1986). By 1835, McWhorter had purchased the eighty-acre tract that was the basis for the town. McWhorter clearly understood that financial freedom was a primary tool for liberation in a capitalist society. He showed that business and social justice do not have to be irreconcilable entities.

Archaeologists have devised a wide range of research questions about New Philadelphia, largely focusing on the post-emancipation history of the town as opposed to the UGRR (Fennell 2009, 2010). What can New Philadelphia's interracial demography tell us about regional U.S. race relations and (anti)racism? What similarities and differences concerning diet and consumption existed between households? How was the town spatially organized during each phase of its existence? Laroche (2004: 200) points out that the family-based clustering of plots at local cemeteries is part of a wider pattern of segregated grave placement that contradicts notions of interracial harmony.

A variety of field strategies have been employed by University of Maryland and University of Illinois researchers, including surface reconnaissance, remote sensing, and subsurface excavation. The National Science Foundation supported archaeological field schools that have exposed college students to the fundamentals of research at New Philadelphia. The local cemeteries have been avoided in accord with the wishes of descendents. Mundane items such as buttons, toys, tools, fragments of glass bottles, and pottery have been recovered. These items have been observed in aggregations that may indicate former house lots (Laroche 2004: 195). It remains to be seen what research problems or hypotheses can be formulated in order to discover what archaeology can say about the UGRR or people's transition to freedom after emancipation. Finding Frank McWhorter's house would be a good place to start, because oral traditions (Walker 1983) state that it was a refuge for UGRR passengers.

Rocky Fork, Illinois

In a hilly part of southwest Illinois, African Americans escaping from slavery found refuge in a community called Rocky Fork. During the early nineteenth century, this small settlement was inhabited by African- and Euro-American families who had antislavery sentiments. The proximity of Rocky Fork to the Mississippi River and its placement on the margin of different regional, political, and ecological boundaries made it somewhat ideal for antislavery resistance (Laroche 2004: 157). African American oral histories state that a white family named the Hawleys allowed people who escaped from enslavement to rest on their property en route to destinations promising freedom. Documentary sources indicating which local residents participated in the UGRR have been almost impossible to find.

A mix of African Americans lived at Rocky Fork, including people who were emancipated by owners (or self-purchased), who escaped from slavery on their own, and who were passengers on the UGRR. Some black residents came as free people from the East Coast; others were short-term visitors transshipped from nearby black towns. By the 1850s, the area was inhabited by almost one hundred residents. The Hawleys and another white family named the Spauldings owned a large proportion of the available land in the area. These families entered into labor agreements with African American migrants, who temporarily worked the land or purchased lots over time (Laroche 2004).

Laroche (2004: 169–71) reports that she assisted archaeologist Gail Anderson (of the Center for American Archaeology) in mapping features, cemeteries, and building foundations at Rocky Fork. Southern Illinois archaeologists such as Bonnie Gums and Mary Lentz have also conducted preliminary investigations in the area. The use of remote sensing (such as the magnetometer) in locating self-liberated African American graves in Iowa and archaeological features at Harriet Tubman's birthplace in Maryland are encouraging signs that technology may one day illuminate the settlement footprint at Rocky Fork (De Vore 2008; compare Laroche 2004: 22, 29, 168–71).

Road building, church vandalism, and other forces obstruct research and preservation at Rocky Fork (Laroche 2004: 145–47). Matching specific African American families with properties and artifacts is difficult, for documents suggest that few were able to formalize land ownership in the mid nineteenth century. Oral and documentary evidence suggests that UGRR escapees and African American immigrants engaged in a transitory residence pattern. This kind of short-term tenancy indicates that any homesteads found will probably exhibit light artifact densities and diffuse household distributions (Laroche 2004: 150). Two other significant challenges facing archeologists include finding funding and dispelling descendents' fears about state intervention (for example, in matters of land ownership).

Lick Creek, Indiana

By the second decade of the nineteenth century, small groups of African and Euro-Americans from the East Coast, mid South, and Midwest were settling in a location known as Lick Creek, Indiana. What they encountered in Indiana was no racial utopia (Rotman and others 1998: 53, 56). As late as the 1850s, Indiana's laws reflected the voting majority's wishes to prohibit the immigration of African Americans and curtail the rights of people racially categorized as Negro. White antislavery sympathizers in the area included a small number of Quakers who came with some African Americans from North Carolina. By the 1830s, free black and white families purchased spatially integrated forty-acre (and larger) tracts of land that are now collectively known as Lick Creek (Krieger 1999: 1; Laroche 2004: 257). By 1850, the number of people of African descent in Orange County reached 251, including a number who resided at Lick Creek. Like some other Indiana settlements with a major black population and church, Lick Creek was on UGRR routes. By 1902, black residents abandoned Lick Creek, gradually leaving behind over fifteen hundred acres of accumulated land.

Lick Creek's links to antislavery initiatives include the service of residents in the United States Colored Troops during the Civil War. Less clear are the UGRR activities of the AME church in Lick Creek, which Laroche (2004) suggests we infer from AME UGRR activities elsewhere. The activism of black (AME) church leader William Quinn—an important organizer of congregations across Indiana and neighboring states—and Quinn's association with abolitionists offer further support for the argument that Lick Creek was a UGRR site. Other factors that seem to implicate Lick Creek as a UGRR haven are the local and regional Quakers' support of Quinn and their wider UGRR activities in the United States. Finally, the location of Lick Creek, sitting one mile north of Chambersburg, a well-known stopover point on escape routes along the Ohio River, also increases the likelihood of its UGRR association (Krieger 1999: 1; Laroche 248, 268–69).

Angie Krieger directed archaeological fieldwork at Lick Creek (1999: 5). These efforts served the primary aim of identifying the role of African American and UGRR history in the Hoosier National Forest (surrounding Lick Creek) for heritage, recreation, and tourism purposes. Other goals included locating farmsteads with the aid of test excavation units, discerning socioeconomic profiles of black and white people in the area, and unearthing evidence of interracial relations. In her investigations, Kreiger used evidence such as oral histories (such as descendants' discussions of family participation in the UGRR), 1938 aerial photos, census records, and land ownership documents.

Archaeological field researchers have located a dispersed settlement layout, the edges of which have yet to be clearly demarcated (Laroche 2004: 245). So far twelve locations, spread over roughly five square miles, have yielded evidence of a built environment (Krieger 1999: 14, 16). The human remains of former residents lie in Lick Creek, Danners Chapel, and Lick Creek Friends cemeteries. They contain over 127 graves, a significant portion of which have no markers (Krieger 1999: 9). Remnants of the African American Union Meeting House (circa 1843), the predecessor of the local AME church, include a ten square meter pile of stone, window and container glass, cut nails, and charcoal (Kreiger 1999: 32–34). A small cemetery contains grave markers dating 1858–91 and the remains of the Roberts and Thomas families. It is within one hundred and ten meters of the ruins of the Union Meeting House and Lick Creek AME Church. At a nearby documented farmstead, surface and subsurface testing uncovered rock piles, a dark blue molded and edged whiteware potsherd (circa 1830–1860) and some depressions. Other farmsteads date from the nineteenth and twentieth centuries and contain a range of material culture: corrugated metal roofing, building ruins, machine-made glass, a modern root cellar, twentieth-century appliances, and brick and stone piles. The surface areas of the former farmsteads range from 8 × 10 meters to 100 × 200 meters.

A more in-depth study of the Roberts site, part of the three-hundred-acre property that belonged to Elias (1793–1866) and Nancy Roberts, was sponsored by the USFS (U.S. Forest Service) and the Indiana State Museum. New evidence was brought to light about residents' "solidly rural middleclass lifestyle," which ended in 1876 when Nancy, a widow of ten years, died. Researchers were fortunate to have access to a set of probate records that informed a wide material universe, of which the recovered artifacts comprised a smaller subset. An analysis of functional categories (architectural, tools, and so on) indicates that the artifact assemblage was more informative about clothing and recreation. Wepler, McCullough, McCullough, and Arthur (2001: 35, 75) posed their investigation as a long-term rural community study exploring material wealth, area economics,

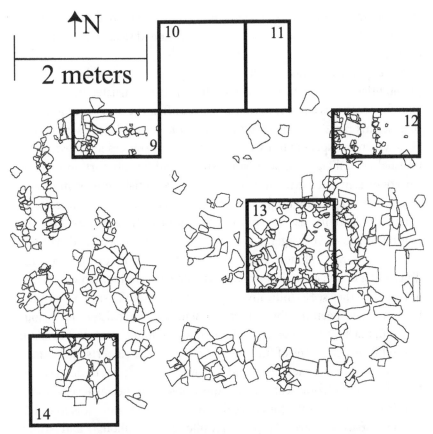

Figure 5.2. Planview map of Roberts site cabin foundation stones. Courtesy of Robert G. McCullough.

ethnicity, and human interactions. They focused on the remains of a log home, outbuildings, and refuse areas. The site was later inhabited by twentieth-century white residents who left behind a paper trail and material culture. The investigation determined that the site was eligible for the National Register of Historic Places.

The study brought to light the 16.5 × 20 foot lime and sandstone foundations of the Roberts cabin (Wepler, McCullough, McCullough, and Arthur 2001: 33–34, 45, 65). Other domestic finds include pottery (ironstone, whiteware, stonewares), nails (cut and wrought iron), scissors, buttons, glass vials, and window glass. Food remains include the bones of wild rabbits and squirrels as well as domesticates such as pigs and chickens. The data suggest that the Roberts employed a variety of agricultural strategies in order to realize a relatively successful existence in an area that lacked the kind of resources that typically generated wealth (in a capitalist economy).

No explicit evidence of UGRR activity was found, although some possibilities exist for future testing. Elias's role as a trustee in the AME church, which was a major player in the UGRR, is the only explicit thread (besides his racial experience) that may indicate antislavery sentiments. However, more specific links via oral or written sources are needed. No unusual assemblage characteristics, such as a high proportion or wide variety of arms, are evident at Lick Creek. Potential signs of militancy or defensive capability might not be the best archaeological indicator of antislavery activity, as stockpiling of arms may have aroused the attention of pro-slavery agents if their structures were searched. Wepler, McCullough, McCullough, and Arthur (2001: 75, 81) discovered two gunflints and a bullet, as well as written evidence of a shotgun and a powder horn, which they see as indicative of subsistence activities such as hunting. Firearms have been notably underrepresented or nonexistent in various east Indiana sites (Wepler, McCullough, McCullough, and Arthur 2001: 85). While expectations of finding cold cellars at the Roberts Homestead went unfulfilled, archaeologists did discover a crawl space under a cabin. No special foundation work or remains suggesting special accommodation (such as extra walls for concealment or food remains) was found in the crawl space, however (Wepler, McCullough, McCullough, and Arthur 2001: 93).

More detailed investigations are needed at Lick Creek to uncover possible hiding places and homes, and their role as nodes or hubs in UGRR networks. The sparse remains of a shed (and some artifacts such as potsherds) found in an outlying area may have provided a hiding spot for UGRR passengers, if the Roberts were personally involved in sheltering escapees. However, this type of space could have also been a more obvious place for slave hunters to search. Other fundamental questions need to be raised in future research. Will nineteenth-century root cellars be found? If they are, what criteria can be used to differentiate their use as places of concealment versus storage areas or later refuse repositories?

A broader consideration of African American cultural resistance occurring within enslavement contexts, such as the covert religious spaces called "hush arbors," reminds us that the natural landscape should be considered in analyses of places like the Roberts' homestead and Lick Creek.

Thus, methodologies could include ways of reconstructing dramatically altered landscapes or assessing the concealment potential of caves, woods, or wetlands (Laroche 2004). Although the UGRR was not their frame of reference for the study of the Roberts homestead, Wepler, McCullough, McCullough, and Arthur's (2001: 95) consideration of regional history suggests a hypothesis that could be tested in the future with comparative site-location data: "The pattern of relatively isolated rural African American settlements in Indiana . . . may indicate a resistance to a white-dominated larger society."

Ramptown, Michigan

By the mid nineteenth century, Cass and Penn townships (Cass County) were destinations and travel routes for thousands of Michigan's UGRR travelers (Campbell and Nassaney 2005: 24). Besides free people of African descent, a Euro-American Quaker population was also active in the local fight against slavery. Underground Railroad passengers and self-liberated people moved to the area, where they settled on the lands of abolitionists. Quaker abolitionists assisted formerly enslaved people by providing them with temporary shelter and land use, by challenging slavery in the courts, by physically confronting slave hunters, and by boycotting businesses and institutions that promoted slavery (Campbell and Nassaney 2005).

The first UGRR archaeological research in Michigan was conducted on a settlement called "Ramptown" (near Vandalia, in Cass County), which was founded by people freed by the UGRR. Archaeologists responded to calls for investigation by the Michigan Historical Center and the Michigan Freedom Trails Program. Archaeologists' goals and methods were driven by the aims of these heritage entities, which sought to locate UGRR homesteads and use them to educate citizens and preserve sites. A portion of Ramptown's artifact assemblages was recovered from archaeological sites spanning nearly two square miles. Some finds have been put on display in venues such as Southwestern Michigan College (Stewart: 2005, 7).

Archaeologists surveyed seven hundred acres of land around Ramptown. A hand-drawn map made from information supplied by a Ramptown descendant in 1964 suggests that it is located where archaeologists have found artifacts (Campbell and Nassaney 2005). Archaeologists streamlined their search for housing remains by identifying abolitionists' or UGRR participants' properties on plat maps. Area residents also assisted archaeologists in locating sites by sharing their knowledge of artifacts that they saw in plowed fields during the 1980s and 1990s.

Various forms of evidence suggest that Ramptown was inhabited from roughly 1846 until 1890. Abolitionist letters from the 1850s and a newspaper obituary of a Ramptown resident provide hints about the settlement and wider UGRR activities. Researchers have concluded that three out of six possible nineteenth-century sites were inhabited by African American settlers who escaped from slavery. These UGRR sites are not located on plat maps from the 1860s or 1870s, as are the structures of Quakers and other landowners. Ceramic sherds (such as sponge-painted wares) are the most prevalent artifact class in an assemblage of over three hundred specimens. Ramptown's material remains also include glass bottle shards, bricks, metal hardware, and cut nails. Collectively, the evidence suggests that all the households shared a humble lifestyle and simple dwellings, which is what one would expect of people who had recently obtained freedom from slavery. Another possible reason for the small material assemblages is that many UGRR refugees who came to the area only stayed on the properties for up to a decade, bringing little with them and leaving little behind. Many fled to Canada, while some stayed in the area, farming the lands of UGRR operators in exchange for rents or shares of the produce. However, as most artifacts were collected on the surface, these suppositions will have to be assessed with more data, particularly excavated materials (Campbell and Nassaney 2005: 36–52).

Distributions of late nineteenth-century building materials and artifact scatters suggest that Ramptown was a settlement of dispersed households, not a nucleated or rectilinear "town" as one might surmise from its name. Like the settlements of most self-emancipated Africans that have been studied by archaeologists, thin clusters of refuse and construction debris constitute the most visible material evidence of structures.

Ripley, Ohio: The John P. Parker House and John Rankin House

By the 1840s, John P. Parker had bought his freedom and moved from the South to Ripley, Ohio. His creativity, entrepreneurial drive, mechanical aptitude, and industriousness served him well. His commitment to ideals such as freedom enriched his family and motivated him to liberate hundreds of enslaved people (Sprague 1996). By 1900, when he passed away, he had run a steel foundry and obtained patents for machines. Parker's home has been examined by Cincinnati Museum Center archaeologists in order to satisfy the house renovation and preservation mission of the John P. Parker Historical Society. Robert Genheimer (2001) led an investigation which sought to locate domestic and industrial remains and evaluate the quality of the Parker family's material culture.

From 1998 to 2000, roughly 5% of the property (80 square meters) was excavated, producing backhoe trenches and standard test units containing over 10,000 artifacts and 51 features. Parker's house and shed were the only standing structures. Maps suggest that Parker's property contained various nineteenth-century functional centers: foundry workspaces, cisterns, a well, a lumber holding area, and a shop. Features that were uncovered during fieldwork include a metal walkway, oven floors, building foundations, piers, brick flooring, prepared clay surfaces, and post molds. A rich assemblage of artifacts was found, including ceramic doorknobs, sheet metal, whiteware pottery sherds, animal bone, wrought nails, eggshell, animal bone, buttons, roofing slate, window glass, doll fragments, limestone, medicine bottles, pins, and ax heads. Some of the most peculiar finds include a cast-iron angel and a dog burial (Genheimer 2001: i–ii, 99, 113–20).

No explicit evidence of UGRR activity was found in the excavations, which was expected based on the researcher's assumptions and observations about Parker's biography and UGRR history: only one recorded incident placed a UGRR traveler at the Parker House; housing people who escaped from slavery would have been dangerous to Parker's personal liberty, business, and his family's well-being; slavery proponents watched Parker; many UGRR passengers were kept on the move; and the areas excavated were not high-probability zones for UGRR activities (Genheimer 2001: 93). These impediments to participation in the UGRR are not surprising or unusual factors for many who investigate its material culture. Further, Genheimer's (2001: 102) research addressed techno-functional and economic questions, not ones exclusive to resistance issues. Analyses of Kentucky's UGRR, a major origination point for enslaved people who escaped to Ohio, suggest that escapees fled with few items (such as clothes, weapons, money, or, rarely, horses [Hudson 2002: 42–46, 127, 156]). Nevertheless, more attention could be paid to discerning whether aspects of the built environment, such as the well and cisterns, were places of concealment for people or objects of the UGRR.

Despite the challenges of finding UGRR evidence at the Parker House, it did not hurt other UGRR archaeology efforts in Ripley. At the Rev. John Rankin House in Ripley, archaeological studies were conducted by the Ohio Historical Society. For over a year, surface surveys sought out evidence of domestic farm life. A barn cellar was alleged to be the hiding place for people escaping from slavery. Fieldwork has uncovered a cistern and summer kitchen, but no clear UGRR hiding place (Hitch 2006).

The Upper South: Camp Nelson, Kentucky

As the Civil War came to a close, many enslaved people, such as John Mason, did not wait for the help of an abolitionist or a liberator. Mason emancipated himself, fought his way out of re-enslavement, and allegedly led thirteen hundred people to freedom on the UGRR (Quarles 1969: 78–80). Thousands of others escaped to Union troops by their own means. In places such as Georgia, Maryland, Missouri, and Tennessee, formerly enslaved people sought freedom in Union war camps, becoming known to chroniclers as "contrabands" (Hunter 1997: 18; Penningroth 2003: 3–4). While many were liberated in this way, a significant number faced problems after their escape, such as being forced to work for Northern troops and having their few possessions pillaged by both Union and Confederate soldiers.

Archaeologists such as Stephen McBride (2008) have examined similar issues at Fort Nelson, Kentucky, where formerly enslaved people fled with the hope of speeding up their emancipation during the Civil War. Union Army officers stationed at Fort Nelson were reluctant to take on the responsibilities of managing formerly enslaved civilians, especially ones whose status forced the troops to make daily decisions about their role as liberators, enslavers, or indifferent soldiers. Many soldiers probably would have rather passed off the challenging ethical, legal, economic, and moral issues to politicians and other citizens.

Hundreds of African Americans arrived at Camp Nelson in 1864, leaving behind bondage in Kentucky and bordering states. The Union Army was more receptive to the male refugees from slavery because of their potential contribution as manual laborers or soldiers. Females, some of whom were relatives and mates of men taken on as soldiers or laborers, were turned away by U.S. officers despite their offers of labor (for example, as washerwomen) and material compensation. While there were some sympathetic U.S. soldiers, the views of officers such as Colonel Clark largely shaped how women were treated. Clark's correspondences illuminate the racist and sexist beliefs that shaped the local military policy of turning African American women away from Camp Nelson. Further pressure was applied by slaveholders, who called on Clark and others to return the former captive laborers. Between two hundred and four hundred African American women persisted in their pleas and their presence in or near Camp Nelson. They and their sympathizers or kin built shelters, but these "shanties" were destroyed by order of the Colonel. Ash and other features provide material evidence of the documented ejection of women and children from the camp. Stephen McBride (2008) recovered traces of these buildings during a 2001 survey. Fortunately, the remains of destroyed structures are not the end of the story, for in 1865, public outrage led to the construction of housing for some women, especially wives of African American soldiers.

Clusters of building material (such as nails) and a few chimney falls indicate that physical structures (not tents) were erected. McBride (2008) suggests that the different house locations also vary greatly in domestic (ironstone pottery, for instance) and architectural debris, hinting at the possibility of wealth differentials between neighbors. Excavations uncovered a stove, iron parts, buttons, and a few needles and thimbles, suggesting that some women spent more time washing clothes than sewing. McBride (2008: 11) draws on Tera Hunter's (1997: 62) analysis of post-emancipation black women in order to explain the social significance of laundering, which in her view created "informal networks of reciprocity" over time as women developed bonds in their neighborhood workplaces.

In post-emancipation situations of dramatic social change, networks played crucial roles in (re)connecting family members and creating new communities (Laroche 2004: ii). Fluidity and informality would have been useful features for networks that may have developed in Civil War-era Camp Nelson, where women and children faced displacement and daily uncertainty (regarding food or the dangers of re-enslavement, for example). Wild fauna remains indicate that the families of formerly enslaved camp inhabitants lived off the land or traded for lean protein sources. This kind of expedient subsistence is seen in other instances of collaborative resistance to slavery, such as in the faunal remains of Fort Mose (Reitz

1994). Despite these and other traumatic challenges, the women and children persisted, and the media eventually shamed the government into aiding them.

Canadian Antislavery Resistance

In classic works on flight from U.S. slavery, Canada is often viewed as the primary destination, though Mexico, Haiti, and Europe were among the many alternative places of refuge from enslavement. Some Quakers, U.S. politicians, and other citizens drew the ire of African Americans for suggesting that they be sent to Africa as part of a colonizing scheme. Nonetheless, the diversity of political views within African American populations ensured that there was a number of willing migrants who went to places such as Liberia and Sierra Leone. The number of self-liberated people who reached Canada is difficult to estimate, but we could at least say that it was in the thousands by the end of the Civil War (Gara 1961: 37–40; Smardz Frost 2008: xv). Their struggles have been commemorated in various ways, such as through the exhibition of a bell that replaced the one which was rung in historic Buxton, Ontario, to signify the arrival of liberated people (OMCI 2007; see other examples in Smardz Frost 2008).

The archaeology of Canadian antislavery heritage has largely been focused on Nova Scotia, where over three thousand people of African descent fled from the British colonies during the American Revolution (Robertson 2000: 16–21). Later waves of immigration involved Jamaican Maroons who were deported there after the "Trelawney Town War" (1796) and escapees and black soldiers who served the British during the War of 1812 (Campbell 1990: 242; Smardz Frost 2008: 259). The British enticed people to escape during the American Revolution with promises of freedom, especially in exchange for military service. Some of these "Black Loyalists" are listed on the "Book of Negroes" (1783), a census that documented migrants and the ships that carried them to Nova Scotia. The migrants on this census included Funky Hancock, age twenty-five, who left enslavement in Virginia; Sukey Dismal, a self-liberated woman who escaped from Norfolk, Virginia, with her two children in 1778; Mimbo Scot, who fled enslavement in Charleston, South Carolina, in 1778; forty-five-year-old John Longstreet, who "left enslaver Derick Longstreet of Princetown, New Jersey," in 1776 (Robertson 2000: 22–100, 45).

The migrants arrived in places such as Port Mouton, Guysborough, Tracadie, and Birchtown. The British did not support these communities solely because of antislavery policies, but they were nonetheless important destinations for some people who escaped from slavery. In the minds of the slaveholders who had formerly controlled the migrants, their existence in Nova Scotia was an ongoing act of rebellion. A number of African descendents who inhabited eighteenth-century Nova Scotia continued to migrate, eventually leaving for Africa (Campbell 1993). This outmigration may have been the result of adversities such as the existence of slavery in the region until 1834 and local racist hostility, as well as better economic opportunities, weather, and land elsewhere (Powell and Niven 2000: 10).

Archaeological research that was carried out in Tracadie (1787–present) and Birchtown (1783–1796) uncovered thousands of artifacts (Powell and Niven 2000: 4–5). Archaeologists tested a small spatial sample of Birchtown, which was comprised of over seven hundred acres of land at its peak. Residents such as Joe Blair obtained lots measuring sixty by one hundred and twenty feet. In 1993 and 1998, fieldwork at Birchtown located features such as a cellar, a wall, a depression, and twenty-two stone mounds (Niven 1994; Powell and Niven 2000: 10–17). The function of the mounds is still a mystery. Excavations revealed that residents lived in semi-subterranean houses. These residences formed part of a settlement that also contained documented buildings such as religious "meeting houses" and a school. Excavations of a four-meter-wide depression produced fragments of cream and gray stoneware pottery, clay pipes, and spirits bottles which suggest that one structure was inhabited in the eighteenth century. These temporally diagnostic artifacts agree with documents which describe fifteen hundred Birchtown residents inhabiting the settlement during the 1780s. Many left for Sierra Leone by 1791.

An archaeological survey was also conducted on a tract believed to be owned by Stephen Blucke, a local leader and a veteran of the American Revolution. He opposed migration to Sierra Leone by remaining in Birchtown until its decline around 1796 (Niven 2000: 17). Blucke's house location was inferred from a twentieth-century minister's local history. This historical work stated that the house was on the land of a family who still owned the property at the time of its excavation in 1998. Archaeologists placed test excavation units in locations where the landowners remembered seeing nineteenth-century structures (which were demolished in the twentieth century). No ruins or traces of an ancient built environment existed on the property. Shovel test units uncovered nine hundred artifacts that dated from the eighteenth to the twentieth century (Niven 2000: 24). A brief historical document's description of Blucke's house indicates that it was spacious and superior to the meager structures that housed most Birchtown residents. Blucke lived there with his wife, mother-in-law, and two servants. Of the nearly sixteen thousand total artifacts discovered at the Blucke site, eighty percent were food preparation and consumption items (such as hand-decorated pearlware), and eighteen percent were architectural (such as nails). Military buttons, metal utensils, buckles, locks, a bayonet, a mouth harp, and a spur are among the other remnants of Blucke's possessions. Researchers believe that the variety and volume of artifacts reflect the remains of a middle-class family. Laird Niven, the project director, cautions that the evidence does not prove beyond a doubt that Blucke actually lived at the exact spot (Niven 2000: 36). In order to move beyond the evidence gaps that Niven alludes to, future researchers will have to broaden the excavated area so that they can discern whether the remnants of other houses, which could be alternative candidates for Blucke's home, exist on the property. Postholes and other features would also provide stronger evidence for a home.

The original Tracadie land grant (1787) was negotiated by individuals such as Thomas Brownspriggs, a former resident of St. Augustine, Florida, who secured a three thousand-acre tract for himself and seventy-three grantees (Robertson 2000: 18). Today, many descendants still live in the area. Stephen Powell, archaeologist for the Nova Scotia Museum, conducted a pedestrian survey and limited test excavations which sampled sixteen sites, including parts of Birchtown. He located rock-lined pits, stone burial markers, cellar depressions, and wells that date to the nineteenth and twentieth centuries. One of the best examples of early loyalist-period finds is a stone house foundation, near which artifacts including pearlwares (edged and hand-painted), animal bones, bottle shards, wrought nails, bricks, and a gunflint were found. This presents archaeologists with the future possibility of tracing the community's transition to the post-slavery period.

The extent to which Tracadie's residents were free or liberated was affected by the political obligations placed on them (as Crown land grantees): requirements to clear land, drain swamps, pasture cattle, build houses of a certain size, or mine rocky lands (see transcription in Robertson 2000: 116). These obligations limited the inhabitants' rights to merely subsist or use the land for inns or other entrepreneurial activities. Such government impositions affected both individuals' free choices (to select more lucrative pursuits) and collectivist practices (like using land for the common good). Archaeologists could use these land grant terms as hypotheses that could be tested by excavating material residues of grantees' behaviors. For instance, did most Tracadie homes conform to the 16 × 20-foot standard size mentioned in the 1787 grant? The government-granted lands were also sites of conflict because some Euro-Americans contested the black loyalists' claims, arguing that they had been granted some of the land (Robertson 2000: 20, 118). Thus, archaeologists could use the built environment to explore government-sponsored relocation and contested land rights. Philosophers might characterize this as an opportunity to examine "negative freedom."

Research at Birchtown and Tracadie has demonstrated that generations of African descendents left behind a variety of structural and domestic remains. Like a number of other archaeological sites of the African diaspora, no explicit material expressions of African practices have been found (Niven 2000). Rather than searching for overt symbols or forms indicating African influences, future researchers might try looking at how African cultural practices facilitated the uses or meanings of material culture. The Anglican and Methodist churches of Birchtown may have muted the physical expression of African practices or transformed them into less obvious emblematic forms. It remains to be seen if cultural or social differences (such as people coming from the Caribbean versus the United States) were visible in the local material culture. More household remains need to be examined in order to address whether the accumulation of wealth achieved by settlers such as Colonel Blucke lead to inequalities, class structures, possessive individualism, or exploitation. Conversely, researchers might discover whether archaeological remains can speak to the development of communalism and a unique African Nova Scotian identity.

Other studies of African Canadian life also touch on the issue of self-liberation from slavery (Fennell 2010: 30–32). In Toronto, Smardz Frost (2008: xi–xii, 54, 264–67, 350) excavated the eight hundred-square-foot shotgun home, root cellar, and outbuildings of Lucie and Thornton Blackburn, a couple who had escaped from enslavement in Kentucky during

1831 (Smardz 1995: 3). Excavations at the Blackburn site uncovered kitchen implements, pipe fragments, glass shards (from wineglasses or preserve jars), buttons, pins, transfer-print pottery sherds, and salvaged bricks. These remains attest to over fifty years of consumer access and frugality. The physical remains of the barn pinpoint the location from which the Blackburns ran their taxi company, the first established in Toronto. The wealth generated from this company and Lucie Blackburn's domestic work allowed them to acquire items such as a pearl-handled pocketknife, silver-plated spoons, a brass watch, and jewelry, possessions that hint at the couple's prosperous adjustment to a new society. The Blackburn's victorious physical and legal battles against slavery and their entrepreneurial achievements in Canada contrast with the harsher existence of other escapees in places like Nova Scotia. Their story is one of many that dispelled the misinformation that some slaveholders circulated about Canada being a barren and unbearable place (Gara 1961: 35). Like at other sites discussed in this chapter, public engagement has been an important aspect at each stage of the research (Smardz 1995).

From Resistance to Colonial Compromise at Amapa, Mexico

People of African descent acted in various periods to end their enslavement in colonial Mexico. During the sixteenth century, almost half of all enslaved people who were brought to Spanish colonies ended up in Mexico. Around one hundred and fifty thousand people had been shipped to Mexico by 1650 (Palmer 1976, 1993). Over the next 180 years, slavery expanded very slowly, though it never compared in scope with other major slave societies in the hemisphere. This fact did not lessen the brutality of punishments, violations, and dehumanization felt by those whose labor was forcibly extracted to enrich mine and sugar plantation owners and create a life of ease for slaveholding households. Under these conditions, it is not surprising that Africans rebelled and *cimarron* settlements emerged. As elsewhere, self-liberated Africans were not a uniform group in terms of their age, ethnic origins, or sex.

Mexico became a destination for people of African descent fleeing nineteenth-century U.S. slavery and racism. Because slavery was abolished in Mexico nearly thirty years before U.S. emancipation, enslaved and free people of African descent from Texas and other states sought refuge in Mexico. Anthropologists and the general public have begun to realize the important role of Africans in Mexican culture, building on the works of community activists and scholars such as Aguirre Beltran in the preceding decades. Archaeologists working for INAH (Mexico's National Institute of Archaeology and History) have surveyed plantations in the state of Veracruz, and U.S. students and established scholars are also developing projects in the area.

One of the most famous self-liberated Africans is Yanga, a man who escaped from enslavement and established a mountain enclave with the help of west and central Africans who built seventy homes there. He later led a settlement supported by the colonial government, who signed a treaty protecting inhabitants from re-enslavement. Yanga's fame and the efforts of people like him to establish free communities helped stimulate research on self-emancipated Africans in the northeastern and Veracruz regions of Mexico (Weik 2008).

During the summer of 2003, Weik (2008) did preliminary fieldwork in Veracruz in order to assess *cimarron* and slavery sites in the area south of the city of Cordoba. In the eighteenth century, this region was dotted with hundreds of ranches and plantations that were worked by over one thousand enslaved Africans. Brief archaeological surface inspections were conducted at plantations near the modern town called Yanga, including the Senora de la Concepcion, San Joachim, and Palmillas plantations. Red-brown, coarse earthenware and majolica pottery, glass shards, brick, and metal fragments were found at some of these plantations amid the ruins of churches, walls, manor houses, work spaces, fields, and storage buildings.

The pueblo called Amapa became the focal point of Weik's 2003 fieldwork in Veracruz. The field research goal was to assess the integrity and scope of material culture, structures, and other evidence of Amapa so that the potential for future archaeological research could be determined. Amapa was founded around 1743 by *cimarrones* (Maroons) who Spanish authorities convinced to descend from the mountains of Mazateopan (Winfield Capitaine 1988, 1992). Amapa was founded in a manner similar to Yanga's San Lorenzo de los Negros and the Florida settlement called Fort Mose, two places where Spanish colonists supported the establishment of free black towns in exchange for the military assistance of black troops against colonial adversaries (such as France or Britain). In Mexico, colonists also requested that the former *cimarrones* help capture future self-liberated Africans. Fort Mose's archaeological remains suggest that life in these communities was a product of social diversity, Afro-European collaboration, self-sufficiency, and opportunistic consumption (Deagan and MacMahon 1999).

From its formation until 1827, Amapa's population grew from over 20 to nearly 150 persons (Carroll 1977: 500). By the 1760s, over thirty houses and a church existed at Amapa (Pereira 1994: 103). Today, modern houses, a clinic, a store, and a church all surround a central paved and fenced public space in the small settlement. While most buildings are made of cinderblock and corrugated roofing, a few have thatched roofs. The church is in the far eastern part of the town, in a position similar to the church that appears on an eighteenth-century map of Amapa's rectilinear layout (Winfield Capitaine 1992). Abbreviated surface collection and pedestrian survey were carried out in the yard of a store and public spaces, as well as on a couple private properties. A resident whose ancestors were among the founders of Amapa was briefly interviewed (Weik 2008: 7–8). Physical remains were noted, photographed, and then left in place, as Mexican law prohibits removing artifacts from archaeological sites and transporting them out of the country (Weik 2008: 6–9).

Amapa's material culture hints at eighteenth and nineteenth century habitation. The judgmental sample of artifacts that was encountered included fragments of clear glass medicine bottles, dark green beverage bottles, unidentified metal containers and tools, and thin, red-brown brick. Some of the eighteenth- and nineteenth-century pottery that was found is part of the Majolica tradition that was produced in Puebla, Mexico City, and Oaxaca. The Majolica sherds were decorated with blue and white, polychrome, or green and white hand-painted designs (compare Deagan 1987, Lister and Lister 1974, and Charlton and Fournier 1993: 209–18). The surfaces of the Majolica sherds had clear glazes and the pastes were pink or orange. Few semi-porcelaneous, hand-painted, English pearlwares were observed. A bell from the historic church was stored in one of the buildings. It is not apparent whether the bell dates to the eighteenth century or later, as it was locked up and inaccessible.

The brief fieldwork in western Veracruz reported above suggests that there are various lines of evidence and questions worth pursuing in the study of Mexican *palenques*, plantations, and free African towns. Research could help explain the costs (such as political autonomy) and opportunities (such as access to manufactured items) that transformed self-liberated

Figure 5.3. Church at Amapa, Mexico. Photo by Terrance Weik.

Africans into interdependent colonial subjects. Many interesting questions remain: What kind of impact did missionaries—whose presence was a requirement of the treaty that established Amapa—have on inhabitants' ability to find spiritual guidance or their willingness to convert to Christianity? Did Amapans Africanize Christianity? Hopefully archaeological investigations at Amapa will also be of use to researchers, publics, and descendant communities (in other towns in the states of Veracruz, Guererro, and Oaxaca) who are working to preserve the cultural resources of Afro-Mexican heritage (Silva Castillo 2007: 122).

Conclusion

Although there is some overlap in their features, the places discussed in this chapter could be classified in the following way: ten long-term settlements inhabited for more than a year; one short-term settlement inhabited for less than a year; one battlefield; and four hiding places. The Parvin House site and some sites that have been linked with the UGRR in Randolph County, Indiana, are not included in this typology, as they have not been linked to tangible or strong evidence of antislavery actors or escapees (Rotman, Mancini, Smith and Campbell 1998: 1–6). Many more sites remain to be found, and known or alleged antislavery locations need more attention.

What researchers of the UGRR and collaborative antislavery resistance are bringing to light is the continual need to read between the lines, do detailed biographical profiles, understand the intricacies of antislavery networks, move between different scales of analysis, and devise analytical techniques sensitive to the material traces of liberatory activities. One of the clearest patterns for African American settlements that aided escapees was a dispersed layout and placement at a considerable distance from slave-owning or white communities (for example, see Laroche 2004: 151). Methodological challenges such as the need to work around farmers' cultivation cycles must also be addressed in the early stages of research designs (Campbell and Nassaney 2005: 35; compare Weik 2002: 106).

The assemblages of many resistance and UGRR sites contain artifacts commonly found in sites of enslaved people and the masses of U.S. society, such as low-cost pottery, glass bottles, architectural remains, and metal debris. Much remains to be done to discern whether there are other material patterns that inform resistance events or acts. Micro-level studies are needed to generate artifact databases amenable to formal comparative analysis, especially at the intra-site scale where more can be discovered about social differentiation (for example, related to identity or wealth differentials) or shared material culture. However, as the archaeology of an underground hideout at the Stevens-Smith property suggests, researchers have to remain open to the value of subtle or negative artifact evidence.

Future archaeology could examine the nature of buildings, layout of homesteads, and dimensions of environments (such as landscapes or topography), thereby discerning defensive features or clues to the organization of social spaces. It may become possible to observe material residues of antislavery resistance at particular places once intensive household- or activity-level scales become the focus. For instance, clothing remains (such as buttons) or caches of domestic artifacts (such as inexpensive ceramics or bottle glass) found in unlikely places of domestic activity (workspaces or outbuildings, for example) and organic concealed spaces (like caves or depressions) could trigger an examination of those locations for their use as hideouts.

Some archaeologists who have investigated the UGRR and collaborative antislavery resistance have focused more on life after enslavement.

However, the communities where people settled were never fully places where people could afford to assume they were beyond the reach of enslavers or oppression. The implication for archaeologists is that they have the ability to examine the long-term processes and transformations of racism and inequality across the chronological divide marked by official U.S. emancipation. Did the residents (including escapees) of towns that actively supported antislavery resistance leave a different kind of material record than their neighbors? If so, was this divergent material record a result of the ways residents were aided or hampered by labor and land agreements they made with white farmers who supported abolition? To what extent did the race, class, and gender attitudes of neighbors, merchants, or government officials affect residents' ability to draw on economic networks or protect their human rights?

In order to advance the discourse, some types of generalizations need to be examined on a case-by-case basis, with specific evidence or carefully constructed inferential leaps. For example, some generalizations about black churches being active participants in the UGRR are plausible. However, threats to the survival of churches are likely to have affected some congregations' willingness to aggressively or extensively participate in the UGRR. Similarly, the history of the Quakers, who are widely associated with antislavery resistance, also contains contradictions, such as members who were not supportive of antislavery or antiracist actions. The existence of antislavery activity in a region did not always mean that networks existed. Further, the initiative of lone escapees and those offering random acts of aid are downplayed in grand UGRR narratives more concerned with demonstrating organized, courageous, interracial or intra-ethnic collaboration. Archaeology is bringing to light the material presence of buildings, settlements, and behaviors that constituted nodes of resistance networks and branches of escape routes. Churches have been highlighted in this chapter, which attests to the potential of places of worship to serve as safe houses regardless of their congregations' level of support for antislavery activities.

Extant architectural remains, such as can be found at the aforementioned Tubman, Parker, and Parvin Houses, should not be ignored by archaeologists. Most buildings that were part of the UGRR—homes, churches, schools, mills, warehouses, stables, and outbuildings—were unassuming structures that blended into the everyday landscape (Vlach 2004: 109), and escapees likely stayed in common spaces in these structures.

Figure 5.4. Adobe house at Nacimiento. Photo by Terrance Weik.

Researchers who have tested properties in Ohio and the Northeast for (architectural, and in a few cases archaeological, evidence of the UGRR have challenged assertions about the presence of tunnels and secret in-house hiding places (Fruehling and Smith 1993; Vlach 2004: 108, 318). While it is reasonable to closely examine claims about UGRR hiding places, it would seem premature to cast doubt on all claims until systematic, large-scale research is done which assesses a statistically robust range of buildings and geographic locations.

Even Larry Gara (1961), whose highly skeptical book called attention to the uncritical use of oral and other sources of UGRR history decades ago, gives us cause to remain cautiously optimistic. He cited a study done by the Western Reserve Historical Society which investigated rumors of tunnels beneath Cleveland's St. John's Episcopal Church. Although Gara (1961: 181–82) does not elaborate on the investigators' methods and results, he suggests that they found no tunnels. However, the researchers acknowledged the possibility that the church's belfry could have been used to conceal escapees. Thus, ambiguous evidence, unconventional methods, and new questions are a part of research on collaborative resistance.

This chapter has largely focused on collaborations between European and African descendants who worked to free enslaved people. Although archaeologists have largely been seeking material traces of these antislavery efforts in the Midwest and Northeast, research on Buffalo Soldiers and towns in the Great Plains has the potential to contribute much more to the story (King 2006). More southern parts of the United States, as well as Meso-American and South American sites of resistance also deserve attention in future archaeological research. For instance, Nacimiento, Mexico, was a refuge for African Seminole, people who escaped from slavery in Texas, and indigenous people (such as the Kickapoo and Seminole).

6

Coalitions, Community-Building, and Conflict in Seminole Territory

For people of African descent, life in Native American territories provided opportunities to realize various forms of liberty which shaped their cultural identities, power relations, and sociocultural transformations. By allying with Native Americans, some African escapees joined indigenous opposition to European (American) colonial control. While self-liberated Africans may have symbolized the potential for resistance in the minds of some enslaved people, escapees may have also found inspiration in the more aggressive acts of enslaved Africans in Florida who rose up against bondage during regional conflicts (compare Bird 2005 with Campbell 1990: 1). The continental relevance of antislavery resistance can be seen in Native American studies such as Wright's (1986: 314) *Creeks and Seminole*, which made reference to "Florida's Underground Railroad."

This chapter examines social processes and cultural identities that shaped ethnogenesis at a nineteenth-century African Seminole settlement called Pilaklikaha. Regional interactions between Africans, Native Americans, and colonists will be explored in order to understand how they shaped antislavery resistance, exchange, and communal participation. African diaspora and Native Americanist literature offer analogues that can be compared with African Seminole history in order to build a model of the society at Pilaklikaha. Archaeology is an important approach to African Seminole settlements because it has uncovered material evidence of daily life, such as reliance on local raw materials in building construction. The archaeological data take on a greater importance as they become analyzed in conjunction with various lines of evidence in pursuit of a more refined understanding of the ethnogenetic dynamics at work in the material universe, social relations, and cultural products of Pilaklikaha.

Nuances of Seminole Identities

The word "Seminole" is the product of colonists' and U.S. citizens' ethnonymies—reductive labels that collapsed numerous Southeastern groups who had different languages, beliefs, interests, and trajectories into a single sociocultural entity. Nevertheless, the people who became Seminole also shared worldviews and cultural practices (such as ball games) with people who spoke related Muskogean and Mikasuki languages (Hass 1941; Hardy 2005: 70). Descendants carry forth these languages and historical legacies as members of the Seminole and Miccosukee tribes of Florida and the Seminole Nation of Oklahoma (Weisman 1989: 170). I differentiate certain Seminole in this chapter by using the adjective "indigenous" (a word which has its own baggage) to distinguish a subgroup who primarily associated with or claimed Native American identities and worldviews. Alternative labels such Muskogean or Maskoki have been used to name people and traditions that had native Southeastern origins, as well as to challenge the usage of colonial constructs such as "Seminole" (Martin 1991; Wickman 1999; Wright 1986).

The group that I refer to below as "African Seminole" are people of African descent who had significant social or cultural connections with Native Americans (especially indigenous Seminole). African Seminole included people who were affected by one or more of the following conditions: escaped from slavery; served the labor demands of indigenous Seminole; had both African (American) and Native American parents; lived in territories controlled by indigenous Seminole. Scholars, documents, and descendants use other terms to describe them, such as black Seminole, Afro-Seminole, freedmen, Seminole Maroons, and self-emancipated Africans (Mulroy 1993; Ogunleye 1996; Opala 1980). A nineteenth-century letter that is part of the congressional record regarding the Second Seminole War uses the term "African Seminole." I prefer African Seminole because the term recognizes African and Native American heritage. I also seek to avoid merely reproducing documentary descriptions that uncritically assign racial identities to people (such as "Seminole Negroes"). Though many were self-liberated Africans, I do not always use "Seminole Maroon" to describe them because, according to chroniclers, a significant number were enslaved and a number were freeborn. We ultimately lack specific oral or written sources that indicate that they had a widespread term of self-definition.

My usage of certain identity labels is not an argument that the past or present people to whom they refer embrace(d) these terms of self-definition. My "African" and "indigenous" qualifiers differentiate between idealized groups that were linked by collective concerns and cultural influences. No one term of self-identification is likely to find acceptance among scholars, descendants, or laypersons (Weik 2007: 316). In cases that involve both African and indigenous peoples, I will refer to them as "Seminole," without qualification.

Africans Meet Native Americans in Colonial Florida

Outside of older "diffusionist" arguments about lost tribes and mythic events, or Afrocentric explorations of pre-Columbus contact, the dominant paradigm in academia asserts that African and Native American interactions occurred throughout the Americas during colonialism and slavery (Forbes 1993; Sertima 1992). In North America, Florida offers one of the most instructive cases of antislavery resistance involving African-Native American interaction. This contact took place within a context where Native Americans (such as the Calusa) faced destruction in Florida because of a range of factors: colonial conquests, missionary assaults on native worldviews, conflicts between indigenous peoples, catastrophic deaths from diseases, and lack of awareness or denial of long-term consequences of colonialism (Milanich 1995).

A group known as "Creeks" or Maskoki, people who shared ancestors with the Seminole, traveled through Florida in the eighteenth century. These journeys allowed them to seek resources and relationships that fostered kinship, successful hunting, war victories, and wealth (Wickman 1999; Wright 1986). The soldiers, travelers, colonists, and officials—writers whose voices are loudest in historical documents—recognized some cultural distinctions within indigenous Seminole, such as the Mikasuki, Tallasees, and Topekayligays (Covington 1993; Weisman 1989: 105).

After British forces from the Carolina colony destroyed Spanish missions (1704) and the towns of groups such as the Apalache, Maskoki migration occurred with greater magnitude. As the Atlantic slave trade accelerated in the eighteenth century, Florida's African populations rose from the hundreds to the thousands. A small number escaped from plantations and cities devastated both by ongoing battles between British and Spanish colonial forces and by the American Revolutionary War (Landers 1999; Rivers 2000).

By the end of the eighteenth century, Florida was part of a colonial frontier and an expanding U.S. border. During the second decade of the nineteenth century, U.S. citizens and armies were engaged in conflicts with Spanish, British, and Seminole forces. After the War of 1812, a failed invasion by Georgian settlers, and the First Seminole War (1816–1817), the United States had gained enough victories to control North Florida. In 1821, the Spanish signed a treaty granting colonial lands to the United States. The Treaty of Moultrie Creek (1823) envisioned U.S. containment of the Seminole on a central Florida reservation (Covington 1993; Mahon 1985). American forts, settlements, and "Indian agencies" expanded across northern Florida, pressing into Seminole lands. American settlers took lands that Seminole valued for residences, hunting grounds, agricultural fields, burial plots, ceremonial spaces, and shrines. However, despite the conflicts that wrecked human relations, there were still numerous exchanges between Euro-Americans, Africans, and Native Americans in and around Fort Brooke and Fort King. These two U.S. military installations fostered frontier markets (McCall 1974; Mahon 1985: 55).

A range of relations existed between Africans and Native Americans in Seminole territory. Beneficial interactions consisted of military alliances, economic exchanges, and collective participation in ceremonies. Some formerly enslaved Africans had linguistic skills and knowledge of Euro-Americans that made them capable diplomatic liaisons. Inequality was evident in cases where Native Americans enslaved Africans (Americans) or collected tribute from them (Covington 1993; Landers 1999; Miller 2003; Porter 1996; Weik 2007, 2009; Weisman 1989).

One particularly complicated type of Seminole interaction that deserves closer inspection is slavery. From a cross-cultural and long-term perspective, slavery is a human institution that exhibited a great diversity of labor requirements, restrictions, meanings, and statuses. Servitude in African and Native American societies was not the same as American chattel slavery (Miers and Kopytoff 1977). In colonial Florida, documents portrayed people of African descent largely as slaves, although paperwork or oral sources substantiating slave sales and ownership for the majority

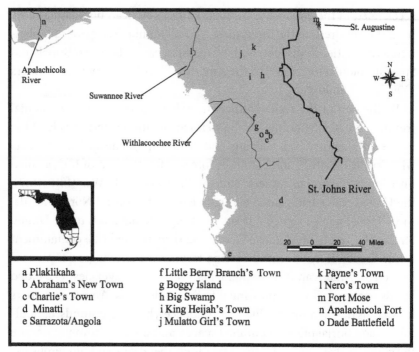

a Pilaklikaha
b Abraham's New Town
c Charlie's Town
d Minatti
e Sarrazota/Angola

f Little Berry Branch's Town
g Boggy Island
h Big Swamp
i King Heijah's Town
j Mulatto Girl's Town

k Payne's Town
l Nero's Town
m Fort Mose
n Apalachicola Fort
o Dade Battlefield

Figure 6.1. African Seminole towns, Maroon communities, and African-colonial forts. Illustration by Terrance Weik.

of enslaved African Seminoles has not been extensively examined. Further, most African Seminoles who were described as "slaves" had minor labor requirements and freedom of movement. Therefore, one could question the appropriateness of labeling all Africans living among the Seminole as mere slaves (compare Landers 2010). This is not to say that there were not cases similar to chattel slavery. For example, a group of Africans was forced to work for an indigenous Seminole known as Philip, tending his fields and building his plantation under the watch of armed guards (Weisman 2000). However, many indigenous Seminole did not own slaves (Miller 2003).

African Seminoles realized freedom in various ways. A significant proportion of their population was born free, while others were granted freedom by Native Americans. Many people of African descent living in central Florida during the nineteenth century had fled from Southeastern slavery. It seems unlikely that people who had suffered under years of enslavement would have escaped to an area where they would be forced to endure harsh conditions similar to those in Euro-American slave societies. Some twentieth-century African Seminole oral traditions also contradict the idea that African Seminole service was the same as chattel slavery. For example, descendents emphasize their ancestors' skills in warfare, agriculture, and interpreting. In reference to his Florida ancestors' status, a descendant from Oklahoma explained, "A slave don't carry no gun" (Jones 1990). Historian Kenneth Porter (1996) argued that gun possession was one of the key factors that enabled "Seminole Negroes" to attain autonomy in Florida.

By 1835, U.S. activities in Florida were part of an "Indian Removal" policy which would lead to two subsequent wars (Porter 1943a). In the Second Seminole War (1835–1842), the U.S. military fought to a truce and captured enough Seminole forces to convince most Native Americans and about half of the African Seminole to resettle in Oklahoma reservations. A number of African Seminole had escaped to the Bahamas in the years leading up to this war. During a lesser, final military conflict (1855–1860), the small group of primarily indigenous Seminole fought with U.S. forces in South Florida. After this last war, a few hundred Seminole were left in Florida. U.S. control of Florida was gained at the cost of millions of dollars and thousands of lives. The U.S. military was aided by a considerable number of Native American troops assembled from groups such as the Shawnees and Creeks. In addition, some Africans and indigenous Seminole served as guides for U.S. troops, though a portion of these guides were coerced war captives. A letter sent by General Thomas Jesup to the commissioner of Indian Affairs illustrates why captive guides would have cooperated in actions against their comrades: "The Seminole negro prisoners are now all the property of the public. I have promised Abraham the freedom of his family if he be faithful to us; and I shall certainly hang him if he be not faithful" (25th Congress 1838: 22, 25). At times, these guides were unreliable and willing to betray forces that pressed them into service.

By the end of the nineteenth century, the few remaining Florida Seminole settlements were mostly in the southern, Everglades region. Late nineteenth- and early twentieth-century observers documented few people of African descent living among indigenous Seminole, and few interracial Seminole marriages (Covington 1993). Twentieth-century indigenous Seminole oral histories describe a small number of interactions with African Americans in schools or on farms (Jumper and West 2001). The oral histories of African Seminole descendents celebrate their ancestors' military service in Mexico, family relations in various states, and life in Oklahoma (Jones 1990; Porter no date). An indigenous group led by Coacoochee joined African Seminoles in their exodus to Mexico, which was spurred by the attempts of pro-slavery Seminole and Creek factions in Oklahoma to impose harsh servitude on African Seminole (Mulroy 1993, 2007). Archaeologists have conducted a minor survey of a community that formed at Fort Clarke, Texas, an outpost where some Afro-Mexican Seminole known as *Mascogos* returned to the United States in the early 1900s (Davis and Botelier Mock 1996; Porter 1996). By 2000, African Seminole descendants from Oklahoma had reconnected with their Florida ancestors by visiting ceremonies related to the Seminole Wars (Weik 2002). Members of the Seminole Tribe of Florida have also taken steps to recognize the historical importance of the African Seminole by reaching out to descendants in the Bahamas (Howard 2002).

An Archaeological Model of African Seminole Ethnogenesis at Pilaklikaha

Pilaklikaha is one of the few places where archaeologists have found material evidence of a documented African Seminole "town" (as historical records refer to them) in Florida. Over four hundred archaeological sites and nearly one hundred documented settlements, the vast majority related to indigenous Seminole, have been identified in Florida (Carr and Steele 1993; Mykell 1962). Military officers and U.S. officials estimated that nearly five thousand indigenous Seminole and fourteen hundred African Seminole lived in Florida by the nineteenth century. Past scholarship has pieced together glimpses of various settlements in regional historical narratives (Mulroy 1993; Porter 1996; Riordan 1996). By focusing on one settlement, we can build a more coherent theory of African Seminole life. I employ model-building with the understanding that my conception of Pilaklikaha is not a universal, normative, one-size-fits-all explanation for every African Seminole settlement. Unique actions and processes affected the nature and rhythms of each location. More case studies are needed at different locations before strong arguments can be made about regional similarities and patterns.

Archaeological Fieldwork

From 1998–2006, brief periods of fieldwork were conducted in order to explore African Seminole ethnogenesis and African—Native American interaction (Weik 2002, 2009). Subsurface excavation and surface collection methods were employed, expanding the coverage area of previous surface collections (Herron 1994; Carr and Steele 1993; Weisman, personal communication, 1997). In addition, pedestrian surveys were conducted on select properties adjacent to Pilaklikaha, within a mile radius and largely to the south and east. Nearly two hundred small shovel test pits, 30 square centimeters and up to 100 centimeters deep, were placed at 10-meter intervals on a Cartesian grid covering the primary settlement area. Shovel test pits containing the highest number of Seminole-period artifacts (similar to what is found in archival sources or archaeological reports) were identified on distribution maps. Then, 23 larger test units (1 × 1 meter, 1 × 2 meters, and 2 × 2 meters) were excavated individually or in contiguous units at locations having the most artifact-laden shovel test pits. A few locations, largely in the far eastern or central parts of the study area, could not be excavated because they contained tree stumps, dense clay, standing water, or rocks. Likewise, the southern portion of the settlement was destroyed by a paved road. Some properties to the west of the main artifact concentrations were inaccessible due to landowners' wishes. Wetlands also prevented the testing of areas ringing the site.

Dating Pilaklikaha

Most descriptions of Pilaklikaha date to the 1820s and were written by Anglo officials and soldiers (McCall 1974). One of the earliest known writings that mention Pilaklikaha is a letter by Captain John Bell describing the "state of Indians in Florida" for the U.S. Congress (reproduced by Morse 1822). Bell recorded lists of settlements that Native Americans such as "Mulatto King," "Blount," and Nea-moth-la" provided to Andrew Jackson at a meeting in Pensacola during 1821. One of Bell's entries mentions "Pe-lac-le-ka-ha, the residence of Miccanopa, chief of the Seminole nations, situated by one hundred and twenty miles south of Alachua" (Morse 1822: 307). Military maps dating to the 1820s and 1830s also indicate the presence of Pilaklikaha, other black towns, and Native American settlements.

Figure 6.2. "Burning of Pilaklikaha by Gen. Eustis." Lithograph by R. F. Gray (1836). Courtesy of the Library of Congress.

Robert Williams refers to the location of Pilaklikaha as "Abraham's Old Town" in his permit (#79), granted by the Florida Armed Occupation Act (AOA) (Boyd 1951). In 1842, this act gave free land to settlers who bore arms, settled at a distance from U.S. forts, cleared the land, and lived on it for several years. General Abraham Eustis, whose troops burnt the town in 1836, documented Pilaklikaha's destruction (Eustis 1836). A few years later, U.S. soldiers camped at Pilaklikaha and engaged African and indigenous Seminole in the vicinity (Sprague 1848). Present-day topographic maps can be connected to features on 1840s AOA records. The location of current archaeological remains is near Pilaklikaha River and Palatlakaha Prairie. There are various explanations for the meanings and origins of Pilaklikaha (and its variant spellings). Native American languages and chroniclers suggest that Pilaklikaha means "wetlands," while a few scholars see possible central African etymologies that suggest the word connotes a posture of militancy (Weik 2007, 2009).

Around thirteen hundred (out of over two thousand) artifacts, including pipe stems, beads, and dark green glass fragments, have been recovered from Pilaklikaha (Weik 2002: 112–39). These items are comparable to relics found in late eighteenth- and early nineteenth-century Seminole archaeological sites. Mean ceramic dating determined that Pilaklikaha was founded in 1811 (2002). It is likely that a significant proportion of the pottery (which includes thickly glazed stoneware and semi-porcelaneous wares) and medicine bottle shards were deposited by later settlers such as Robert Williams, who is listed as a property owner on the earliest area plat maps. He may have also left behind a penny produced in 1843, seven years after Pilaklikaha's destruction.

Founding Moments

The first African and indigenous Seminoles that came to Pilaklikaha arrived from north and northeast Florida, especially areas around the Alachua Prairie, the Suwannee River, and the Apalachicola River. U.S. expansion into this region brought an end to the political influences, economic benefits, and military alliances that Seminoles negotiated with Spanish and British colonists.

The most explicit statement about the residents of Pilaklikaha comes from a soldier named McCall (1974 [1868]), who described one hundred "runaways" from Georgia. Other chroniclers' population estimates vary from 75 to 160, which may reflect their different motives (for making population estimates), levels of training (in observation techniques, or lack of them), concerns for precision, and lengths of visitation. Alternatively, each enumeration could represent a time slice in a fluctuating population. Some inhabitants could have hidden during chroniclers' visits as a mode of resistance, or out of fear of being noticed and having their whereabouts reported to their previous masters.

A comparative perspective supports the argument for an intricate settlement trajectory at Pilaklikaha. Oral history and archival sources suggest that self-emancipated Africans in Jamaica and Suriname escaped alone and in groups, at different times, forming new societies or joining preexisting communities of Native Americans or African escapees. In some cases, Native Americans escaped from the same plantations as Africans (Patterson 1993; Price 1983: 48–58). To date, no clear evidence demonstrates whether residents came *directly* from Georgia to Pilaklikaha, or if escaping individuals lived in Alachua settlements first, as most scholars suggest (Mulroy 1993). The nonlinear patterns of group formation, dissolution, splitting, and joining that ethnogenetic theorists have observed in historical societies suggest that more evidence is needed to discern how Pilaklikaha was established (Hudson 1999; Moore 1994; Perez 2002; Sturtevant 1971). It may have been settled by a single group who undertook one in-migration at a particular point in time, by multiple migrations, by seminomadic inhabitants, or by a combination of these foundational scenarios.

Clues about the built environment at Pilaklikaha are present in works such as the depiction of the town's destruction by J. F. Gray, a South Carolina soldier who served in the U.S. army campaigns against the Seminole (1835–1842). His sketch entitled "Burning of Pilak-Li-ka-ha By Gen. Eustis" was advertised in the *Charleston Mercury* on July 11, 1836. The lithograph depicts square cabins. Another soldier, who served in a military unit from Tennessee that helped destroy "Abraham's town" (another name for Pilaklikaha), noted that the settlement had small, pine houses that contained items in the rafters such as beef (Irwin 1836: 33). The grandest home at the settlement was a two-story structure occasionally inhabited by the indigenous Seminole leader called Micanopy. African Seminole settlements elsewhere are rarely discussed in documents. One description from a military engineer claimed that they were well built and larger than neighboring Native Americans cabins. Descendants in Texas, Mexico, and Oklahoma inhabited rectangular adobe or timber and daub structures.

African Seminole resistance to slavery necessitated various defensive strategies. Maroons and free black soldiers at Apalachicola's "Negro Fort" (circa 1816), Fort Mose (circa 1730–50s), and a Maroon town on the Chattahoochee River (1790) all attest to the use of palisades and fortifications (Landers 1990; Mulroy 2007: 11; Griffin 1960). The lack of evidence for large walls in excavation units and archival descriptions seems to indicate that settlement-wide and household fortifications were not employed at Pilaklikaha. General Abraham Eustis ordered his troops to burn Pilaklikaha's "houses and fences" in 1836, but he gave no indication that there were formidable barricades (Weik 2009: 217). The wetlands surrounding Pilaklikaha may have been valued for their moatlike defensive potential, and for the cultivation of documented crops such as rice (McCall 1974). However, the occurrence of dry seasons would limit the strength of an organic moat hypothesis (Weik 2009). Pilaklikaha's residents had been gone for weeks before General Eustis' troops arrived, which is a circumstance comparable to what Euro-American soldiers found in 1813, when they attacked some empty Seminole villages in northern Florida. It is likely that

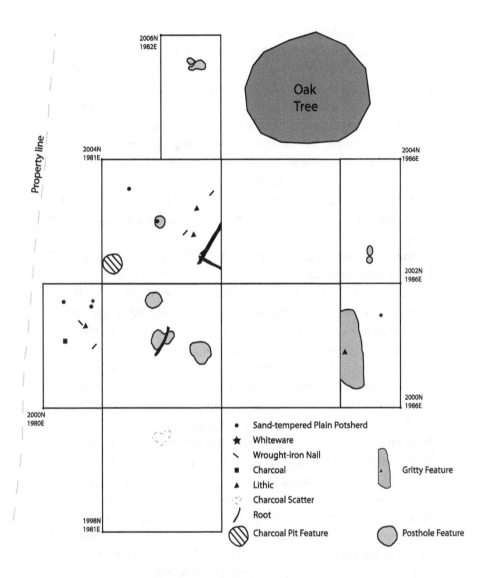

2006N
1982E

Oak
Tree

Property line

2004N
1981E

2004N
1986E

2002N
1986E

2000N
1986E

2000N
1980E

1998N
1981E

●	Sand-tempered Plain Potsherd
★	Whiteware
＼	Wrought-iron Nail
■	Charcoal
▲	Lithic
⌣	Charcoal Scatter
⁄	Root
⊘	Charcoal Pit Feature

Gritty Feature

Posthole Feature

Figure 6.3. Structural remains from Pilaklikaha.
Illustration by Terrance Weik.

N

0 ▬▬▬▬▬▬ 1m

Artifacts not drawn to scale

Pilaklikaha's residents considered flight a more viable option than forti-
fication in light of the advantages (technological and numerical) held by
U.S. troops (and their Native American allies) and the historical lessons
learned from the destruction of the "Negro Fort." More research is necessary to discover whether the residents of Pilaklikaha were connected to
communication networks like the ones that gave early warning to Creeks
and Seminoles (and Africans) during 1813, helping them avoid the attacks
of Euro-American forces who burned their north Florida settlements
(Potter 1836: 100; Weik 2002: 144–45). Similar actions occurred in other
parts of the African diaspora, such as Brazil, where Portuguese colonists
were accused of warning Palmares residents of attacks (Carneiro 1966;
Orser 1996: 47).

Some archaeological data exists for buildings constructed at Pilaklikaha. Based on the number of inhabitants (one hundred people living in
households of five to ten) and a sketch of the town, it is likely that there
were somewhere between eleven and twenty buildings in the settlement.
The posthole stains uncovered in excavation units reveal a portion of one
building that is nearly square in form. Fragments of pottery (such as sand-
tempered and brushed earthenware or blue-edged pearlware) and green
glass shards were excavated from the posthole area. A long ovoid feature
on the eastern edge of these structural remains (test unit 2000N1985E) had
a gritty consistency, charcoal specs, and grasslike impressions. It ranged
from one to three centimeters thick and seemed like it could have been
the remnant of a thatched roof or mat. Clay daub and wrought iron nails
constitute a tiny portion of the total artifact assemblage, suggesting that
most buildings were constructed largely with local materials. Middens,
structure floors, and Seminole-period ground surfaces were not identifi-
able from profile maps, photos, or visual inspections of the excavated site
stratigraphy. Excavation units contained thin lenses of artifacts ranging
from ground level to sixty centimeters below the surface. Most artifact
concentrations are nineteen to twenty-five centimeters below the surface
(figure 6.3).

Artifacts, feature patterns, and documentary sources produce a picture of social complexity at Pilaklikaha. The pattern of thin artifact sheets
could support the argument that Pilaklikaha underwent various migrations of new residents. A greater density of artifacts would be expected for
settlements having long-term occupation by a highly stationary population. However, yard sweeping and selective trash disposal are factors that

Figure 6.4. Bisected feature, southern half of test unit 2000N1985E. Photo by Terrance Weik.

could also have produced such an artifact distribution. Gray's depiction of the burning town suggests that structures covered the hill upon which the settlement was built. In contrast, archaeological remains are concentrated in the westernmost section of the ridge. This artifact distribution may be the result of residents avoiding clay and limestone deposits on the east part of the hammock. This area would have been harder to build in and uncomfortably wet on rainy days due to the impermeability of the clay.

The preceding discussion of site formation processes raises a fundamental question about the nature of the settlement layout. Gray's painting of Pilaklikaha does not provide a clear indication of whether the houses are aligned or configured in a nongeometrical distribution. More work needs to be done to conceptualize the landscape in order to understand the role of motivation, memory, and perspective (theoretical and directional) in Gray's depiction, and the relation of these aspects to Pilaklikaha's spatial dynamics. A soldier who helped destroy Pilaklikaha stated that it was "laid out like the towns in a civilized country" (Irwin 1836: 33). The author was a white Tennessee soldier who probably associated "civilization" with European, colonial, and U.S. towns having

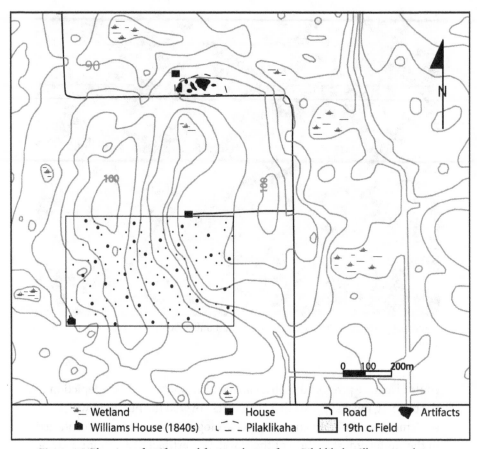

Figure 6.5. Planview of artifact and feature clusters from Pilaklikaha. Illustration by Terrance Weik.

symmetrical, rectilinear, or geometrical layouts (compare Deagan 1996). Some residents may have based their ideas about the built environment on their memories of a wide assortment of African settlement strategies and architectural traditions from the numerous west or central African societies that they (or their ancestors) once resided in: camps, rural farmsteads, or urban areas; geometric or irregular structural configurations; courtyard complexes and interconnected modules; royal compounds and palaces (Agorsah 1985; Ogundiran 2007: 81–82). Maroon histories elsewhere suggest that both rectilinear and unaligned settlement layouts were common (Agorsah 1985; Weik 2004: 40–42). Residents who were born into American slavery had memories of "slave rows." Unless they were deeply indoctrinated with a dependency mindset, it seems likely that they would have used their freedom to explore some settlement layout that did not remind them of their enslavement. The few indigenous Seminole residents at Pilaklikaha may have sought to create one of two Maskoki settlement plans: a central space surrounded by four structures and satellite housing, or a family homestead containing one or two open-sided pole and thatch structures (called *chickees*). In either case, tables, central fires, food preparation structures, and storage sheds filled in settlement spaces.

Clusters of surface and subsurface remains seem to be indicated by the distribution of Pilaklikaha's artifacts and features (Weik 2009: 218). However, the systematic and judgmental sampling strategies that were employed to locate material remnants do not provide enough contiguous coverage to discern a clear settlement plan (Weik 2009). The faintness and rarity of artifacts and features such as postholes also make it difficult to infer a definitive settlement layout (Weik 2002, 2009). For now, we can hypothesize that four of the clusters represent groups of buildings or activity areas that surround a cleared space.

The People: Traces of Identity

The theme of identity is important because it establishes a point of departure for discussing group origins and situating socially constructed beliefs about individuals or communities. Identity has major implications for freedom and liberation when one considers the importance of self-definition in helping people reject dehumanization and declare a communal vision of well-being. Ideas about race have had one of the strongest influences on the ways origins and identities have been constructed in archival sources. Maps, travelers' accounts, military records, and government reports racialize people and space through the use of qualifiers such as "negro town." These labels fail to consider how self-liberated people defined themselves, and whether they saw race as the primary or primordial basis of their collective identity.

Another form of evidence identifying residents of Pilaklikaha is the lists of "prisoners" and "emigrants" from the Second Seminole War (1835–1842) that were generated by military officers and reproduced in the U.S. congressional record (25th Congress 1838). The lists feature names of both Africans and Native Americans who were captured or who agreed to truces during the war (see discussions in Bateman 2002, Kly 2006, Littlefield 1977, and Weik 2009). A subset of people on these lists provides a profile of the inhabitants of Pilaklikaha. The lists describe African and indigenous Seminole first names, ages, sexes, and their associated "tribe, town, or owner." The Seminole leader Micanopy and African Seminole leader Abraham are among the listed inhabitants of Pilaklikaha. The lists are not without weaknesses, for some individuals who are listed in other chroniclers' descriptions, such as July and August, are not on the military's lists. Another ninety-nine African Seminole are associated with the "owner" Micanopy. Micanopy lived at Pilaklikaha as well as at a neighboring settlement called Okehumpke, a practice that varied widely from the separate African and Native American residence pattern noted by most chroniclers.

A number of things can be discerned from the ninety-nine listed African Seminole. Most of the recorded individuals are female, which is significant because of the paucity of discussions about women in primary sources and histories. In cases where they are mentioned, the information is focused on women's labor or their relation to men and children. The majority of African Seminoles listed are children or teenagers, suggesting that the society was able to reproduce itself. The names provide clues to identities, kinship, and transcontinental origins. Most are English names, but Spanish and Middle Eastern (Jewish or Arabic) links are also evident (Weik 2009). More research is necessary to discern how these names were ascribed (that is, by slaveholders or kin) and whether self-definition was at work. Did some African Seminoles rename themselves, as have others who redefined themselves to resist racialization and enslavement, forget painful experiences, or indicate their status change? Narratives of formerly enslaved people and studies of "runaway" advertisements show that some people changed their appearance and used aliases to avoid detection and capture. Similarly, it is plausible that some African Seminoles whose names were recorded by the military for the congressional record gave alternative names to avoid being discovered by the slaveholders who visited military camps.

Studies of African Seminole and other Maroon descendents indicate that they have received and transmitted African names and naming traditions into the present day (Bateman 2002; Jones 1990; Price and Price

1972; R. Price 1983: 77). Discerning cultural origins from names on the congressional lists can be complicated. For instance, it is possible that the name "Tena," that of a woman associated with Micanopy on the lists, derived from central and/or west African languages (Kongo or Twi, respectively) based on comparisons with African names (Weik 2009).

African Seminole societies such as Pilaklikaha were heterogeneous places, inhabited by different groups of Africans, African Americans, and Native Americans, all co-influencing each other, and thus inviting an exploration of ethnogenetic processes such as amalgamation that were identified by Hudson (1999). This cultural heterogeneity necessitated the development of individual or social methods of compromise, tolerance, and conflict resolution.

Perpetuating Pilaklikaha: Organizing Principles

The diverse motivations and cultural practices of the residents presented challenges for Pilaklikaha, whose citizens needed to find common ground in order to perpetuate society, fight wars, and ensure daily survival. If these challenges are not considered, our conceptualization of African Seminole ethnogenesis will fail to account for the internal agents of action, change, and continuity that animate this social process. Diaspora and Afrocentric approaches have pointed out the importance of collective interests, common heritage, and similar experiences (for example, of racism) in explanations of social identities (Hamilton 2007). Similarly, the relation between cultural identity and efforts to promote social solidarity deserves attention. Many inhabitants of Pilaklikaha were described as "runaways," and their memories of enslavement provided them with shared histories of abuse and exploitation that facilitated ties to the region's enslaved population and strengthened their resolve to remain free. The available evidence seems to speak most loudly to the familial, political, and spiritual dimensions of these issues.

Family Relations

Families are essential units of social reproduction, labor, and residence in most societies. In slavery, families provided a refuge from the abuses and exploitations that accompanied dislocations and violence. Archaeologists and other scholars have discovered that a number of families and households were able to carve out autonomous spaces within plantation life (Battle-Baptiste 2007). Small numbers of people who escaped from bondage discovered opportunities to affirm preexisting and new family bonds. While unrelated individuals and groups made up a large portion of the population that fled from slavery, a small number were composed of families (Franklin and Schweninger 1999). Oral and written histories of formerly enslaved people tell of the dismemberment of families due to sale and escape, of African and Native American relatives, and of ways that captive plantation laborers provided food and supplies to self-emancipated Africans (Rawick 1976).

At least fourteen family units have been located on the 1838 U.S. government lists associated with Pilaklikaha (25th Congress 1838; Weik 2009). It would be hasty to assume that the 1838 group was comprised of the same one hundred people who lived there in the 1820s (McCall 1974) without taking into account documented census or biographical information. Forty individuals in the 1838 group were born after 1824, the date at which McCall claimed one hundred people lived in Pilaklikaha. In addition, factors such as wars, illnesses, and re-enslavement threatened to depopulate African Seminole communities. These factors, along with the various population estimates, indicate that significant demographic shifts may have occurred at Pilaklikaha, which ethnogenesis theoreticians would predict. Native Americans such as Micanopy and African Seminoles such as John Horse had familial ties that moved them between settlements and placed them in kinship networks linking Pilaklikaha to towns such as Okehumpke (Micanopy's other settlement) or Thonotosassa and (later) the Oklawaha River (the site of John Horse's residences) (Rivers and Brown 1996).

African Seminoles engaged in a variety of kinship forms in nineteenth-century Florida and nineteenth- to twentieth-century Oklahoma, including polygamy and monogamy (Bateman 1990: 26–27; Mulroy 1993, 2004). African Seminole polygamy was a result of either their African heritage or their willingness to borrow indigenous Seminole practices. Matri-focal households and patrilineal descent practices were also found in (African) Seminole and African societies (Miller 1988; Mulroy 2004, 2007; Vansina 1990; Wilks 1993). This diversity in family forms is not reflected in the 1838 lists related to Pilaklikaha, which point to pairs of adults and their children.

Politics and Power

According to documents, the political practices and expressions of power in self-liberated African communities were as varied as their environments, sizes, cultural beliefs, and ethnic constituencies. In addition to concerns about the extent of social hierarchy, centralization, and formal organization, it is important to consider cultural beliefs about politics and power that led to the selection of rules and leaders, group aspirations, and interests.

Various ideas exist on the political organization of African Seminole settlements. Many view African Seminoles communities as largely led by powerful male leaders who negotiated a semi-independent life with the indigenous Seminoles (Landers 1999; Mulroy 2004; Porter 1996; Riordan 1996). Ogunleye (1996) viewed the "self-emancipated Africans of Florida" as "Pan-African Nationalists" who carved out an autonomous existence. However, she does not address the process or chronology by which this pan-Africanist nationalist ideology emerged or tangible manifestations of it in any location. The late John Henrik Clarke (in Swanston 2003: 212) laid out criteria defining collective freedom from a nationalist, pan-Africanist perspective: ethno-racial blocks controlling lands (especially Africa); an equal position at international economic negotiations; self-determined political positioning; a state of expanding freedoms for others around the world; the ability to (re)claim heritage (especially ancient African) and resources without taking what belongs to others. We should not take for granted that Africans in Seminole territory automatically established a formal or nationalist government. The complexities of coordinating multiple interests, reconciling egos, and sustaining collective political movements need to be considered. The timing of what appears today as a collective African Seminole identity and its impact on the definition of collective policies is not clear for nineteenth-century Florida. To date, evidence of nationalist or uniform beliefs and material or textual traces of nationalistic land claims are lacking.

On the other hand, Ogunleye's conceptualization raises important issues undeveloped by previous scholarship. As she suggests (1996), enslaved Africans benefitted from reflecting on their collective interests. Similarly, Yai (2001: 254) notes that an important gap in our knowledge of Brazilian *quilombos* and other antislavery enclaves concerns the mechanism by which various Africans fostered communication and cooperation in plural language and religious situations. Conversely, the multilingualism and cultural plurality of many African societies, as well as regional pan-cultural religious traditions, may have fostered linkages that made cultural barriers less formidable in the Americas (Yai 2001; compare Kent 1979). In a study of "Black Seminole" names, Bateman (2002: 233) discusses an individual named Lotty, whose name has a Kongo (central African) origin, and his daughter, Cumba, whose name appears to have a Mandinka (west African) source (compare derivations established by Turner 2002 [1949]). Likewise, other Africans had to work out compromises regarding what aspects of ancestral traditions such as naming (and associated rituals) were to be passed on and what new practices would be created or borrowed. In the wider context of African American resistance to slavery, common ground was also found on issues besides African culture, such as the development of a critical consciousness about racial identities and racism (Gomez 1998).

As in self-liberated societies elsewhere, African Seminole leaders commonly had qualities such as military skills, multilingual abilities, and powerful relatives (Bilby 1996). Individuals such as Abra(ha)m, August, July, and Billy John are the most visible leaders that chroniclers associate with Pilaklikaha. Biases that highlight men and military or logistical issues have shaped many of the histories and archival records of "Black Seminole" life, although oral histories of female descendents in Texas are helping change this representational imbalance (Davis and Botelier Mock 1996; Mock 2010; Weik 2009: 30). A few documents describe towns in Florida named for female leaders such as "Mulatto Girl." U.S. and colonial leaders of the Americas have contributed to this bias through their attempts at shaping the policies and leadership of indigenous and resistant groups. Archives that represent the gendered division of labor (that is, that women had greater influence over settlement matters and men greater roles in defense and dealings with outsiders) may be impeding our ability to recognize the impact of women on governance and to see the full range of gendered leadership practices.

A level of decentralization and accessibility to decision-making bodies existed at places like Pilaklikaha, suggesting one person did not monopolize leadership. In a rare description by a U.S. military engineer, it was noted that African Seminole rulers were only able to keep their position by maintaining the admiration and esteem of their comrades (Young 1818). Ethnographic and historical studies of African Seminole descendants in

Oklahoma, Texas, and Mexico suggest that they maintained a high level of settlement autonomy (Bateman 1991). This type of check on power, as well as people's ability to "vote with their feet," probably kept tyrants from ruling Pilaklikaha or establishing pan-settlement hierarchies (compare similar observations on histories of American Maroon societies in Thompson 2006). The ethnic diversity at Pilaklikaha was not a disruptive factor as it was in some other antislavery initiatives (Gomez 1998: 3). Conversely, anthropological studies of some modern civil rights and liberation theology movements suggest that "segmentary," decentralized leadership aided movements against oppressive national and racist policies (Gerlache and Hine 1970). Segmented or multiple leadership was beneficial for some resistance groups because it facilitated the emergence of various leaders who were able to take over if other leaders were captured, co-opted (by money or threats) into betraying their peers, or killed in battle. Parallel issues existed in indigenous Seminole settlements, where coresident family groups maintained their independence despite attempts to force them into treaties or pan-ethnic policies (Wickman 1999).

The expression of power at Pilaklikaha was interrelated with indigenous Seminole political formations. Indigenous Seminoles maintained some aspects of ancestral Maskoki (what chroniclers referred to as "Creek Indians") political practices (Weisman 1989; Wickman 1999). By the nineteenth century, most indigenous Seminole settlements were clan-centered camps, although some recognition was afforded to traditions of pan-settlement, hereditary leadership. Another dimension of Maskoki and Seminole life was the rise of rulers who increased their power through entrepreneurship, military prowess, intermarriage with outsiders, and international diplomacy. One of the few indigenous residents of Pilaklikaha, a man called Micanopy, came from a lineage that placed him in a hereditary leadership position. However, chroniclers suggest that Micanopy did not exercise great power in Seminole territory.

A soldier who visited Pilaklikaha stated that Micanopy received tribute in the form of one-third of the agricultural products of his neighbors at Pilaklikaha. If the aforementioned discussion of slavery is valid, then there may have been heterogeneity of meaning and practice informing "tribute" relationships (Mulroy 2007; Sattler 1987; Weik 2002, 2009). Chroniclers state that Africans gave crops—somewhere between several bushels to half of a crop—to indigenous Seminole in Florida and Oklahoma as tribute (see, for example, Williams 1837 [1976: 45]). These historical practices seemed similar to Seminole communal precedents of stockpiling food for lean times or showing allegiance (Weik 2009). Tribute also existed among other indigenous groups of the Southeast. African Seminoles who were born across the Atlantic may have had a similar frame of reference based on memories of politics in their natal land. From an African perspective, tribute was a means by which some regional powers related to smaller or conquered groups and towns. The U.S. congressional record listing hundreds of African Seminoles in Florida includes names with origins from the area in and around modern Ghana, such as Kofi and Cudjo. In this part of west Africa, polities such as Gonja gave tribute to the Asante kings, who promoted the conquest of many ethnic groups and settlements in the eighteenth and nineteenth centuries (Wilks, Levtzion, Haight 1986: 190, 197; Wilks 1993).

Exchange, Subsistence, and Economy at Pilaklikaha

Work at African Seminole settlements was conducted according to a division of labor, as it was at some other documented self-liberated communities. Women were the primary domestic and agricultural laborers according to Horatio Dexter (in Boyd 1958: 88), who traveled through the area in 1823 as an agent for the U.S. government. Visitors noted that rice, beans, oranges, and corn were raised at Pilaklikaha during the 1820s. Native root crops used by indigenous Seminoles may have also been part of African Seminole's subsistence. A dish made from corn called *soffkee* continues to be made by Seminole descendents. Honey and other wild foods and game, the last of which was largely procured by men, also played a role in their diet. The importance of food security should not be underestimated. Historical narratives of the Underground Railroad mention how some people were re-enslaved because they could not combat hunger on the run (Chapman 1971). During campaigns against self-liberated Africans, bounty hunters and Euro-American forces made a point to destroy their crops. Dexter noted how he provided some sugarcane to African Seminoles, who successfully grew it near their settlement twenty miles to the west of Pilaklikaha. He lamented at the "idleness" of the African Seminoles at Pilaklikaha, and claimed that they only "occasionally" hunted.

Women's roles were as important in war and resistance as they were in peace. Mathurin (1975) reminds us that African women who joined self-liberated communities may not have always fought directly with the

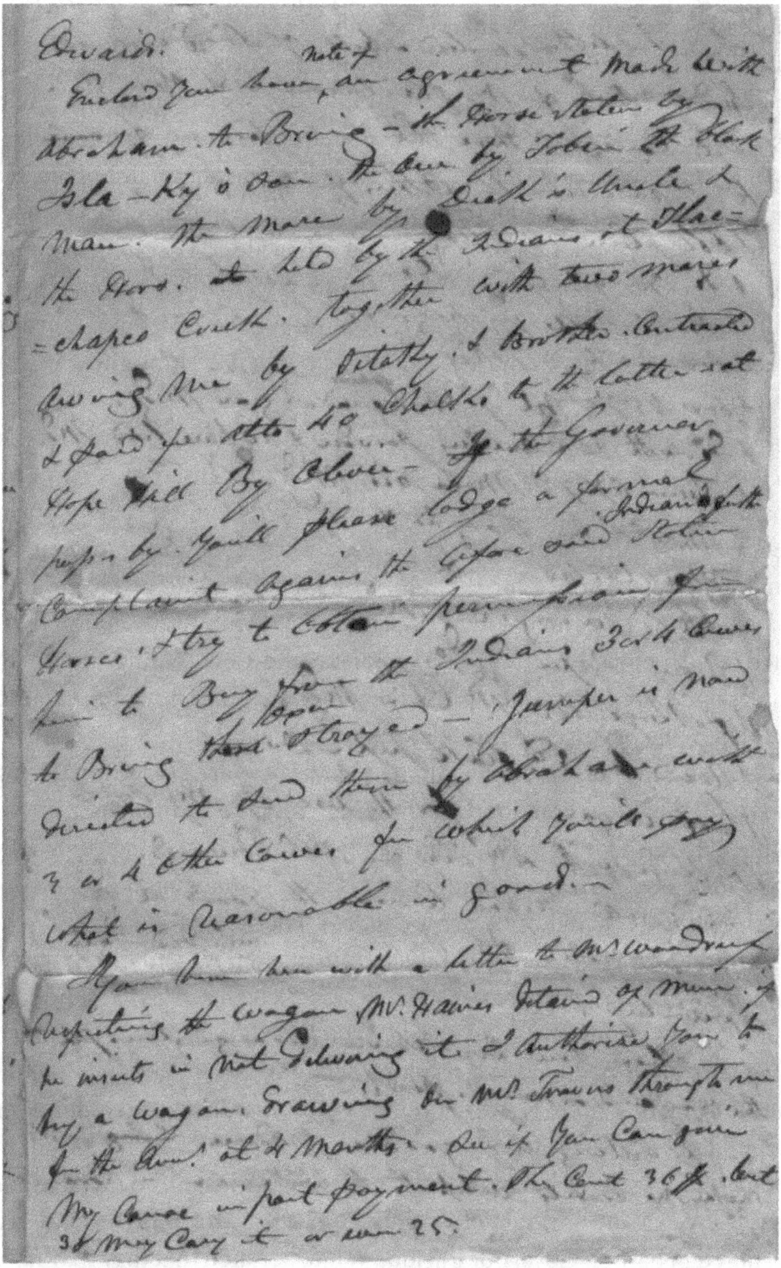

Figure 6.6. Letter to an agent of an Alachua County slave owner permitting payment to Abraham for cattle. Courtesy of Special Collections, George A. Smathers Library, University of Florida.

enslaving armies sent after them, but they played vital roles in carrying off spoils of war, setting fire to abandoned villages, and cultivating crops that sustained the rebel effort. The complementary efforts of men and women at Pilaklikaha were reinforced by communal work practices (Bateman 1991; Porter 1996). Descendants perpetuated this commitment to collective labor, as co-wives and different families provided mutual support. No clear evidence speaks to whether formalized communal practices evident in archival and ethnographic sources on other Florida settlements were part of Pilaklikaha's belief systems or if more informal philosophies were cultivated by organic intellectuals. Communalism was part of a range of ideas (including hierarchy) shaping self-liberated communities in the Americas.

African Seminoles were involved in regional economic interactions as well as subsistence and local productivity. Free and enslaved Africans of Spanish Florida had long been cowboys in the region, servicing dependent colonial settlements (Parker 2000). An overseer and some traders would exchange money for the return of runaway cattle or for animals that they bought from Pilaklikaha (Charles 1825; Mulroy 2007). The presence of U.S. officials, settlers, and soldiers who were willing to pay for guides and interpreters also infused Seminoles with currency. Similar to the gift-giving practices of preceding colonial agents, the U.S. government subsidized Seminole resettlement on a central Florida reservation during the 1820s, providing both food and money to indigenous inhabitants (Mahon 1985; Weisman 1989). In addition, Euro-Americans, enslaved people, and Seminoles (African and indigenous) bartered, bought goods, and exchanged gifts (Covington 1993; McCall 1974; Mahon 1985).

A number of items that were raided from plantations and invading militias' supplies during the eastern Florida conflicts that raged around 1813 still circulated. Some enslaved Africans, such as those held by Zephaniah Kingsley, found freedom as a result of Seminole raids on Anglo plantations during that time. However, bond persons hardly waited around for Seminole liberators. A case in point occurred in 1806, when a group of eight enslaved, armed people of African descent escaped from plantations near St. Augustine and raided various supplies and a canoe from a ship anchored in harbor. Governor Enrique White declared that they may have been led by an Englishman (White 1806). Dexter (in Boyd 1958: 92) mentioned that the Spanish seaman who visited coastal towns supplied bayonets, muskets, bullets, gunpowder, lead, molasses, and rum in exchange

Figure 6.7. Lead shot, bullet, and molten mass recovered from Pilaklikaha. Photo by Terrance Weik.

for cattle. No Spanish colonial artifacts have been found at Pilaklikaha except for one fragment of an "olive jar" vessel that Herron (1994) found in his surface collection survey. Only three specimens excavated from Pilaklikaha represent weaponry: a piece of lead shot, half of a lead bullet, and a piece of molten lead (Weik 2002: 127). The arms implied by these remains could have come from either coastal or interior trade networks. The need for weaponry is one of the factors that prevented self-emancipated Africans from taking an isolationist stance in regards to politics, economics, and cultural contact. After 1821, when U.S. forces destroyed coastal Maroon settlements and dispersed the remaining vestiges of Spanish and British power in west and north Florida, inland suppliers became more prominent in the lives of Seminole. This geopolitical fact had regional spatial implications for people resisting enslavement. Archaeological site distributions and archival maps for the 1820–1830s suggest that African Seminole settlements were the most southern and interior of all villages in each regional Seminole settlement cluster. This positioning was likely the result of a calculated decision by self-liberated people to use distance and buffer zones of indigenous Seminole settlements to protect themselves from enslavers' attacks.

African Seminoles in Florida engaged in covert, underground economies linked to wider slave societies of the Southeast and the Caribbean (Porter 1943; compare Egerton 2006, Parris 1983, Usner 1999). Laws and white supremacist ideologies motivated slaveholders, colonists, and U.S. citizens to limit enslaved and free people of African descent from fully realizing profits and access to resources. Nevertheless, tobacco pipe

Figure 6.8. Euro-American pottery sherds from Pilaklikaha. Photo by Terrance Weik.

fragments, bullets, beads, and porcelain buttons excavated from Pilak-likaha were acquired by residents who engaged in raids, underground trade, or barter (Porter 1943; Usner, 1999: 24–37). Markets were dangerous places for self-liberated Africans, because slaveholders, slave traders, and their agents patrolled these locations in search of new or formerly captive laborers (Weik 2009). Government documents concerning St. Augustine describe a group of African Seminoles who were captured after being supplied with cloth, needles, tobacco, and weapons. Pilaklikaha's artifact assemblage suggests that residents were willing to face the risk of re-enslavement so that they could benefit from regional exchanges. The relative frequency of fragments from Pilaklikaha's artifact assemblage suggests that nearly fifty-five percent of the material culture was manufactured in European or Euro-American shops and factories (Weik 2009: 35). This proportion should be viewed with caution, as this assemblage statistic was derived from artifact fragments (which are subject to bias from differential breakage) as opposed to a minimum vessel count. In addition, many of the items manufactured by Europeans and Americans were produced over a long period, making them difficult to date. Finally, whiteware, ironstone, and pearlware pottery have no clearly visible date stamp or dateable maker's marks. A proportion of the Euro-American-made items were probably used by the Euro-American settler who took over the lands around Pilaklikaha in the 1840s.

There is evidence that the African Seminoles used their economic dealings to gain leverage with their indigenous peers. From one U.S. soldier's perspective,

> The negro is also much more provident and ambitious than his master, and the peculiar localities of the country eminently facilitate him in furnishing the Indian with rum and tobacco, which gives him a controlling influence over the latter, and, at the same time, affords him an immense profit. (Potter 1836: 45–47)

Fragments of dark green bottles, remnants of spirits and rum bottles, have been found throughout Pilaklikaha, amounting to over ten percent of the total artifact assemblage. This type of material culture has also been found at many other colonial and Seminole sites (see Jones 1991: 96; Weisman 1989). Similarly, the U.S. military traded cash, supplies, and clothing to underground merchants, such as an African American man who soldiers blamed for supplying the liquor that led to one of their brawls (Weik 2002).

It is not clear whether African Seminoles gained leverage over each other. Individuals like Abraham were able to accumulate money, dishes, blankets, livestock, and other items. According to the above-mentioned congressional lists, "Abram" owned an individual named Tenebo (or Charles) (25th Congress 1838: 76). If the Abram on the congressional list is the same as Abraham of Pilaklikaha, then it is likely that the influential African Seminole leader was a slave owner. It remains to be seen whether Abram became an "owner" in order to purchase a peer or kinsman out of slavery, or whether Abram saw Tenebo as a bond laborer. Since other people who are listed as "free" or "claims to be free" on the congressional lists are not named as (slave) "owners," it would seem that African Seminole slaveholders were few. It is unlikely that inequalities based on the accumulation of property led to significant class differences in African

Figure 6.9. Seminole and locally made pottery from Pilaklikaha. Photos and illustration by Terrance Weik.

Seminole society. The beliefs that fostered communalism at settlements may have also prevented the development of significant social stratification or slaveowning. At the same time, communalism did not impede pursuit of individual wealth, which manifested itself in forms such as the large herds of cattle amassed by African Seminole leaders.

Handmade pottery was traded and produced in Seminole territory. Most Seminole pottery is brownish-gray, 5–8 millimeters thick, sand tempered, smooth on the interior surface, and imprinted with brush marks on the exterior (Fairbanks 1961; Goggin 1953; Weisman 1989). The vessel rims exhibit various types of incised and geometrically punctated decoration. Pottery forms consist of small bowls, lozenge-shaped jars, large globular pots, and carinated (angled at the shoulder) bowls. The pottery is connected to similar wares produced by Maskoki populations hundreds of years prior. Assuming that artifacts broke and were fragmented at similar rates, this type of pottery constitutes the majority of the excavated ceramics and nearly twenty percent of all nineteenth-century artifacts from Pilaklikaha. A local clay sample taken to a University of Florida ceramicist suggests that the clay had qualities conducive to pottery production.

More research comparing excavated pots with local clays is necessary to demonstrate whether pots were made at Pilaklikaha. Excavations at Jamaican and Brazilian Maroon settlements suggest that they made their own pottery. Ethnographic and archival sources describe Maroons who used locally made pots (Agorsah 1993; Allen 2004; King 1979; Price 1983: 60, 66). For instance, a Saramaka Maroon oral tradition describes the value they placed on their pots, which they carried with them even during crises when they had to quickly abandon their camps (Price 1983: 85). One pottery variant found at Pilaklikaha that has no parallel in other regional Seminole sites is a dense, black, thin ware that exhibits carination; some similar sherds have triangular punctations (Weik 2002; compare Weisman 1989). It could thus be an original African or Seminole cultural ceramic expression or the product of an individual potter's creativity that diverged from the usual Seminole potting conventions. Moreover, this new form may have been a material consequence of ethnogenetic social transformations. In addition to pottery, other items that do not show up in the archaeological record were probably also used at Pilaklikaha, such as baskets or wooden bowls like those made by Bahamian descendants (Howard 2002).

African and Seminole Spirituality

Spiritual beliefs informed Native American and African thinking, practices, and material culture in Seminole territory. African and indigenous
cosmologies, as well as those of some Maroon descendants, held that daily
human life is directly affected by an omnipotent creator, ancestral spirits, and various nature divinities (Martin 1991: 17; Price 1983: 85; Thornton 2002). Herbalists, spirit devotees, and diviners facilitated worship at
shrines, healed people, played central roles in communal decision-making, and facilitated socialization in Seminole territory (Dexter [in Boyd
1958]; Ogunleye 1996). Spiritual beings were shown reverence and offered
sacrifices during rituals, rites of passage, and public ceremonies. Indigenous Seminole and their Maskoki ancestors believed that purification and
reciprocity had to be maintained to ensure success in legal proceedings,
hunting, and warfare (Bear Heart and Larkin 1999; Martin 1991; Sprague
1848: 328; Weisman 1989: 127; Wickman 1999: 44).

Indigenous Seminole and African societies (such as Yoruba and Akan)
that contributed to African Seminole culture engaged in a practice called
divination to make decisions about war, settlement locations, healing,
and other major issues. Studies of divination have shown that it involves
systems of spiritual communication, guidance, and philosophy (Winkelman and Peek 2004). Diviners in nineteenth-century Seminole territory
included a woman of African descent and an indigenous Seminole man
(Young 1954 [1818]: 94). Divine revelation and inspiration are also present
in Underground Railroad narratives. The material culture of Seminole
divination includes a "medicine bundle," which, according to ethnographers, contained beads, pipe fragments, stone flints, and organic materials
(Weik 2009). Descriptions of other southeastern medicine bundles mention similar items, which makes for an interesting parallel with the sacred
bundles attributed to Africans that have been found by Leone (2005) in
the mid-Atlantic and archaeologists in other regions of the United States
(Fennel 2008). Other self-liberated societies employed divination, such
as those in Suriname, where oral traditions tell of a spiritual entity that
convinced Africans that they were to be free (Price 1983: 83–85).

In the African diaspora, self-liberated Africans were attuned to their
environment in ways that benefitted them strategically. According to a
verse of Saramaka Maroon oral tradition, a nature spirit protected the Maroons that hid in its territory from enslavers sent against them (Price 1983:

75). No oral or written accounts of African Seminoles discuss specific engagements with nature deities. However, it is clear from documented and oral histories that African Seminoles were attuned to the environment in other ways that may have protected them from enslaving bounty hunters. For example, one chronicler discussed how an African Seminole named Cudjo was alerted to an approaching Euro-American traveler by the behavior of animals in the vicinity. African Seminole descendants speak of their ancestors' skills in learning about their enemies from the tracks they left in the ground (Porter no date; compare a Jamaican case in Campbell 1993: 153).

A soldier who helped destroy Pilaklikaha reported finding ball sticks, an "Indian flute," and turtle shell rattles. These items could have been used for entertainment, but they are described in ethnohistoric sources as implements used during Busks—annual, multiday ceremonies that included acts of divination, healing, purification, dispute resolution, criminal punishment, and spiritual reverence. Florida oral histories of formerly enslaved African Americans and historic accounts concerning the Afro-Maskoki (Creek) suggest that people of African descent participated in Busks (Weik 2009: 43; Wright 1986). Christianity also played a role among African Seminoles. A nineteenth-century traveler reported witnessing a Christmas celebration at an African Seminole settlement. African Seminole descendants have become largely Christians, though some also take part in the synthetic practices of Native American churches (Mulroy 1993b, 2007).

Conclusion

Archaeological evidence from Pilaklikaha has brought to light undocumented information about African Seminole architecture (for example, the shape and dimensions of a structure), unique ceramic stylistic attributes (vessel symbols not found elsewhere on Seminole pottery), and more predictable aspects of adornment (such as faceted glass beads), weaponry, and beverage storage (dark green spirits bottles). The sparseness of architectural remains contrasts with what one might retrodict from the dense building distribution appearing on a soldier's sketch of Pilaklikaha. Archaeology has demonstrated that there are geological reasons (for example, the shallow clay strata) why the settlement was more concentrated on one part of the ridge than the sketch would suggest. The light artifact distribution also may hint at short-term or intermittent site use by different households, which fits patterns seen in ethnographic and documentary data on self-liberated and indigenous groups in the hemisphere (Bilby 1996; Campbell 1990; Hill 1996; Moore 1994; Perez 2000; Sturtevant 1971). However, other explanatory factors may also be relevant. For instance, the settlement was only inhabited for approximately twenty years (a short period in archaeological terms). Because residents had weeks to evacuate (likely taking much with them) before U.S. soldiers attacked the empty town, the small artifact assemblage is unsurprising. The use of organic materials (like wooden utensils) lowers the probability of some things being preserved. Finally, the liability created by the accumulation of bulky or numerous possessions—for people who had to remain inconspicuous to enslavers and ever-ready for flight—might have discouraged residents from amassing objects.

Even though a few African Seminoles suffered under conditions of harsh bond labor, most realized numerous freedoms. But the price of freedom at places like Pilaklikaha included a range of responsibilities and a high level of tolerance. Residents had to grapple with social heterogeneity and untested newcomers who brought different cultural practices. They also had to adjust to demographic changes (due to births and deaths) and some inhabitants' multiple residence practices (such as Micanopy), factors that heightened ethnogenetic fluidity and change. Though Pilaklikaha's population was small, it was larger than those of many neighboring indigenous settlements, which could be a result of African Seminoles needing to take advantage of safety in numbers. Extended family ties, communalism, multiple leadership, and mixed subsistence (paid work and agriculture) gave shape to the fortunes of the hundred people who lived in the town.

African Seminole entrepreneurship (including ranching, hunting, and trade) demonstrated the contradictions of a wider geopolitical situation where even enemies (U.S. soldiers and plantation managers) were willing to conduct business during lulls in Euro-American expansion. Maps by officials such as Horatio Dexter illustrate how Pilaklikaha was physically connected to central Florida settlements. Similarly, it was also linked to regional networks that facilitated the global movements of people, goods, and knowledge. Inexpensive undecorated stoneware, ironstone, and whiteware pottery constitute the biggest portion of imported goods found at Pilaklikaha, which suggests that the inhabitants did not invest much in imported goods or become dependent on foreign suppliers. Locally made items like pottery are more numerous and may hint at a level of self-sufficiency.

Even though Pilaklikaha would eventually be demolished by invading U.S. armies, its existence demonstrates that resistance could produce a fairly long-term community in a region where slavery was the common experience for many people of African descent. The wars that punctuated the period convinced indigenous Seminoles and U.S. soldiers that Africans were formidable foes and shrewd intermediaries. However, wartime alliances were only part of a continuum of African and indigenous relations. Ultimately, most African—Native American relations in Florida Seminole territory were mutually beneficial, resulting in bidirectional influences affecting practices such as foodways, crafts, and oral traditions. This complementary relationship and the relative ambivalence toward slavery that many indigenous Seminole felt (compared to other Native American societies) worked against the development of imposing labor demands or burdensome levels of "tribute" taking. These factors allowed the development of African Seminole autonomy, as did their own militancy and mobility.

While many found refuge within Seminole-controlled territory, there were some self-liberated Africans who established villages further away. Angola, a town near Tampa, was one such outlier, though it was eventually destroyed by slave-raiding Creeks who captured many of the people unable to relocate to the Bahamas or an interior settlement called Minatti (Brown 2005). Archaeologists are now at work on land and underwater "looking for Angola," as their project suggests (Baram 2008). Perhaps one day an archaeologist will look for Minatti as well.

A transatlantic comparative perspective is crucial for understanding African Seminoles, for the relations and cultural practices they engaged in transcended localities and populations. African Seminoles were not mere subsets of slaveholding or Native American societies, nor were they just Africans seeking to perpetuate ancestral traditions. They were related to all these things and sovereign entities that underwent sociocultural metamorphoses in political, economic, familial, spiritual, and other realms of life.

The archaeological approach to African Seminoles taken in this chapter sought to draw on both the social process and identity versions of ethnogenesis theory. Without a body of documents or oral histories that provide insiders' views on identity, or a complete account of community-building acts, it is difficult to provide robust, empirically grounded explanations about the African Seminoles. While military and political records provide valuable glimpses of people's lives, they have to be used cautiously due to their racializing slants on identities and settlements. For example, many officials' and soldiers' accounts were motivated in part by the writers' desires to distinguish between people who were to be returned to slavery and those who were to be forced into Western borderlands during "Indian Removal." In light of this shortcoming, it is useful to create a broader conceptualization of community transformations and genesis that employs ethnographies, archives, and material culture.

The explanations set forth in this chapter are one of many possible perspectives. The presence of Native Americans (occasional visitors and part-time residents) adds to the challenge of understanding the personal or cultural beliefs that shaped the use of artifacts such as the silver conical earring found at Pilaklikaha. Even with all the time and effort that went into collecting the above evidence, much more could be said after undertaking further research. Only a small portion of Pilaklikaha's total area has been covered by archaeological fieldwork. Future investigations have the potential to greatly improve our understanding of the material variations or similarities between households, the settlement layout, and the full range of activities at Pilaklikaha. Preservation is also necessary so that threats from the expansion of a neighboring mine and area home construction do not obliterate the settlement's delicate archaeological remains.

7

▒▒▒▒▒▒

Conclusion

The archaeology of antislavery resistance continues to emerge, building on decades of study. Political initiatives and legislation devoting millions of dollars to investigations and preservation efforts have also fostered public engagement with remnants of the UGRR and self-liberated African communities. Recent conference symposia (for example, those hosted by the Society for Historical Archaeology and the American Anthropological Association) have contributed to data, methods, and theories concerning flight from slavery, plantation rebellions, and antislavery coalitions. Archaeology at various locations has demonstrated how this discourse has transcended Eurocentric, racist, document-centric models. Researchers have moved beyond earlier concerns with supplementing documented events to more robust views of community transformation, materialized identities, and landscapes of defiance.

As a result, archaeologists are helping to challenge monolithic notions such as the idea that the "American experience" was the story of founding fathers in search of freedom. The experience also involved the denial of freedoms and the struggles of Africans, native societies, the working class, and poor people (of different cultures) to regain their dignity and rights in colonial and modern societies.[1] The discourse can help people move toward a postcolonial present by encouraging them to challenge opportunists who marshal notions of freedom and resistance as convenient rallying cries that feed global domination and ideologies of privilege.

Archaeology at places such as Camp Nelson has helped to expand older conceptualizations that largely focused on rebellions, the UGRR, or marronage. Now scholars also consider similarities and direct links in phenomena that were once considered completely distinct in the traditional intellectual division of labor. For example, European and African cooperation is a theme that cross-cuts various instances of defiance, rebellion, and liberated community-building (Parris 1983). Smardz Frost (2008) underscores this point methodologically in her study of the U.S. birthplaces (in Kentucky), enslavement sites, and temporary residences of a couple who found their final sanctuary in Canada. The implication is that one cannot understand resistance by focusing on destinations alone, for there are various points of refuge and conflict on journeys toward freedom. Although common labels that differentiate forms of resistance are useful for introducing the subject, the classificatory function served thereby may also over-compartmentalize antislavery phenomena. In other words, one should use new or extent labels (like "contrabands," self-liberation, or the UGRR) carefully, keeping in mind that the modes of collaboration, goals, and social proximity of escapees to free people who aided them are among the factors that defy simple comparisons or typologies.

Despite the difficulties of doing fieldwork in rugged terrains and locating ephemeral material evidence, successful site location efforts have outnumbered failed searches. Remote sensing techniques contribute to the success of archaeologists. Decades ago, Deagan demonstrated the powerful role that remote sensing could play by using thermal imagery generated by NASA to locate part of Fort Mose. Various methods of geophysical prospecting have been employed in a few other studies with success. However, ephemeral sites like Pilaklikaha, where a fifty-square-meter portion was unsuccessfully examined with ground-penetrating radar, serve as a reminder that some remote sensing methods may be inappropriate for particular types of locations. Certain places and evidence will always prove ambiguous. But vagueness and a lack of patterning may be part of the very structure of data for some antislavery phenomena (Weik 2004).

Archaeologists have made a number of contributions to the study of African resistance to enslavement. The lack of extensive documentation for many settlements makes it possible for fieldwork to yield original results, particularly regarding artifacts used every day, such as the locally made smoking pipes decorated by Africans in Brazil, the Dominican Republic, and Cuba. Work needs to be done to uncover the significance of the pipes' geometric decorations and similar decorative motifs elsewhere (such as triangular punctates and incisions on Pilaklikaha's pottery). Were they expressions of identity or consumer-oriented decorations? Items such as copper bracelets, metal conical earrings, and beads found at different sites suggest that African escapees maintained the ability to express their tastes in adornment even on the run. Self-liberated Africans' ability to make their own ceramics (such as pots) and weapons (such as blades or bullets) and obtain their own subsistence (as indicated by wild fauna bones) suggests that the foundation for freedom was laid by skills, self-sufficiency, and access to raw materials.

Goods from American and European manufacturers are present in all self-liberated African and UGRR communities. This presence begs for attention in the future as it could inform a number of fundamental issues: the volume and regularity of exchange between self-liberated, free, and enslaved persons; the number of kitchenwares, arms, jewelry, and other items that escapees were able to take with them when they fled captivity; and resisters' relative success in (retributive or offensive) raiding, bartering, or trade. Archaeologists have discovered that many settlements were located at a distance from Euro-American neighbors or predominately white towns. Hopefully, future analyses of environmental features, travel routes, settlement patterns, and landscape features will teach us more about the networks and tensions connecting homesteads, plantations, Native American settlements, and communities of resistance.

For a few UGRR and self-liberated African sites that have been studied thus far, there is some evidence of dispersed settlement. Many people employed relaxed spatial organization and environmentally adaptive home-building and village-placement strategies. However, clear patterns of settlement layout continue to elude archaeologists at most locations. This gap will be addressed by multiyear, large-scale projects that conduct horizontally extensive sampling and block excavation strategies. Mechanical stripping may be an alternative in places, as its utility was demonstrated at the John P. Parker House site. By discerning the material culture of unique households or intra-settlement groups, archaeologists will be able to say more about themes such as African American communal redefinitions of freedom. One could strengthen arguments for communalism—which have largely been based on documentary anecdotes or modern ethnographic works—by examining whether the artifact evidence speaks to resource sharing or disparities between individual and group possessions. As material culture spatial distributions become clearer, the opportunity for more formal approaches to the social organization of space and defensive techniques become possible. Research at Pilaklikaha illustrates that assumptions about people maximizing their use of all available space are unfounded at some sites. Bumping up the unit of analysis and taking more regional approaches may be helpful, especially for materially sparse activity areas.

Besides archaeology, students of material culture may take other directions in pursuit of their interests in antislavery resistance. For instance, a lively debate has emerged concerning the meaning of quilt motifs (such as zigzag lines) associated with written or oral sources on the UGRR. Scholars have produced some anecdotal and circumstantial evidence in support of arguments that quilts contained coded geographic messages or that they were secret signals used to mark safe houses on the UGRR (Vlach 1978; Tobin and Dobard 1999). Skeptics point to the existence of similar motifs among numerous quilters, while other commentators note the implications of the debates for issues such as representation and Afrocentricity (Klassen 2009). Protest media such as flags, decorated plates, and monuments have materialized the beliefs of abolitionists and Africans resisting enslavement (Fischer 2005; see also Guyatt 2000 and various contributions in Blight 2004). Thus, there are ample opportunities to study artifacts that have not yet entered the subterranean part of the archaeological record.

Another direction future studies could take is to address the significant gap in the reach of antislavery archaeology in regions outside of North America, the Caribbean, and northeastern Brazil. Work could be done on the role of sites used by mutual aid societies in Latin America. Another example of alternative archaeological research includes the investigations that have been done on the Garifuna, or "Black Caribs," who settled in the islands and coastal areas of Honduras and Belize after escaping from slavery and allying with Native Americans in the Lesser Antilles (Cheek 1997; Cheek and Gonzalez 1986). Research in Africa and other parts of the world is also adding new breadth to the geographic scope of antislavery archaeologies (see, for example, Wilson Marshall 2009).

There are various stakeholders in the research process and many publics which stand to gain from antislavery archaeology. For instance, artists are creating archaeological illustrations as well as generating their own narratives on history and material culture that fall outside of traditional academic venues. Archaeologists and material culture researchers have important roles to play in human encounters with the past: as public-engagement facilitators; as anthropological knowledge producers on resistance, freedom, and liberation; as gatekeepers for access to artifacts and other evidence; as professional funding locators and grant writers. Tabloids, radio interviews, documentary films, newspaper articles, Web sites, and government pamphlets are also educating many people. Public archaeology initiatives such as the one at Poke Patch—where the National Forest Service supported a program that engages HBCU (Historically Black College or University) students in field research—have arisen from studies of the UGRR (USFS 2001).

Yet descendants could use more specific programs tailored to the needs of cultural survival and communal liberation (Weik 2007). National education curriculums and textbooks need to integrate the findings of antislavery researchers to ensure that children are exposed to the breadth of global African and diasporic experiences. Many archaeologists working on antislavery resistance have donated educational packets to grade schools, providing exercises for youth, some of whom could be the next generation of cultural resource managers and scholars.

The future of ongoing programs is a cause for concern. By 2003, the Bush administration had made cuts to the national funding for UGRR programs begun in the 1990s (Laroche 2004: 166). Cemetery and church vandalism, unmarked graves, artifact selling, and building construction are major concerns that shape the state of preservation for many settlements (Allen 2001: 75–77; Laroche 2004). In addition, wars threaten the existence of heritage resources and the very people who carry on the legacy of antislavery resistance around the world (Price 1998).

Despite these challenges, there are reasons to remain optimistic about the survival of descendants and the cultural resources of antislavery resistance. The history of rebellions, protest, and escape show that no matter how brutally a regime enforces its agenda, hegemony does not paralyze every member of a subject population (Beaudry and others 1991: 156–59; Scott 1985). The seeds of hope can be found in reflection on the historical evidence, oral traditions, and archaeological remains of antislavery defiance, which continue to educate people and provide inspiration for social movements (Hilliard 1994; Abrahams 2007). Direct action, collaboration, and applied scholarship are also needed in the present, where they can contribute new chapters to ongoing struggles and traditions of resistance (see White 2009a, 2009b).

Note

1. Some members of "First Nations" struggle against being labeled "American" because of the colonial roots of this construct (named for a European) and the presumptuous way that it stamps continents with a single Eurocentric label. Thus, the trope of an "American Experience" invites debate in realms of theory and identity politics.

References

Abrams, Leonard, and D. Chuck. 2006. *Quilombo Country*. New York: Quilombo Films.

Abu-Lughod, Lila. 1990. "The Romance of Resistance: Tracing Transformations of Power Through Bedouin Women." *American Ethnologist* 17 (1): 41–55.

Acosta Saignes, Miguel. 1967. *Vida de los esclavos negros en Venezuela*. Caracas: Hespérides.

Agorsah, Kofi E. 1985. "Excavation in the North Volta Basin." *West Africa Journal of Archaeology* 15: 11–40.

———. 1993. "Archaeology and Resistance History in the Caribbean." *African Archaeological Review* 11: 175–96.

———. 1994. "Archaeology of Maroon Settlements in Jamaica." In *Maroon Heritage: Archaeological, Ethnographic, and Historical Perspectives*. Kingston, Jamaica: Canoe Press.

———. 1997. "Locational and Spatial Transformation Patterns of Maroon Settlements in Suriname: A Preliminary Report." Report submitted to National Geographic Society and the Suriname National Museum. Portland, Oregon: Portland State University.

———. 1999. "Archaeological Considerations of Social Relationships and Settlement Patterning among Africans in the Caribbean Diaspora." In *African Sites Archaeology in the Caribbean*, edited by Jay Haviser, pp. 38–64. Kingston, Jamaica: Ian Randle.

———. 2001. *Freedom in Black History and Culture*. Middletown, Cal.: Arrow Point Press.

———. 2006. "The Other Side of Freedom: The Maroon Trail in Suriname." *African Re-Genesis: Confronting Social Issues in the Diaspora*, edited by Jay Haviser and Kevin C. MacDonald, pp. 191–203. Abingdon, UK: Taylor & Francis.

Allen, Richard. 2004. "A Serious and Alarming Daily Evil: Marronage and its Legacy in Mauritius and the Colonial Plantation World." *Slavery and Abolition* 25 (2): 1–17.

Allen, Scott J. 1995. *Africanisms, Mosaics, and Creativity: The Historical Archaeology of Palmares*. M.A. thesis. Providence, Rhode Island: Brown University.

———. 2001. *Zumbi nunca vai morrer: History, the Practice of Archaeology and Race Politics in Brazil*. Ph.D. dissertation. Providence, Rhode Island: Brown University.

Alpers, Edward. 2003. "Flight to Freedom: Escape from Slavery among Bonded Africans in the Indian Ocean World, c. 1750–1962." *Slavery and Abolition* 24 (2): 51–68.

———. 2004. "The Idea of Marronage: Reflections on Literature and Politics in Re´union." *Slavery and Abolition* 25 (2): 18–29.

———. 2007. "The African Diaspora in the Northwestern Indian Ocean: Reconsideration of an old Problem and New Directions for Research." In *Routes of Passage: Re-*

thinking the African Diaspora, edited by Ruth Simms Hamilton, ADRP series. East Lansing: Michigan State University Press.

Alpers, Edward A., Gwyn Campbell, and Michael Salman, eds. 2005. *Resisting Bondage in Indian Ocean Africa and Asia*. London: Routledge.

Andah, Bassey. 1988. *African Anthropology*. Ibadan, Nigeria: Shaneson C. I. Ltd.

Ani, Marimba. 1994. *Yurugu: An African-Centered Critique of European Cultural Thought and Behavior*. Trenton, New Jersey: Africa World Press.

Aptheker, Herbert. 1939. "Maroons Within the Present Limits of the United States." *Journal of Negro History* 24 (2): 167–84.

———. 1972. *A Documentary History of the Negro People in the United States Volume 2, From the Reconstruction Era to [the Founding of the N.A.A.C.P.] in 1910*. New York: Citadel Press.

Armstrong, Douglas. 2003a. "Faces in the Basement." *Dig* 5 (1): cover, 16–19.

———. 2003b. *Creole Transformation from Slavery to Freedom: Historical Archaeology of East End Community, St. John, Virgin Islands*. Gainesville: University Press of Florida.

———. 2009. "Excavating Inspiration: Archaeology at the Harriet Tubman Home, Auburn, New York." Paper presented at the Archaeology of the Recent African American Past conference, South Carolina Institute of Archaeology and Anthropology, University of South Carolina, Columbia, February 27.

Armstrong, Douglas, and Anna Hill. 2009. "Uncovering Inspiration: Current Archaeology Investigations of Harriet Tubman in Central New York." *The African Diaspora Newsletter*. http://www.diaspora.uiuc.edu/news0609/news0609.html (Accessed June 2009).

Armstrong, Douglas, and Lou Ann Wurst. 2003. "Clay Faces in an Abolitionist Church: The Wesleyan Methodist Church in Syracuse, New York." *Historical Archaeology* 37 (2): 19–37.

———. 1998. "'Faces' of the Past: Archaeology of an Underground Railroad Site in Syracuse, New York." *Syracuse University Archaeological Report* 10 (with Lou Ann Wurst).

Arrom, Jose Juan, and Manuel A. Garcia Arevalo. 1986. *Cimarron*. Santo Domingo, Dominican Republic: Fundacion Garcia Arevalo.

Ascher, Robert, and Charles Fairbanks. 1971. "Excavation of a Slave Cabin: Georgia, U.S.A." *Historical Archaeology* 5: 3–17.

Ashmore, Wendy. 2002. "'Decisions and Dispositions': Socializing Spatial Archaeology." *American Anthropologist* 104 (4): 1,172–83.

Aswani, Shankar, and Peter Sheppard. 2003. "The Archaeology and Ethnohistory of Exchange in Precolonial and Colonial Roviana: Gifts, Commodities, and Inalienable Possessions." *Current Anthropology* 44 (5): 51–78.

Baram, Uzi. 2008. "A Haven from Slavery on Florida's Gulf Coast: Looking for Evidence of Angola on the Manatee River." *African Diaspora Archaeology Newsletter* (June 2008): 1–18.

Barile, Kerri S. 1999. *Causes and Creations: Exploring the Relationship between Nineteenth Century Slave Insurrections, Landscape and Architecture at Middleburg Plantation, Berkeley County, South Carolina*. M.A. thesis. Columbia: Department of Anthropology, University of South Carolina.

Barth, Fredrik. 1969. *Ethnic Groups and Boundaries. The Social Organization of Culture Difference*. Bergen, Norway: Universitetsforlaget.

———. 2000. "Reflections on Theory and Practice." In *The Unity of Theory and Practice in Anthropology: Rebuilding a Fractured Synthesis*, edited by Carole E. Hill and Marietta L. Baba. NAPA bulletin 18: 147–63. Arlington, Virginia: American Anthropological Association.

Bateman, Rebecca. 1990. "Africans and Indians: A Comparative Study of the Black Carib and Black Seminole." *Ethnohistory* 37: 1–24.

———. 2002. "Naming Patterns in Black Seminole Ethnogenesis." *Ethnohistory* 49 (2): 227–57.

Battle-Baptiste, Whitney. 2007. "'In This Here Place': Interpreting Enslaved Homeplaces." In *Archaeology of Atlantic Africa and the African Diaspora*, edited by Akinwumi Ogundiran and Toyin Falola, pp. 233–48. Bloomington: Indiana University Press.

Bear Heart and Molly Larkin. 1996. *The Wind is My Mother: The Life and Teachings of a Native American Shaman*. New York: Clarkson Potter/Publishers.

Bell, Alison. 2005. "White Ethnogenesis and Gradual Capitalism: Perspectives from Colonial Archaeological Sites in the Chesapeake." *American Anthropologist* 107 (3): 446–60.

Bidney, David. 1963. *The Concept of Freedom in Anthropology*. Studies in General Anthropology 1. The Hague, Netherlands: Mouton.

Bilby, Kenneth. 1996. "Ethnogenesis in the Guianas and Jamaica: Two Maroon Cases." In *History, Power, and Identity*, edited by Jonathan Hill, pp. 119–41. Iowa City: University of Iowa Press.

———. 2005. *True-Born Maroons*. Gainesville: University Press of Florida.

Billingsley, Andrew. 2007. *Yearning to Breathe Free: Robert Smalls of South Carolina and His Families*. Columbia: University of South Carolina Press.

Bird, J. B. 2005. "Rebellion." http://www.johnhorse.com. (Accessed June 4, 2009).

Blakney-Bailey, Jane Anne B. 2007. *An Analysis of Historic Creek and Seminole Settlement Patterns, Town Design, and Architecture: The Paynes Town Seminole Site (8Al366), A Case Study*. PhD Dissertation. University of Florida and UMI/Proquest, Ann Arbor, Michigan.

Blight, David W. 2004. *Passages to Freedom: The Underground Railroad in History and Memory*. Washington, D.C.: Smithsonian Books in association with the National Underground Railroad Freedom Center.

Boas, Franz. 1940. "Liberty Among Primitive People." In *Freedom: Its Meaning*, pp. 375–80. New York: Harcourt, Brace, and Company.

Boteler-Mock, Shirley, and Mike Davis. 1997. "Seminole Black Culture on the Texas Frontier." *CRM* 20 (2): 8–10.

Bourdieu, Pierre. 1977. *Outline of a Theory of Practice*. Cambridge Studies in Social Anthropology, 16. Cambridge, UK: Cambridge University Press.

Boyd, Mark F. 1951. "The Seminole War, Its Background and Onset." *Florida Historical Quarterly* 30: 3–115.

———. 1958. "Horatio Dexter and Events Leading to the Treaty of Moultrie Creek with the Seminole Indians." *Florida Anthropologist* 11 (3): 65–95.

Bradley, K. R. 1994. *Slavery and Society at Rome.* Cambridge, UK: Cambridge University Press.

Branton, N. 2009. "Landscape Approaches in Historical Archaeology: The Archaeology of Places." In *International Handbook of Historical Archaeology,* edited by T. Majewski and D. Gaimster, pp. 51–65. New York: Springer.

Brooks, James F., ed. 2002. *Confounding the Color Line: The Indian-Black Experience in North America.* Lincoln: University of Nebraska Press.

Brown, Canter, Jr. 2005. "Tales of Angola: Free blacks, Red Stick Creeks, and International Intrigue in Spanish Southwest Florida, 1812–1821." In *Go Sound the Trumpet!: Selections in Florida's African American History,* edited by D. H. Jackson Jr. and C. Brown Jr., pp. 5–21. Tampa, Fla.: University of Tampa Press.

Brown, Christopher L. 2006. "The Arming of Slaves in Comparative Perspective." In *Arming Slaves: From Classical Times to the Modern Age,* edited by Christopher Leslie Brown and Philip D. Morgan, pp. 330–54. New Haven, Conn.: Yale University Press.

Brown, Michael F. 1998. "On Resisting Resistance." *American Anthropologist* 98 (4): 729–35.

Cabral, Amilcar. 1973. *Return to the Source: Selected Speeches by Amilcar Cabral.* Edited by the African Information Service. New York: Monthly Review Press.

Campbell, Gwyn, and Edward A. Alpers. 2004. "Introduction: Slavery, Forced Labour and Resistance in Indian Ocean Africa and Asia. *Slavery and Abolition* 25 (2): ix–xxvii.

Campbell, Mavis C. 1990. *The Maroons of Jamaica, 1655–1796.* Trenton, New Jersey: Africa World Press.

———. 1993. *Back to Africa: George Ross and the Maroons From Nova Scotia to Sierra Leone.* Trenton, New Jersey: Africa World Press.

Campbell, Amanda, and Michael S. Nassaney. 2005. *The Ramptown Project: Archaeological and Historical Investigations of Underground Railroad Activities in Southwest Michigan.* Kalamazoo, Mich.: Department of Anthropology, Western Michigan University.

Cardoso, Gerald. 1983. *Negro Slavery in the Sugar Plantations of Veracruz and Pernambuco 1550–1680: A Comparative Study.* Washington, D.C.: University Press of America.

Carneiro, Edison. 1966. *O quilombos dos Palmares.* Rio de Janeiro, Brazil: Editôra Civilização Brasileira.

Carr, Robert, and Willard Steele. 1993. *Seminole Heritage Survey: Seminole Sites of Florida.* Miami, Fla.: Archaeological and Historical Conservancy.

Carroll, Patrick J. 1977. "Mandinga: The Evolution of a Mexican Runaway Slave Community: 1735–1827." *Comparative Studies in Society and History* 19 (4): 488–505.

———. 1991. *Blacks in Colonial Veracruz: Race, Ethnicity, and Regional Development.* Austin: University of Texas Press.

Carter, Ian, Matthew H. Kramer, and Hillel Steiner. 2007. *Freedom: A Philosophical Anthology.* Malden, Mass: Blackwell Publishers.

Castaño, Ana Mª Mansilla. 2000. "Patrimonio Afroamericano en Brasil: Arqueologica de los Quilombos." *Artículos* 2 (2): September. www.ucm.es/info/arqueoweb/numero2_2b/articulo2_2C.htm.

Castells, Manuel. 1996. *The Rise of the Network Society*. Malden, Mass., and Oxford: Blackwell Publishers.

Chapman, Abraham. 1971. *Steal Away; Stories of the Runaway Slaves*. New York: Praeger.

Charlton, Thomas H., and Patricia Fournier. 1993. "Urban and Rural Dimensions of the Contact Period: Central Mexico, 1521–1620." In *Ethnohistory and Archaeology: Approaches to Postcontact and Change in the Americas*, edited by J. Daniel Rogers and Samuel M. Wilson, pp. 201–16. New York: Plenum Press.

Cheek, Charles D. 1997. "Setting an English Table: Black Carib Archeology on the Caribbean Coast of Honduras." In *Approaches to the Historical Archaeology of Mexico, Central & South America*, edited by Janine Gasco, Greg Charles Smith, and Patricia Fournier-Garcia, pp. 101–10. Monograph 38. Los Angeles: The Institute of Archeology, University of California.

Cheek, Charles D., and Nancie L. Gonzalez. 1986. "Black Carib Settlement Patterns in Early 19th Century Honduras: The Search for a Livelihood." *Studies in Third World Societies* 35: 403–29.

Comaroff, Jean. 1985. *Body of Power, Spirit of Resistance: The Culture and History of a South African People*. Chicago: University of Chicago Press.

Comaroff, Jean, and John L. Comaroff. 1991. *Of Revelation and Revolution*. Chicago: University of Chicago Press.

Cooper, Carolyn. 1994. "Resistance Science: Afrocentric Ideology in Vic Reid's Nannytown." In *Maroon Heritage*, edited by E. Kofi Agorsah, pp. 109–18. Kingston: Jamaican Canoe Press.

Covington, James. 1993. *The Seminoles of Florida*. Gainesville: University Press of Florida.

Craton, Michael J. 1982. *Testing the Chains: Resistance to Slavery in the British West Indies*. Ithaca: Cornell University Press.

Davis, David Brion. 2006. *Inhuman Bondage: The Rise and Fall of Slavery in the New World*. Oxford, UK: Oxford University Press.

Davis, Natalie Zemon. 2000. *Slaves on Screen: Film and Historical Vision*. Cambridge, Mass.: Harvard University Press.

Deagan, Kathleen. 1987. *Artifacts Of The Spanish Colonies Of Florida And The Caribbean, 1500–1800: Ceramics, Glassware, and Beads, Volume 1*. Washington, D.C.: Smithsonian Institute.

———. 1996. "Colonial Transformation: Euro-American Cultural Genesis in the Early Spanish American Colonies." *Journal of Anthropological Research* 52 (2): 135–61.

———. 1998. "Transculturation and Spanish American Ethnogenesis: The Archaeological Legacy of the Quincentenary." In *Studies in Culture Contact: Interaction, Culture Change, and Archaeology*, edited by J. G. Cusick, pp. 23–43. Carbondale, Illinois: Southern Illinois University.

Deagan, Kathleen, and Jane Landers. 1999. "Fort Mose: Earliest Free American Town in the United States." In *I, Too, Am America*, edited by Theresa A. Singleton, pp. 261–82. Charlottesville, Virginia: University of Virginia Press.

de Barros, Philip. 2001. "The Effect of the Slave Trade on the Bassar Ironworking Society." In *West Africa During the Atlantic Slave Trade: Archaeological Perspectives*, edited by C. DeCorse, pp. 59–80. London and New York: Leicester University Press.

DeCorse, Christopher R. 1992. "Culture Contact, Continuity, and Change on the Gold Coast, AD 1400–1900." *African Archaeological Review* 10: 163–96.

Deive, Carlos Esteban. 1980. *La Esclavitud del Negro en Santo Domingo (1492–1844).* Santo Domingo, Dominican Republic: Museo del Hombre.

———. 1985. *Los Cimarrones del Maniel de Neiba. Historia y Etnografia.* Santo Domingo, Dominican Republic: Publicaciones del Banco Central de la Republica Dominicana.

Delle, James A. 1998. *Archaeology of Social Space: Analyzing Coffee Plantations in Jamaica's Blue Mountains.* New York: Plenum Press.

———. 1999. "'A Good and Easy Speculation': Spatial Conflict, Collusion and Resistance in Late Sixteenth-Century Munster, Ireland." *International Journal of Historical Archaeology* 3 (1): 11–35.

Delle, James A., and Mary Ann Levine. 2004. "Excavations at the Thaddeus Stevens and Lydia Hamilton Smith Site, Lancaster, Pennsylvania: Archaeological Evidence for the Underground Railroad?" *Northeastern Historical Archaeological* 33: 131–52.

Delle, James A., and Jason Shellenhamer. 2008. "Archaeology at the Parvin Homestead: Searching for the Material Legacy of the Underground Railroad [Berks County, Pa.]." *Historical Archaeology,* 42 (2): 38–62.

De Vore, Steven L. 2008. "Geophysical Investigations of the North Liberty Cemetery (13CD158), Cedar County, Iowa." Submitted to the archeologist of the State Historic Preservation Office, State Historical Society of Iowa, Department of Cultural Affairs.

Drake, St. Clair. 1987. *Black Folk Here and There, Volume 1.* Los Angeles: Center for African American Studies, University of California.

DuBois, Page. 2003. *Slaves and Other Objects.* Chicago: University of Chicago Press.

DuBois, W.E.B. 1915. *The Negro.* New York: Holt and Company.

Egerton, Douglas R. 2006. "Slaves to the Marketplace: Economic Liberty and Black Rebelliousness in the Atlantic World." *Journal of the Early Republic* 26: 617–39.

Ejstrud, Bo. 2008. "Maroons and Landscapes." *Journal of Caribbean Archaeology* 8: 1–14.

Englund, Harri. 2006. *Prisoners of Freedom: Human Rights and the African Poor.* Berkeley: University of California Press.

Fabian, Johannes. 1998. *Moments of Freedom: Anthropology and Popular Culture.* Charlottesville: University Press of Virginia.

Fairbanks, Charles. 1958. "Some Problems of the Origin of Creek Pottery." *Florida Anthropologist* 11 (2): 53–63.

Fennell, Christopher C. 2010. "Early African America: Archaeological Studies of Significance and Diversity." *Journal of Archaeological Research* 1: 1–49.

———. 2009. "Archaeological Perspectives on Structural Racism in the Jim Crow Era of the American Midwest." Paper presented at the Archaeology of the Recent African American Past conference, South Carolina Institute of Archaeology and Anthropology, University of South Carolina, Columbia.

———. 2007. *Crossroads and Cosmologies: Diasporas and Ethnogenesis in the New World.* Gainesville: University Press of Florida.

Ferguson, Leland. 1991. "Struggling with Pots in Colonial South Carolina." In *The Archaeology of Inequality,* edited by Robert Paynter and Randall H. McGuire, pp. 28–39. Oxford, U.K.: Basil Blackwell.

———. 1992. *Uncommon Ground*. Washington, D.C.: Smithsonian Institution Press.

Fischer, David Hackett. 2005. *Liberty and Freedom*. Oxford: Oxford University Press.

Fitts, Robert. 1996. "The Landscapes of Northern Bondage." *Historical Archaeology* 30 (2): 54–73.

Flory, Thomas. 1979. "Fugitive Slaves and Free Society." *Journal of Negro History* LXIV (2, Spring): pp. 116–30.

Forbes, Jack. 1993. *Africans and Native Americans: The Language of Race and the Evolution of Red-Black Peoples*. Chicago: University of Illinois Press.

Franklin, John Hope, and Loren Schweninger. 1999. *Runaway Slaves: Rebels on the Plantation*. New York: Oxford University Press.

Fraser, George C. 2004. *Success Runs in Our Race: The Complete Guide to Effective Networking in the Black Community*. New York: Amistad.

Fruehling, B. D., and R. H. Smith. 1993. "Subterranean Hideaways of the Underground Railroad in Ohio: An Architectural, Archaeological and Historical Critique of Local Traditions. *Ohio History* 102: 98–117.

Funari, Pedro Paulo. 1995. "The Archaeology of Palmares and its Contribution to the Understanding of the History of African-American Culture." *Historical Archaeology in Latin America* 7: 1–41.

———. 1999. "Maroon, Race and Gender: Palmares Material Culture and Social Relations in a Runaway Settlement. In *Historical Archaeology: Back from the Edge*, edited by P. P. Funari, M. Hall, and S. Jones, pp. 308–27. London: Routledge.

Furlonge, Nigel D. 1999. "Revisiting the Zanj and Re-visioning Revolt: Complexities of the Zanj Conflict." *Negro History Bulletin* 62: 7–14.

Gara, Larry. 1961. *The Liberty Line; The Legend of the Underground Railroad*. Lexington: University of Kentucky Press.

Geggus, David. 1982. "Slave Resistance Studies and the St. Domingue Slave Revolt." *Occasional Papers Series* (4, Winter): 1-36. Latin American and Caribbean Center, Florida International University, Miami.

Genheimer, Robert A. 2001. "A Report on Preliminary Archaeological Testing and an Archaeological Development Plan for the John P. Parker House and Foundry Site, Ripley, Ohio." Prepared for the John P. Parker Historical Society, Ripley, Ohio, and the National Park Service, Midwest Region, Omaha, Nebraska. Prepared by the Cincinnati Museum Center, Cincinnati, Ohio.

Gerlach, Luther P., and Virginia H. Hine. 1970. "The Social Organization of a Movement of Revolutionary Change: Case Study, Black Power." In *African American Anthropology: Contemporary Perspectives*, edited by Norman E. Whitten Jr. and John F. Szwed. New York: The Free Press.

Giddens, Anthony. 1979. *Central Problems in Social Theory: Action, Structure, and Contradiction in Social Analysis*. Berkeley: University of California Press.

Gilroy, Paul. 1993. "The Black Atlantic as a Counterculture of Modernity." Introduction, *The Black Atlantic: Modernity and Double Consciousness*, pp. 1–19. Cambridge: Harvard University Press.

Glaude, Eddie S. 2004. "A Sacred Drama: 'Exodus' and the Underground Railroad in African American Life." In *Passages to Freedom: The Underground Railroad in History and Memory*, edited by David W. Blight, pp. 291–304. Washington, D.C.: Smithsonian Books in association with the National Underground Railroad Freedom Center.

Goggin, John M. 1953. "Seminole Archaeology in East Florida." *Southeastern Archaeological Conference Newsletter* 3 (3): 16, 19.

Gomez, M. A. 1998. *Exchanging our Country Marks: The Transformation of African Identities in the Colonial and Antebellum South*. Chapel Hill: University of North Carolina Press.

Gonzalez, Nancie L. Solien. 1988. *Sojourners of the Caribbean: Ethnogenesis and Ethnohistory of the Garifuna*. Urbana: University of Illinois Press.

Gray, T. F., and James 1836. "Burning of the Town Pila-kli-ka-ha." Print: Lithographic Color. Library of Congress.

Green, Sarah, Penny Harvey, and Hannah Knox. 2005. "Scales of Place and Networks: An Ethnography of the Imperative to Connect through Information and Communications Technologies." *Current Anthropology* 46 (5): 805–26.

Griffin, John W. 1950. "An Archaeologist at Fort Gadsden." *Florida Historical Quarterly* 28 (4): 255–61.

de Groot, Silvia W. 1979. "The Bush Negro Chiefs Visit Africa: Diary of an Historic Trip." In *Maroon Societies: Rebel Slave Communities in the Americas, Second Edition*, edited by Richard Price, pp. 389–98. Baltimore: Johns Hopkins University Press.

———. 2003. *Surinam Maroon Chiefs in Africa in Search of their Country of Origin*. Amsterdam: [de auteur].

Guimaraes, Carlos Magno. 1990. "O Quilombo do Ambrosio: Lenda, Documentos e Arqueologia." *Estudos Ibero-Americanos* 16: 161–74.

Gundaker, Grey. 2000. "Discussion: Creolization, Complexity, and Time." *Historical Archaeology* 34 (3): 124–33.

Guyatt, Mary. 2000. "The Wedgwood Slave Medallion Values in Eighteenth-Century Design." *Journal of Design History* 13 (2): 93–105.

Haas, Mary. 1941. "The Classification of the Muskogean Languages." In *Language, Culture, and Personality: Essays in Memory of Edward Sapir*, edited by Leslie Spier et al., 41–56. Menasha, Wisconsin: Banta Publishing.

Handler, Jerome. 1997. "Escaping Slavery in a Caribbean Plantation Society: Marronage in Barbados, 1650s–1830s." *Nieuwe West-Indische Gids* (New West Indian Guide) 71: 183–225.

Harding, V. 1981. *There is a River: The Black Struggle for Freedom in America*. San Diego, Cal.: Harcourt Brace.

Hardy, Heather K. 2005. "Introduction." In *Native Languages of the Southeastern United States*, edited by Heather K. Hardy and Janine Scancarelli, pp. 69–74. Lincoln: University of Nebraska Press.

Harris, C.L.G. 1994. "The True Traditions of my Ancestors." In *Maroon Heritage: Archaeological, Ethnographic, and Historical Perspectives*, edited by Kofi Agorsah pp. 36–63. Kingston, Jamaica: Canoe Press.

Harris, Joseph E. 1971. *The African Presence in Asia; Consequences of the East African Slave Trade*. Evanston, Ill.: Northwestern University Press.

Harrison, Faye Venetia. 2005. "Introduction: Global Perspectives on Human Rights and Interlocking Inequalities of Race, Gender and Related Dimensions of Power." In *Resisting Racism and Xenophobia: Global Perspectives on Race, Gender, and Human Rights*, edited by Faye V. Harrison, pp. 1–31. Walnut Creek, Cal.: Alta Mira Press. .

Hauser, M. W. 2008. *An Archaeology of Black Markets: Local Ceramics and Economies in Eighteenth-Century Jamaica*. Gainesville: University Press of Florida.

Hegland, Mary Elaine. 2003. "Shi'a Women's Rituals in Northwest Pakistan: The Shortcomings and Significance of Resistance." *Anthropological Quarterly* 76 (3): 411–42.

Herron, Jordon. 1994. *Black Seminole Settlement Pattern*. Unpublished M.A. thesis. Columbia: University of South Carolina.

Herskovitz, M. and F. Herskovitz. 1934. *Rebel Destiny*. New York: McGraw-Hill Book Company, Inc.

Hill, Jonathan. 1996. *History, Power, and Identity: Ethnogenesis in the Americas, 1492–1992*. Iowa City: University of Iowa Press.

Hilliard, Asa G. 1995. *The Maroon Within Us: Selected Essays on African American Community Socialization*. Baltimore, Maryland: Black Classic Press.

———. 1998. *SBA: The Reawakening of the African Mind*. Gainesville, Fla.: Makare Publishers.

History News Network (H.N.N.). 2007. *Found? Ship that Carried Escaped Slaves and Was Sunk by Slavers*. http://www.post-trib.com (September 19, 2007). http://hnn.us/roundup/archives/41/2007/9/#429371.

Hollander, Jocelyn A., and Rachel L. Einwohner. 2004. "Conceptualizing Resistance." *Sociological Forum* 19 (4): 533–54.

Howard, Rosalyn. 2002. *Black Seminoles in the Bahamas*. Gainesville: University Press of Florida.

Hudson, Mark. 1999. *Ruins of Identity: Ethnogenesis in the Japanese Islands*. Honolulu: University of Hawaii Press.

Humez, Jean McMahon. 2003. *Harriet Tubman: The Life and the Life Stories*. Madison: University of Wisconsin Press.

Hunter, Tera W. 1997. *To 'Joy My Freedom: Southern Black Women's Lives and Labors after the Civil War*. Cambridge: Harvard University Press.

Ingold, Tim. 1993. "The Temporality of Landscape." *World Archeology* 25 (2): 152–74.

Irwin, John R. 1836. "Memoir." Folder entitled "Irwin, John R. Memoir (photocopy) 01, 007. P. K. Yonge Library of Florida History, University of Florida Special Collections.

James, C.L.R. 1963. *The Black Jacobins; Toussaint L'Ouverture and the San Domingo Revolution*. New York: Vintage Books.

James, Cynthia. 2002. *The Maroon Narrative: Caribbean Literature in English Across Boundaries, Ethnicities, and Centuries*. Portsmouth, New Hampshire: Heinemann.

Jones, Howard. 1987. *Mutiny on the* Amistad: *The Saga of a Slave Revolt and its Impact on American Abolition, Law, and Diplomacy*. New York: Oxford University Press.

Jones, Vinnie. 1990. *Black Warriors of the Seminole*. WUFT.

Jumper, Betty Mae Tiger, and Patsy West. 2001. *A Seminole Legend: The Life of Betty Mae Tiger Jumper*. Gainesville: University Press of Florida.

Karenga, Malauna. 2006. "Philosophy in the African Tradition of Resistance: Issues of Human Freedom and Human Flourishing." In *Not Only the Master's Tools: African-*

American Studies in Theory and Practice. Cultural Politics & the Promise of Democracy, edited by Lewis R. Gordon and Jane Anna Gordon, pp. 243–71. Boulder, Col.: Paradigm.

Katz, William Loren. 1986. *Black Indians: A Hidden Heritage.* New York: Ethrac Publication, Inc.

Kent, R. K. 1965. "Palmares: An African State in Brazil." *Journal of African History* 6: 161–75.

King, Eleanor. 2006. "Archaeology and the Warriors Project: Exploring a Buffalo Soldier Campsite in the Guadalupe Mountains of Texas." In *People, Places, and Parks: Proceedings of the 2005 George Wright Society Conference on Parks, Protected Areas, and Cultural Sites*, edited by David Harmon, pp. 475–81. Hancock, Mich.: The George Wright Society.

King, Johannes. 1979. "Guerilla Warfare: A Bush Negro View." In *Maroon Societies: Rebel Slave Communities in the Americas*, edited by Richard Price, pp. 298–304. New York: Anchor Books.

Klassen, Teri. 2009. "Representations of African American Quiltmaking: From Omission to High Art. *Journal of American Folklore* 122 (485): 297–334.

Kly, Y. N. 2006. *The Invisible War: African American Anti-Slavery Resistance from the Stono Rebellion through the Seminole Wars.* Atlanta: Clarity Press.

Knappett, Carl. 2005. *Thinking through Material Culture: An Interdisciplinary Perspective. Archaeology, Culture, and Society.* Philadelphia: University of Pennsylvania Press.

Kondo, Dorinne K. 1990. *Crafting Selves: Power, Gender, and Discourses of Identity in a Japanese Workplace.* Chicago: University of Chicago Press.

Krieger, A. R. 1999. "Initial Report of Phase I Survey of the Lick Creek African American Settlement, Orange County, Indiana, 1817–1911." Culture Resource Reconnaissance Report No. 09-12-04-170. USDA, National Forest Service, Hoosier National Forest.

La Rosa Corzo, Gabino. 2003. *Runaway Slave Settlements in Cuba: Resistance and Repression.* Chapel Hill: University of North Carolina Press.

———. 2005. "Subsistence of *Cimarrones*: An Archaeological Study." In *Dialogues in Cuban Archaeology*, edited by L. A. Curet, S. L. Dawdy, and G. La Rosa Corzo, pp. 163–80. Tuscaloosa: University of Alabama Press.

Laidlaw, James. 2002. "For an Anthropology of Ethics and Freedom." *Journal of the Royal Anthropological Institute* 8 (2): 311–32.

Landers, Jane. 1992. "Fort Mose: Gracia Real de Santa Teresa de Mose, A Free Black Town in Spanish Colonial Florida." *American Historical Review* 95 (1):9–30.

———. 1998. "Black Communities and Culture in the Southeastern Borderlands." *Journal of the Early Republic* 18 (1): 117–34.

———. 1999. *Black Society in Spanish Florida.* Chicago: University of Illinois Press.

———. 2002. "The Central African Presence in Spanish Maroon Communities." In *Central Africans and Cultural Transformations in the American Diaspora*, edited by Linda M. Heywood, pp. 227–42. New York: Cambridge University Press.

LaRoche, C. J. 2004. *On the Edge of Freedom: Free Black Communities, Archaeology, and the Underground Railroad.* Ph.D. dissertation, College Park: University of Maryland.

Law, John, and John Hassard, eds. 1999. *Actor Network Theory and After.* Oxford: Blackwell.

Lee, Dorothy. 1959. *Freedom and Culture*. Englewood Cliffs, New Jersey: Prentice Hall.

Leone, Mark P. 2005. *The Archaeology of Liberty in an American Capital: Excavations in Annapolis*. Berkeley: University of California Press.

Leone, Mark P., Cheryl Janifer LaRoche, and Jennifer J. Babiarz. 2005. "The Archaeology of Black Americans in Recent Times." *Annual Review of Anthropology* 34: 575–98.

Liebmann, Matthew. 2008. "The Innovative Materiality of Revitalization Movements: Lessons from the Pueblo Revolt of 1680." *American Anthropologist* 110 (3): 360–72.

Lister, F. C., and R. H. Lister. 1974. "Majolica in Colonial Spanish America." *Historical Archaeology* 8: 17–52.

Littlefield, Daniel F. Jr. 1977. *Africans and Seminoles, From Removal to Emancipation*. Westport, Conn.: Greenwood Press.

Lockley, Timothy James. 2009. *Maroon Communities in South Carolina: A Documentary Record*. Columbia: University of South Carolina Press.

de Lomnitz, Larissa Adler. 1977. *Networks and Marginality: Life in a Mexican Shantytown*. New York: Academic Press.

Lovejoy, Paul E. 1983. *Transformations in Slavery: A History of Slavery in Africa*. Cambridge: Cambridge University Press.

———. 2000. *Transformations in Slavery: A History of Slavery in Africa*. Second edition. Cambridge: Cambridge University Press.

Mackie, Erin. 2005. "Welcome the Outlaw: Pirates, Maroons, and Caribbean Countercultures." *Cultural Critique* 59: 24–61.

Mahon, John K. 1985 [1967]. *History of the Second Seminole War*. Gainesville: University Presses of Florida.

Malcom, Corey. 2002. "A Collection of Artifacts Recovered from the Shipwreck *Henrietta Marie*." Report submitted in accordance with Florida Keys National Marine Sanctuary Permit 01–046. Mel Fisher Maritime Heritage Society.

Malinowski, Bronislaw. 1944. *Freedom and Civilization*. New York: Roy Publishers.

Martin, Joel W. 1991. *Sacred Revolt: The Muskogees' Struggle for a New World*. Boston: Beacon Press.

Mathurin, Lucille. 1975. *The Rebel Woman in the British West Indies During Slavery*. Kingston: The African-Caribbean Institute of Jamaica.

Matthews, Gelien. 2006. *Caribbean Slave Revolts and the British Abolitionist Movement*. Baton Rouge: Louisiana State University Press.

McBride, Stephen. 2008. "African American Women, Power, and Freedom in the Contested Landscape of Camp Nelson, Kentucky." Paper presented in the Power Dynamics in the Preservation and Public Interpretation of Gendered Landscapes symposium, Society for Historical Archaeology conference.

McCall, George A. 1974 [1868]. *Letters from the Frontiers*. Gainesville: University Presses of Florida.

McDonald, J. Douglas, L. J. Zimmerman, A. L. McDonald, William Tall Bull, and Ted Rising Sun. 1991. "The Northern Cheyenne Outbreak of 1879." In *The Archaeology of Inequality*, edited by Randall H. McGuire and Robert Paynter, pp. 64–78. Oxford: Basil Blackwell.

McGary, Howard, and Bill E. Lawson. 1992. *Between Slavery and Freedom: Philosophy and American Slavery*. Blacks in the Diaspora Series. Bloomington: Indiana University Press.

Mendelsohn, I. 1946. "Slavery in the Ancient Near East." *The Biblical Archaeologist* 9 (4, December): pp. 74–88.

Miers, Suzanne. 2004. "Slave Rebellion and Resistance in the Aden Protectorate in the Mid-Twentieth Century." *Slavery and Abolition* 25 (2): 80–89.

Miers, Suzanne, and Igor Kopytoff, eds. 1977. *Slavery in Africa: Historical and Anthropological Perspectives*. Madison: University of Wisconsin Press.

Milanich, Jerald T. 1995. *Florida Indians and the Invasion from Europe*. Gainesville: University Press of Florida.

Miles, Tiya, and Sharon P. Holland, eds. 2006. *Crossing Waters, Crossing Worlds: The African Diaspora in Indian Country*. Durham: Duke University Press.

Miller, J. C. 1988. *Way of Death: Merchant Capitalism and the Angolan Slave Trade 1730–1830*. Madison: University of Wisconsin Press.

Miller, Susan. 2003. *Coacoochee's Bones: A Seminole Saga*. Lawrence: University Press of Kansas.

Mintz, Sidney Wilfred. 1996. *Tasting Food, Tasting Freedom: Excursions into Eating, Culture, and the Past*. Boston: Beacon Press.

Mock, Shirley. 2010. *Dreaming with the Ancestors: Black Seminole Women in Texas and Mexico*. Race and Culture in the American West series, volume 4. Norman: University of Oklahoma Press.

Moore, John H. 1994. "Ethnogenetic Theory." *National Geographic Research and Exploration* 10 (1): 10–23.

———. 2001. "Ethnogenetic Patterns in Native North America." In *Archaeology, Language, and History: Essays on Culture and Ethnicity*, edited by John E. Terrell, pp. 31–56. Westport, Conn.: Bergin and Garvey.

Morrison, Tara. 1998. "The UGRR Archeology Initiative." *CRM*: (4): 46–47.

Morse, Jedediah. 1822. "A Report to the Secretary of War of the United States on Indian Affairs." St. Clair Shores, Michigan: Scholarly Press. Reprinted in 1972.

Mullin, Gerald W. 1972. *Flight and Rebellion; Slave Resistance in Eighteenth-Century Virginia*. New York: Oxford University Press.

Mullins, Paul R. 1999. *Race and Affluence: An Archaeology of African America and Consumer Culture*. New York: Kluwer Academic/Plenum Publishers.

Mulroy, Kevin. 1993a. "Ethnogenesis and Ethnohistory of the Seminole Maroons." *Journal of World History* 4 (2): 287–305.

———. 1993b. *Freedom on the Border: The Seminole Maroons in Florida, the Indian Territory, Coahuila, and Texas*. Lubbock: Texas Tech University Press.

———. 2004. "Seminole Maroons." In *Handbook of North American Indians: Southeast*, edited by William C. Sturtevant, pp. 465–77. Washington, D.C.: Smithsonian Institution Press.

———. 2007. *The Seminole Freedmen: A History*. Race and Culture in the American West series, volume 2. Norman: University of Oklahoma Press.

Murakami, Kyoko, and David Middleton. 2006. "Grave Matters: Emergent Networks and Summation in Remembering and Reconciliation." *Ethos* 34 (2): 273–96.

Mykell, Nancy. 1962. "The Seminole Towns—A Compilation Prepared for Sociology 630." Unpublished manuscript on file at the Florida Museum of Natural History, Gainesville, Florida.

Nassy Brown, Jacqueline. 2000. "Enslaving History: Narratives on Local Whiteness in a Black Atlantic Port." *American Ethnologist* 27 (2): 340–70.

Ngwenyama, Cheryl N. 2007. *Material Beginnings of the Saramaka Maroons: An Archaeological Investigation.* Ph.D. dissertation, University of Florida and UMI/Proquest, Ann Arbor, Michigan.

Nichols, Elaine. 1988. *No Easy Run to Freedom: Maroons in the Great Dismal Swamp of North Carolina and Virginia, 1677–1850.* Unpublished M.A. thesis. Columbia: Department of Anthropology, University of South Carolina.

Niven, L. 1994. "Black Loyalists in Nova Scotia." *African American Archaeology Newsletter,* number 11, summer. http://www.newsouthassoc.com/newsletters/Summer1994.html.

———. 2000. "Testing Two Sites in Birchtown." In *Archaeological Surveys in Two Black Communities, 1998.* Nova Scotia Museum curatorial report no. 92. Halifax: Nova Scotia Museum. (Can be purchased at NS Museum bookstore.)

———. 2000. "Was This the Home of Stephen Blucke?" In *The Excavation of AkDi-23, Birchtown, Shelburne County.* Nova Scotia Museum curatorial report no. 93. Halifax: Nova Scotia Museum.

Norton, Holly, and Chris Espenshade. 2007. "The Challenge in Locating Maroon Refuge Sites at Maroon Ridge, St. Croix." *Journal of Caribbean Archaeology* 7: 1–17.

Ogundiran, Akinwumi. 2007. "Living in the Shadow of the Atlantic World: Material Life, History and Culture in Yoruba-Edo Hinterland, ca. 1600–1750." In *Archaeology of Atlantic Africa and the African Diaspora,* edited by Akinwumi Ogundiran and Toyin Falola, pp. 77–99. Bloomington: Indiana University Press.

Ogunleye, Tolagbe. 1996. "The Self-Emancipated Africans of Florida: Pan-African Nationalists in the 'New World.'" *Journal of Black Studies* 27 (1): 24–38.

Ohadike, Don C. 2007. *Sacred Drums of Liberation: Religions and Music of Resistance in Africa and the Diaspora.* Trenton, New Jersey: Africa World Press, Inc.

Okihiro, Gary Y. 1986. *In Resistance: Studies in African, Caribbean, and Afro-American History.* Amherst: University of Massachusetts Press.

Omi, Michael, and Howard Winant. 1988. *Racial Formation in the United States: From the 1960s to the 1990s.* London: Routledge.

Ontario Minister of Citizenship and Immigration. 2007. "Historic Underground Railroad Liberty Bell on Display at Queen's Park for Black History Month." http://www.citizenship.gov.on.ca/english/news/2007/n20070214.shtml. (Accessed June 3, 2009.)

Opala, Joseph A. 1980. *A Brief History of the Seminole Freedmen.* Norman: Department of Anthropology, University of Oklahoma.

Orser Jr., Charles E. 1992. *In Search of Zumbi: Preliminary Archaeological Research at the Serra da Barriga, State of Alagoas, Brazil.* Normal, Ill.: Illinois State University.

———. 1998. "The Archaeology of the African Diaspora." *Annual Review of Anthropology* 27: 63–82.

———. 1996. *A Historical Archaeology of the Modern World.* New York: Plenum Press.

Orser Jr., Charles E., and Pedro P. A. Funari. 2001. "Archaeology of Slave Resistance and Rebellion. *World Archaeology* 33 (1): 61–72.

Ortiz, Fernando. 1940. *Contrapunteo Cubano del Tobaco y Azucar*. Havana: Ediciones Ciencias Sociales.

Ortner, Sherry B. 1995. "Resistance and the Problem of Ethnographic Refusal." *Comparative Studies in Society and History* 37 (1): 173–93.

———. 1997. "Thick Resistance: Death and the Cultural Construction of Agency in Himalayan Mountaineering." *Representations* 59: 135–62.

Osagie, Iyunolu Folayan. 2000. *The* Amistad *Revolt: Memory, Slavery, and the Politics of Identity in the United States and Sierra Leone*. Athens: University of Georgia Press.

Painter, Nell Irvin. 1995. "Slavery and Soul Murder: Toward a Fully Loaded Cost Accounting." In *U.S. History as Women's History: New Feminist Essays*, edited by Alice Kessler Harris and Kathryn Kish Sklar, pp. 125–46. Chapel Hill: University of North Carolina Press.

Palmer, Colin. 1976. *Slaves of the White God: Blacks in Mexico, 1570–1650*. Cambridge: Harvard University Press.

———. 1993. "Afro-Mexican Culture and Consciousness During the Sixteenth and Seventeenth Centuries." In *Global Dimensions of the African Diaspora*, edited by Joseph Harris, pp. 125–35. Washington, D.C.: Howard University Press.

Parker, Susan. 2000. "The Cattle Trade in East Florida, 1784–1821." In *Colonial Plantations and Economy in Florida*, edited by Jane Landers, pp. 150–167. Gainesville: University Press of Florida.

Parris, S. V. 1983. "Alliance and Competition: Four Case Studies of Maroon-European Relations." *Nieuwe West-Indische Gids* 55 (3): 172–222.

Passy, Florence. 2003. "Social Networks Matter, But How?" In *Social Movements and Networks: Relational Approaches to Collective Action*, edited by Mario Diani and Doug McAdam, pp. 21–48. Oxford: Oxford University Press.

Patterson, Orlando. 1993 [1979]. "Slavery and Slave Revolts: A Sociohistorical Analysis of the First Maroon War, 1665–1740." In *Maroon Societies: Rebel Slave Communities in the Americas*, edited by Richard Price, pp. 246–92. New York: Anchor Books.

———. 1991. *Freedom in the Making of Western Culture*. New York: Basic Books.

Paynter, Robert, and Randall H. McGuire, eds. 1991. "The Archaeology of Inequality: An Introduction." In *The Archaeology of Inequality*, edited by Robert Paynter and Randall H. McGuire, pp. 1–11. Oxford, UK: Basil Blackwell.

Peerthum, Satyendra. 2001. "Determined to be Free: Marronage and Freedom in Mauritius." In *Freedom in Black History and Culture*, edited by E. Kofi Agorsah, pp. 104–27. Middleton, Cal.: Arrow Point Press.

Penningroth, Dylan C. 2003. *The Claims of Kinfolk: African American Property and Community in the Nineteenth-Century South*. Chapel Hill: University of North Carolina Press.

Pereira, Joe. 1994. "Maroon Heritage in Mexico." In *Maroon Heritage: Archaeological, Ethnographic, and Historical Perspectives*, edited by Kofi Agorsah, pp. 94–108. Kingston, Jamaica: Canoe Press.

Pérez, Berta E. 2000. "The Journey to Freedom: Maroon Forebears in Southern Venezuela." *Ethnohistory* 47 (3–4): 611–34.

Poe, Stephen. 1963. "Archaeological Excavations at Fort Gadsden, Florida." *Notes in Anthropology* 8.

Poplin, Eric, and Gordon Watts. 2010. "Draft Report: Crossing the Combahee Mitigation of the Combahee Ferry Historic District, Beaufort and Colleton Counties, South Carolina." Prepared by Brockington and Associates, Inc. and Tidewater Atlantic Research, Inc. for TRC Solutions, Inc. and the South Carolina Department of Transportation.

Popovic, Alexandre. 1998. *The Revolt of African Slaves in Iraq in the III/IX Century.* Princeton, New Jersey: Markus Weiner.

Porter, Kenneth W. No date. "Freedom Over Me." Kenneth Wiggins Porter Papers, Schomburg Center for Research in Black Culture, New York Public Library.

———. 1943a. "Florida Slaves and Free Negroes in the Seminole War, 1835–1842." *Journal of Negro History* 28 (4): 390–421.

———. 1943b. "Osceola and the Negroes." *Florida Historical Quarterly* 33 (3&4): 235–39.

———. 1971. *The Negro on the American Frontier.* New York: New York Times and Arno Press.

———. 1996. *The Black Seminoles.* Revised and edited by Alcione M. Amos and Thomas P. Senter. Gainesville: University Press of Florida.

Potter, Woodburne. 1966 [1836]. *The War in Florida.* N.p.: Readex Microprint.

Powell, Stephen, and Nevin L. 2000. "Archaeological Surveys in Two Black Communities, 1998: Surveying the Tracadie Area and Testing Two Sites in Birchtown." NSM Curator. Report 92.

Price, Richard. 1975. *Saramaka Social Structure: Analysis of a Maroon Society in Surinam.* Rio Piedra: Institute of Caribbean Studies, University of Puerto Rico.

———. 1983. *First-Time: The Historical Vision of an Afro-American People.* Baltimore: The Johns Hopkins University Press.

———. 1989. *Representations of Slavery: John Gabriel Stedman's "Minnesota" Manuscripts.* Minneapolis: Associates of the James Bell Ford Library, University of Minnesota.

———. 1993 [1979]. *Maroon Societies: Rebel Slave Communities in the Americas.* New York: Anchor Books.

———. 1998. "Scrapping Maroon History: Brazil's Promise, Suriname's Shame." *New West Indian Guide* 72: 233–55.

Price, Richard, and Sally Price. 1972. "Saramaka Onomastics: An Afro-American Naming System." *Ethnology* 11: 341–67.

———. 1994. *On the Mall: Presenting Maroon Tradition-Bearers at the 1992 FAF.* Bloomington: Folklore Institute, Indiana University.

Quarles, Benjamin. 1969. *The Negro in the Making of America.* New York: Collier Books.

Raboteau, Albert J. 1978. *Slave Religion: The "Invisible Institution" in the Antebellum South.* New York: Oxford University Press.

Rawick, George P., ed. 1976. *The American Slave: A Composite Autobiography.* Westport, Conn.: Greenwood Publishing Company.

Raz, Joseph. 1986. *The Morality of Freedom*. Oxford: Clarendon Press.

Reed-Danahay, Deborah. 1993. "Talking about Resistance: Ethnography and Theory in Rural France." *Anthropological Quarterly* 66 (4): 221–29.

Reinhardt, Catherine A. 2006. *Claims to Memory: Beyond Slavery and Emancipation in the French Caribbean*. New York: Berghahn Books.

Reis, Joao Jose, and Batriz Gallotti Mamigonian. 2004. "Nago and Mina: The Yoruba Diaspora in Brazil." In *The Yoruba Diaspora in the Atlantic World*, edited by Toyin Falola and Matthew Childs, pp. 77–110. Bloomington: Indiana University Press.

Reitz, Elizabeth J. 1994. "Zooarchaeological Analysis of a Free African Community: Gracia Real de Santa Teresa de Mose." *Historical Archaeology* 28 (1): 23–40.

Reuben Charles Papers, 1816–1832. Letters digitized on CD entitled "The Meta Shaw Coleman Collection of the Reuben Charles Papers, 1816–1832" at the P. K. Yonge Memorial Library of Florida History, University of Florida, Gainesville.

Riordan, P. 1996. "Finding Freedom in Florida: Native Peoples, African Americans, and Colonists, 1670–1816." *Florida Historical Quarterly* 75: 25–44.

Rivers, Larry E. 2000. *Slavery in Florida: Territorial Days to Emancipation*. Gainesville: University Press of Florida.

Rivers, L. E., and Canter Brown. 1997. "'The Indispensable Man': John Horse and Florida's Second Seminole War." *Journal of the Georgia Association of Historians* 18: 1–23.

Robertson, Carmelita. 2000. *Tracing the History of Tracadie Loyalists, 1776–1787*. Halifax: Nova Scotia Museum.

Roosens, Eugeen. 1989. *Creating Ethnicity: The Process of Ethnogenesis*. Newbury Park, Cal.: Sage Publications.

Rotman, D. L., Rachel Mancini, Aaron Smith, and Elizabeth Campbell. *African-American and Quaker Farmers in East Central Indiana: Social, Political, and Economic Aspects of Life in Nineteenth-Century Rural Communities, Randolph County, Indiana*. Muncie, Ind.: Archaeological Resources Management Service, Ball State University.

Sage, Jesse, and Liora Kasten. 2006. *Enslaved: True Stories of Modern Day Slavery*. New York: Palgrave Macmillan.

Salman, Michael. 2004. "Resisting Slavery in the Philippines: Ambivalent Domestication and the Reversibility of Comparisons." *Slavery and Abolition* 25 (2): 30–47.

Sattler, Richard A. 1987. *Siminoli Italwa: Socio-Political Change among the Oklahoma Seminoles between Removal and Allotment, 1836–1905*. PhD dissertation. Norman: University of Oklahoma.

———. 1996. "Remnants, Renegades, and Runaways: Seminole Ethnogenesis Reconsidered." In *History, Power, and Identity*, edited by Jonathan Hill, pp. 36–39. Iowa City: University of Iowa Press.

Sayers, Daniel O. 2004. "The Underground Railroad Reconsidered." *Western Journal of Black Studies* 28 (3): 435–43.

———. 2006. "Diasporan Exiles in the Great Dismal Swamp, 1630-1860." *Transforming Anthropology* 14 (1): 10–20.

———. 2007. "Landscapes of Alienation: An Archaeological Report of Excursions in the Great Dismal Swamp." *Transforming Anthropology* 15 (2): 149–57.

———. 2008. *The Diasporic World of the Great Dismal Swamp, 1630–1865*. PhD dissertation. Williamsburg, Vir.: Department of Anthropology, College of William and Mary; UMI, Ann Arbor.

Sayers, Daniel O., P. Brendan Burke, and Aaron M. Henry. 2007. "The Political Economy of Exile in the Great Dismal Swamp." *International Journal of Historical Archaeology* 11 (1): 60–97.

Schneider, Herbert W. 1940. "Epilogue: The Liberties of Man." In *Freedom: Its Meaning*, edited by Benedetto Croce, Thomas Mann, Jacques Maritain, and Ruth Nanda Anshen, pp. 653–72. New York: Harcourt, Brace, and Company.

Schwartz, Stuart B. 1979. "The Mocambo: Slave Resistance in Colonial Bahia." In *Maroon Societies: Rebel Slave Communities in the Americas*, edited by Richard Price, pp. 202–26. New York: Anchor Books.

———. 1992. *Slaves, Peasants, and Rebels: Reconsidering Brazilian Slavery*. Urbana: University of Illinois Press.

Scott, James C. 1985. *Weapons of the Weak: Everyday Forms of Peasant Resistance*. New Haven: Yale University Press.

———. 1990. *Domination and the Arts of Resistance: Hidden Transcripts*. New Haven: Yale University Press.

Sertima, Ivan Van. 1992. *African Presence in Early America*. New Brunswick, New Jersey: Transaction Publishers.

Shackel, Paul A. 1995. "Terrible Saint: Changing Meanings of the John Brown Fort." *Historical Archaeology* 29 (4): 11–25.

———. 2010. "Identity and Collective Action in a Multiracial Community." *Historical Archaeology* 44 (1): 58.

Shah, Saubhagya. 2008. "Revolution and Reaction in the Himalayas: Cultural Resistance and the Maoist "New Regime" in Western Nepal. *American Ethnologist* 35 (3): 481–99.

Siebert, Wilbur H. 1898. *The Underground Railroad from Slavery to Freedom*. New York: Macmillan.

Silva Castillo, Jorge. 2007. "The Diaspora in Indo-Afro-Ibero-America." In *Routes of Passage: Rethinking the African Diaspora*, edited by Ruth Simms Hamilton, pp. 119–24. East Lansing: Michigan State University Press.

Simms Hamilton, Ruth. 2007. "Rethinking the African Diaspora: Global Dynamics." In *Routes of Passage: Rethinking the African Diaspora*, edited by Ruth Simms Hamilton, pp. 1–39. East Lansing: Michigan State University Press.

Singleton, Theresa A. 2001. "Slavery and Spatial Dialectics on Cuban Coffee Plantations." *World Archaeology* 33 (1): 98–114.

Sivaramakrishnan, K. 2005. "Some Intellectual Genealogies for the Concept of Everyday Resistance." *American Anthropologist* 107 (3): 346–55.

Skinner, Quentin. 1998. *Liberty before Liberalism*. Cambridge: Cambridge University Press.

Smardz Frost, K. 2008. *I've Got a Home in Glory Land: A Lost Tale of the Underground Railroad*. New York: Farrar, Straus, and Giroux.

Smardz, Karolyn E. 1995. "African Americans Who Became African Canadians: The Thornton and Lucie Blackburn House Site." In *African American Archaeology*, newsletter of the African American Archaeology Network, edited by Thomas R. Wheaton, volume 13.

Smith, Frederick H. 2008. *The Archaeology of Alcohol and Drinking.* Gainesville: University Press of Florida.

Smith, Mark M. 2005. *Stono: Documenting and Interpreting a Southern Slave Revolt.* Columbia: University of South Carolina Press.

Soto David, Moises. 1989. "Un Hallazgo Arqueologico: Armas y Objetos Del Negro Cimarron." *Boletin del Museo del Hombre Dominicana* 22 (Ano XVI): 83–100.

Sprague, John T. 1848. *The Origin, Progress and Conclusion of the Florida War.* New York: Appleton and Co.

Sprague, Stuart Seely, ed. 1996. *His Promised Land: The Autobiography of John P. Parker; Former Slave and Conductor on the Underground Railroad.* New York and London: W. W. Norton & Company.

Stahl, Ann. 2001. "Historical Process and the Impact of the Atlantic Trade on Banda, Ghana, 1800–1920." In *West Africa during the Atlantic Slave Trade: Archaeological Perspectives,* edited by C. DeCorse, pp. 38–58. London: Leicester University Press.

Stefansson, Vilhjalmur. 1940. "Was Liberty Invented?" In *Freedom: Its Meaning,* edited by Benedetto Croce, Thomas Mann, Jacques Maritain, and Ruth Nanda Anshen, pp. 384–411. New York: Harcourt, Brace, and Company. .

Stern, Steve J., ed. 1987. *Resistance, Rebellion, and Consciousness in the Andean Peasant World, 18th to 20th Centuries.* Madison: University of Wisconsin.

Stewart, Tamara. 2005. "Fugitive Slave Community Found in Michigan: Discovery is First Archaeological Evidence of Underground Railroad in the State." *American Archaeology* v: 7.

Sturm, Circe. 2002. *Blood Politics: Race, Culture, and Identity in the Cherokee Nation of Oklahoma.* Berkeley: University of California Press.

Sturtevant, William C. 1971. "Creek into Seminole." In *North American Indians in Historical Perspective,* edited by Eleanor Burke Leacock and Nancy Oestreich Lurie, pp. 92–128. New York: Random House.

Swanston, Anna. 2003. "Pan-Africanism as a Priesthood," speech by John Henrik Clarke. In *Dr. John Henrik Clarke: His Life, His Words, His Works,* p. 212. Atlanta: I AM Unlimited Publishing, Inc.

Taylor, Timothy. 2001. "Believing the Ancients: Quantitative and Qualitative Dimensions of Slavery and the Slave Trade in Later Prehistoric Eurasia." *World Archaeology* 33 (1): 27–43.

Thompson, Alvin O. 2006. *Flight to Freedom: African Runaways and Maroons in the Americas.* Mona, Kingston: University of West Indies Press.

Thornton, J. 1993. *Africa and Africans in the Making of the Atlantic World, 1400–1680.* Cambridge: Cambridge University Press.

———. 2001. "Religious and Ceremonial Life in the Kongo and Mbundu Areas, 1500–1700." In *Central Africans and Cultural Transformations in the American Diaspora,* edited by L. M. Heywood, pp. 71–90. New York: Cambridge.

Toban, Jacqueline L., and Raymond G. Dobard. 1999. *Hidden in Plain View: The Secret Story of Quilts and the Underground Railroad.* New York: Doubleday.

Trouillot, Michel-Rolph. 1995. *Silencing the Past: Power and the Production of History.* Boston: Beacon Press.

Turner, Lorenzo. 2002 [1949]. *Africanisms in the Gullah Dialect.* Columbia: University of South Carolina Press. Published in cooperation with the Institute for Southern Studies and the South Caroliniana Society of the University of South Carolina.

25th Congress. 1838. 3rd Session, United States House of Representatives, Reports from War Department. "Negroes, &c., Captured From Indians in Florida &c." Document Number 225, pp. 76–83. Urban, Greg. 2008. "Freedom and Culture." In *Freedom: Reassessments and Rephrasings,* edited by Jose V. Ciprut, pp. 209–32. Cambridge, Massachusetts: MIT Press.

U.S. Forest Service. 2001. "U.S. Secretary of Agriculture Recognizes Wayne National Forest." Forest Service news release dated May 31, 2001. http://www.ohioarchaeology.org/joomla/index.php?option=com_content&task=view&id=119&Itemid=46.

Usner, Daniel. 1999. "Frontier Exchange and Cotton Production: The Slave Economy in Mississippi, 1798–1806." *Slavery and Abolition* 20 (1): 24–37.

Vansina, J. 1990. *Paths in the Rainforests: Toward a History of Political Tradition in Equatorial Africa.* Madison: University of Wisconsin Press.

Vega, Bernardo. 1979. "Arqueologia de Los Cimarrones del Maniel del Bahoruco." *Boletin de Museo del Hombre Dominicana* 12: 11–48.

Vlach, John Michael. 1978. "Quilting." In *The Afro-American Tradition in Decorative Arts,* edited by John M. Vlach, pp. 44–75. Cleveland, Ohio: Cleveland Museum of Art.

———. 2004. "Above Ground on the Underground Railroad: Places of Flight and Refuge." In *Passages to Freedom: The Underground Railroad in History and Memory,* edited by David W. Blight, pp. 95–115. Washington, D.C.: Smithsonian Books.

Voss, Barbara. 2008. *The Archaeology of Ethnogenesis: Race and Sexuality in Colonial San Francisco.* Berkeley: University of California Press.

Walker, Juliet E. K. 1983. *Free Frank: A Black Pioneer on the Antebellum Frontier.* Lexington: University Press of Kentucky.

Washington, Wayne. 2005. "Work Uncovers Site Where Raid Freed 700 Slaves." *The State,* October 16, 2005, pages A1 and A8.

Weik, Terrance. 1997. "The Archaeology of Maroon Societies in the Americas: Resistance, Cultural Continuity, and Transformation in the African Diaspora." *Historical Archaeology* 31 (2): 81–92.

———. 2002. *A Historical Archaeology of Black Seminole Maroons in Florida: Ethnogenesis and Culture Contact at Pilaklikaha.* PhD dissertation. Gainesville: Anthropology Department, University of Florida.

———. 2004. "Archaeology of the African Diaspora in Latin America." *Historical Archaeology* 38 (1): 32–49.

———. 2007. "Allies, Enemies and Kin in the African-Seminole Communities of Florida: Archaeology at Pilaklikaha." In *Archaeology of Atlantic Africa and the Africa Diaspora,* edited by Toyin Falola and Akin Ogundiran, pp. 311–54. Bloomington: Indiana University Press.

———. 2008. "Mexico's Cimarron Heritage and Archaeological Record." *African Diaspora Archaeology* Newsletter, http://www.diaspora.uiuc.edu/news0608.html (accessed June 2008).

———. 2009. "The Role of Ethnogenesis and Organization in the Development of African-Native American Settlements: An African Seminole Model." *International Journal of Historical Archaeology* 13 (1): 206–38.

———. No date. "Maroon Archaeology in the Dominican Republic: A Five-Week Research Project in the Dominican Republic." Unpublished report submitted to the Tinker Foundation and the Center for Latin American Studies. University of Florida.

Weisman, Brent Richards. 1989. *Like Beads on a String: A Culture History of the Seminole Indians in North Peninsular Florida*. Tuscaloosa: University of Alabama Press.

———. 2000. "The Plantation System of the Florida Seminole Indians and Black Seminoles during the Colonial Era." In *Colonial Plantations and Economy in Florida*, edited by Jane G. Landers, pp. 136–49. Gainesville: University Press of Florida.

Wellman, Barry. 1999. *Networks in the Global Village: Life in Contemporary Communities*. Boulder, Col.: Westview Press.

Wepler, William, Dot McCullough, Robert G. McCullough, and Sarah Arthur. 2001. "The Roberts Site: An Initial Investigation of an Antebellum Multicultural Community, Orange County, Indiana." Report prepared for U.S.D.A, Hoosier National Forest.

White, Cheryl. 2009a. "Archaeological Investigation of Suriname Maroon Ancestral Communities." *Caribbean Quarterly* 55: 1–20.

———. 2009b. "Saramaka Maroon Community Environmental Heritage." *Practicing Anthropology* 31 (3): 45–49.

White, Debra Gray. 2004. "Simple Truths: Antebellum Slavery in Black and White." In *Passages to Freedom: The Underground Railroad in History and Memory*, edited by David W. Blight, pp. 33–66. Washington, D.C.: Smithsonian Books in association with the National Underground Railroad Freedom Center.

White, Enrique. 1806. *East Florida Papers*. Section 65, reel 1, May 28. P.K. Younge Library of Florida History, University of Florida.

Whitten, Norman E. 1976. *Sacha Runa: Ethnicity and Adaptation of Ecuadorian Jungle Quichua*. Urbana: University of Illinois Press.

Wickman, Patricia R. 1999. *The Tree that Bends*. Tuscaloosa: University of Alabama Press.

Wiessner, Polly. 2002. "The Vines of Complexity: Egalitarian Structures and the Institutionalization of Inequality among the Enga." *Current Anthropology* 43 (2): 233–69.

Wilks, I. 1993. *Forests of Gold: Essays on the Akan and the Kingdoms of Asante*. Athens: Ohio University Press.

Wilks, Ivor, and Haight Levtzion. 1986. *Chronicles from Gonja: A Tradition of West African Muslim History*. New York: Cambridge University Press.

Williams, Eric Eustace. 1966. *Capitalism and Slavery*. New York: Capricorn Books.

Williams, J. 1962 [1837]. *The Territory of Florida*. Gainesville: University of Florida Press.

———. 1976 [1827]. *A View of West Florida*. Gainesville: University Presses of Florida.

Wilson, Lydia. 2007. "Economic Organization and Cultural Cohesion in the Coastal Hinterland of 19th-Century Kenya: An Archaeology of Fugitive Slave Communities." *African Diaspora Archaeology Newsletter*. http://www.diaspora.uiuc.edu/news0907. html (accessed September 2010).

Wilson-Marshall, Lydia. 2009. "Fugitive Slave Communities in 19th-Century Kenya: A Preliminary Report on Recent Archaeological and Historical Research." *Nyame Akuma* 72: 21–29.

Winfield Capitaine, Fernando. 1988. "La Vida de Los Cimarrones en Veracruz." In *Jornadas de homenaje Gonzalo Aguirre Beltran*, edited by Gonzalo Aguirre Beltran, pp. 85–87. Veracruz: Instituto Veracruzano de Cultura.

———. 1992. *Los Cimarrones de Mazateopan*. Xalapa, Veracruz, Mexico: Gobierno del Estado de Veracruz.

Winkelman, Peek P. M. 2004. *Divination and Healing: Potent Vision*. Tucson: University of Arizona Press.

Wolf, Eric R. 1990. *Freedom and Freedoms: Anthropological Perspectives*. Cape Town: University of Cape Town.

Wright, J. Leitch. 1986. *Creeks and Seminoles*. Lincoln: University of Nebraska Press.

Yai, Olabiyi. 2001. "African Diaspora Concepts and Practice of the Nation and Their Implications in the Modern World." In *African Roots/American Cultures: Africa in the Creation of the Americas*, edited by Sheila Walker, pp. 244–55. Lanham, Maryland: Rowman & Littlefield.

Yelvington, Kevin A. 2006. *Afro-Atlantic Dialogues: Anthropology in the Diaspora*. Santa Fe, New Mexico: School of American Research Press.

Young, H. 1934. "A Topographical Memoir on East and West Florida with Itineraries of General Jackson's Army, 1818." *Florida Historical Quarterly* 13: 16–164.

Ziegenbein, Linda M. 2009. "David Ruggles Center for Early Florence History and Underground Railroad Studies, Florence, MA." *SHA Newsletter* 42 (4): 23.

Index

Page references in italics refer to illustrations

Terrance M. Weik is associate professor of anthropology at the University of South Carolina, Columbia. He has conducted research on African heritage, social identity, community-building, and struggles against slavery in Africa, the Caribbean, and North America. His writings appear in publications such as *Archaeology of Atlantic Africa and the African Diaspora*.